AN ECONOMIC OVERVIEW

OF THE NIGERIAN ECONOMY

Ejiro U. Osiobe

Paperback: ISBN: 978-1-64318-129-5
Hardback: ISBN: 978-1-64318-130-1
Ebook: ISBN: 978-1-64318-131-8

IMPERIUM PUBLISHING

1097 N 400 Rd
Baldwin City, KS, 66006
www.imperiumpublishing.com

AN ECONOMIC OVERVIEW

OF THE NIGERIAN ECONOMY

Ejiro U. Osiobe

IMPERIUM PUBLISHING
CREATE YOUR STORY

CONTENTS

THE NIGERIAN CURRENCY

INTRODUCTION

This chapter delves into the intricacies of the Bilateral Currency Swap Agreement (BLCSA) between Nigeria and China, orchestrated by the Central Bank of Nigeria (CBN) and the People's Bank of China (PBC). The primary objective is to scrutinize the impact of this agreement on Nigeria's economic trajectory. Beginning with an exploration of the rationale behind the agreement's inception, the chapter conducts a thorough review of existing literature, dissecting the benefits and concerns inherent in the BLCSA. Delving deeper, the chapter examines the effects of the currency swap on Nigeria's economic landscape, analyzing its potential to foster foreign exchange stability and mitigate the volatility of the naira over both short and long-term business cycles. While acknowledging the BLCSA's potential to streamline trade between Nigerian and Chinese entities and alleviate the demand for the US dollar, the chapter also recognizes the agreement as a temporary solution to broader economic challenges. As such, it concludes by presenting recommendations to elicit constructive responses from key stakeholders, including the CBN, PBC, and respective governments, towards maximizing the benefits of the BLCSA for both nations.

Currency Reserves and its importance to an economy*:*

Resources needed within an economy are not entirely under the reigns of an independent nation; this statement is not wholly accurate in every situation. If the latter is true, the opportunity cost to function in a closed economy would be overbearing for any nation. To tackle this dilemma, trading with other countries is the best solution to hedge on disadvantages and expand on areas where the economy has absolute and comparative advantages. The US dollar is the hard currency used for international trade by most countries. However, two sovereign nations engaged in commerce can create a BLCSA and diversify their foreign reserve currency2.

In Nigeria, the US dollar has been the primary foreign reserve currency by the CBN since 1967 (CBN, 2017). But in 2011, the CBN decided to add the Chinese Yuan Renminbi (CNY) to its reserves. The decision was driven by the large volume of trade between Nigeria and China; most of Nigeria's imports in 2017 came from China. (OEC, 2019). The statistics on trade between the two countries in 2016 show that it was about $414.7 billion, accounting for 22% of Nigerian imports as of the last quarter of 2017 (Adu & Ahmed, 2018).

Since 2008, the Chinese government has signed thirty-five BLCSA agreements with other countries. Nigeria is the third African country and the thirty-fifth globally to sign a BLCSA with China (Olayiwola and Fasoye, 2019). The Council on Foreign Relations (CFR) in 2015 shared that China's

2

motivation for these swap agreements is to promote trade and investment and to encourage trading with the CNY in the international market. The Nigeria – China BLCSA is proposed for three years, and its terms and agreement(s) is to exchange 15 Billion CNY for ₦ 720 Billion.

Currency swap:

The CBN describes a currency swap as a bilateral agreement between two nations to exchange cash flows in their currencies at a predetermined rate for a specified period. It can also be seen as a swap in a corresponding amount in another currency to smoothen bilateral trade settlements and provide liquidity to financial markets. Swap deals between countries facilitate the sealing of bilateral trade using their national currencies instead of a third-party currency.

There are three types of currency swaps: one is the fixed currency swap, also referred to as the plain vanilla. It consists of an exchange between two parties for a fixed interest rate in one currency in return for a fixed interest rate in another currency. Two is the fixed-floating currency swap, also called circus swap. It is a fusion of plain vanilla and a market-determined interest rate. It involves the payment of a fixed interest rate on one currency and the receipt of a floating interest rate on another. The third is the floating-floating currency swap, which entails market forces determining the interest rates applied to the two currencies to be swapped.

Theoretical and empirical reviews:

According to Van (2014), the effect of China's currency swap agreements with other countries will have a noteworthy impact on the US dollar. The effect would reduce the dependence on the dollar for international trade, thereby threatening the dollar reserve status. The statement is validated by Durden (2014), stating that China's BLCSA may lessen the power of the US dollar as a reserve currency. These currency swap moves by China could lead to imported inflation in nations that hold their reserves in US dollars.

According to Olayiwola and Fasoye (2019), their paper evaluates the impact of Nigeria-China's currency swap agreements on the US dollar to the naira exchange rate. The chapter employed the Robust Least Squares (RLS) technique covering 1999 to 2017. The chapter results showed the BLCSA would make the naira appreciate against the US dollar. However, doubts assail us due to the inadequacy of data and study period adopted for this chapter since BLCSA was introduced and signed on 27th April 2018.

Adhikari (2016) studied the magnitude to which the China – Indonesia currency swap impacted the value of the US dollar. The objective was to appraise the effect of the swap agreement on the rupiah to the US dollar. The chapter used the natural logs of Indonesian and US data; variables include the real Gross Domestic product (GDP), money supply, and a dummy variable for the swap deal. The analysis showed that China-Indonesia BLCSA does not affect the exchange rate relations between the US dollar and the Indonesian rupiah. The author suggests that the principal amount in the BLCSA might be inconsequential compared to Indonesia's annual trade volume.

Oladosu (2018) examines the effects of the BLCSA between Nigeria and China on the two nations. The chapter shows that the deal will smoothen the bilateral trade relationship between the nations, encouraging foreign direct investment in Nigeria. Furthermore, the article appeals to government agencies to monitor trade transactions, prevent the unrestrained inflow of goods, and manage the country's foreign reserves more effectively.

Implementing the BLCSA:

China is one of Nigeria's largest trading partners. The trade value between China and Nigeria in 2017 alone was estimated at ₦ 2 trillion, 8.7% of the total merchandise trade. This makes China Nigeria's third major trading partner after India with 12.5% and the US with 10.8% (National Bureau of Statistics (NBS) in Gbadeyanka, 2018). With the US dollar being one of the hard reserve currencies of the world, it is used for international trade. The inferred idea implies that if Nigeria wants to import from China, Nigeria would have to convert the naira to US dollars, which would later be converted to Renminbi to pay China. Considering the trade volume and value growth between Nigeria and China, using the US dollar to close their trade deals is an uncalled-for hassle and time waste. The BLCSA between the CBN and PBC for ₦ 720 billion for 15 billion CNY would streamline the trade process. That is, it would make access to liquidity easier for people in business and companies from both countries who are engaged in business dealings. Thus, the huddles of obtaining dollars for trades between Nigeria-China is eliminated.

Advantages and concerns of the Nigeria – China BLCSA:

One of the main benefits is access to naira and renminbi by people in business from both countries without converting to US dollars. Therefore, transaction deals/dealings can be closed in the naira or the renminbi. Another advantage of the agreement is that completing business deals becomes more comfortable between businesses in both countries. This is because the troubles of obtaining US dollars have been eliminated. Another benefit of the BLCSA is the adverse effects of the dollar on the naira exchange rate would be hedged. In Nigeria's last recession, there was high volatility of the dollar to the naira exchange relations. As a result, Nigerian businesses' increased demand for the US dollar led to a scarcity of the US dollar. The shortages, in turn, led to the naira's losses against the dollar and inflation. The BLCSA should contribute towards protecting the naira from its vulnerability to the US dollar.

Better foreign reserves management is another advantage of the 2018 BLCSA. The social amenities in Nigeria are in poor condition (Anaeto, 2018); this negatively affects the Nigerian economy's industrial and non-industrial sectors. The stagnant state of the industrial and non-industrial sectors makes the Nigerian economy more import-dependent. The import-dependent nature of the economy brings into play the high demand for US dollars to finalize international transactions. Unfortunately, this has led to the depletion of foreign currency earnings and the reserve of the Nigerian economy. Thus, implementing the BLCSA will decrease demand for the US dollar for international trade, increase foreign reserves, and improve financial stability.

Furthermore, the BLCSA might promote business and FDI flows between China and Nigeria. Currently, Chinese projects are found all over the sub-sectors of the Nigerian economy, and according to Ide-Jetro (n.d), since 2002, China's projects and commitments in Nigeria have amounted to about $ 5.4 billion. Tubel (2018) comments that China is Africa's most significant financial ally, undertaking several projects on the continent. The more accessible the Naira is to Chinese companies, the more likely there will be an increase in the rate of FDI to the Nigerian economy, both in the long and the short run.

Another value of the BLCSA is the possibility of providing an alternative foreign reserve currency to the US dollar. The BLCSA would result in China and Nigeria no longer needing the US dollar while sealing a business deal involving both countries. This is also a positive by-product between Nigeria and other countries that have signed a BLCSA with China. According to Ogwo and Okpara (2015), Nigerians favor foreign goods over domestic goods, and this taste could make the BLCSA deal unfavorable to the Nigerian economy, making the nation a dumping destination for Chinese products. Furthermore, the low-cost and quality of Chinese products compared to Nigerian products might lead to a steep competition for local companies. With the struggling middle class, this could eventually lead to the collapse of the Nigerian industrial sector growth. Lastly, another cause for concern is Nigeria's rising unfavorable trade balance with China. There is fear that this skewed relation could further deteriorate Nigeria's trade position with China.

Implication(s):

Since the inception of the BLCSA, there have been different views on the performance of the agreement so far. Billy Gillis-Harry, the President of the Coalition of South-South Chamber of Commerce, Industry, Mines, and Agriculture, said it is challenging to access CNY to finalize trade transactions with China, and the dollar is still being involved in the process (Nwaoguji, 2019). Contrary to Billy's statement, Ojosipe Ayodele, Head of Enterprise Banking and Trade Finance at Stanbic IBTC, said that the BLCSA has brought about more accessibility of the CNY to Nigerian businesses. Further, the BLCSA has brought about better terms of trade for Africans and Chinese people in business, working on linking the nations (CNBC Africa, 2019). Examining whether the BLCSA has positively impacted the naira US dollar exchange rate is impossible at this point. Still, the two ideologies are of importance in understanding the situation.

From the Nigerian perspective, the BLCSA is an effort by the CBN to achieve foreign exchange stability for the naira. The BLCSA could become a vital tool for realizing this. At the same time, it might open up the economy to the risk of over-dependence on foreign products that the industrial sector could have produced domestically. A deliberate effort at revamping the infrastructure and industrial sector of the Nigerian economy to deliver goods of global standards could be an effective strategy for enduring the naira's stability.

Furthermore, since most of Nigeria's imports are from China, the Nigerian government could consider initiating partnerships with Chinese businesses, which would benefit both parties. Emanating from such connections will be easy access to the Nigerian market and job creation, leading to technological and economic growth. As stated earlier, the BLCSA intends to make the trade deals between Nigeria and China easier and to foster the growth and development of each nation's local economies. The benefits of the BLCSA are impressive, but caution should be applied so as not to be hit by the adverse effects, especially those that hamper the performance of the industrial and non-industrial sectors of the Nigerian economy. In conclusion, all hands should be on deck to ensure that despite Nigeria's imports, the industrial and non-industrial sectors are being developed simultaneously until the sectors operate at their optimum.

A Nation's Reserves

No sovereign body controls all resources it needs for production, and if it does, the opportunity cost to operate as a closed economy would be high as resources are scarce. Countries that engage in international trade have different currencies. Thus, there is a need to find a common currency with which the respective countries can trade. This currency is called foreign reserve currency [Also known as an anchor currency, held in significant quantities by sovereign governments as part of their foreign exchange reserves. The anchor currency is mainly used in international transactions, investments, and all aspects of the global economy]. The USD is commonly used for international trade, as most countries have foreign exchange reserves in US dollars.

Since the CBN introduced the US dollar as a foreign reserve currency in 1967, all international trade transactions have been made using the US dollar (CBN, 2017). Nevertheless, the CBN in 2011 decided to hold a part of its foreign exchange reserves in the CNY. This could be attributed to two reasons: firstly, China is becoming a significant player in international trade, and secondly, China is the highest import origin of Nigeria as of 2017 (OEC, 2019).

Statistically, bilateral trade between Nigeria and China stood at about $414.7 USD-billion in 2016, accounting for 22% of Nigerian merchandise imports in the fourth quarter of 2017 (Adu & Ahmed, 2018). Owing to the high volume of trade between Nigeria and China, the CBN undertook a BLCSA with the PBC to facilitate the ease of doing business together.

Since 2008, the Chinese government has signed thirty-five BLCSA agreements with other countries (see Table 1.)

Subsequently, Nigeria became the third African country to join the league of BLCSA with China (PBC database, 2019). The driving force for these swap agreements is to support trade and investment and encourage trading with the CNY in the international market (Council on Foreign Relations, 2015). The BLSCA between the CBN and the PBC was signed on

Source: *PBC* *Database*

Table 1:
China's BLCSA with Non-African Countries (2008 – 2015)

Country	Swap Agreement Date	Swap Amount (000,000,000 CNY)	Exchange rate as of 2019
South Korea	12 Dec 2008	360	1 CNY=172.8 KRW
Hong Kong	20 Jan. 2009	400	1 CNY=1.15 HKD
Malaysia	8 Feb. 2009	180	1 CNY= 0.61MYR
Belarus	11 March. 2009	7	1 CNY= 0.31 BYN
Indonesia	23 Mar. 2009	100	1 CNY=2107.15 IDR
Argentina	29 March 2009	70	1 CNY= 6.63 ARS
Iceland	9 Jun 2010	3.5	1 CNY = 17.92 ISK
Singapore	23 Jul. 2010	300	1 CNY = 0.20 SGD
New Zealand	18 Apr. 2011	25	1 CNY = 0.22NZD
Uzbekistan	19 Apr. 20131	0.7	1 CNY= 1238.36 UZS
Mongolia	6 May. 2011	15	1 CNY= 392.06 MNT
Kazakhstan	13 Jun 2011	7	1 CNY = 55.71 KZT
Russia	23 Jun 2011	150	1 CNY = 9.61 RUB
Thailand	22 Dec 2011	70	1 CNY = 4.65 THB
Pakistan	23 Dec 2011	10	1 CNY = 20.81 PKR
UAE	17 Jan 2012	35	1 CNY = 0.54 AED
Turkey	21 Feb. 2012	10	1 CNY = 0.91 TRY
Australia	22 Mar. 2012	200	1 CNY = 0.21 AUD
Ukraine	26 Jun 2012	15	1 CNY = 3.84 UAH
Brazil	26 Mar 2013	190	1 CNY = 0.58 BRL
UK	22 Jun 2013	200	1 CNY = 0.11 GBP
Hungary	9 Sept. 2013	10	1 CNY = 42.22 HUF
Albania	12 Sept, 2013	2	1 CNY = 16.10 ALL
EU	9 Oct, 2013	350	1 CNY = 0.13 EUR
Switzerland	21 Jul 2014	150	1 CNY = 0.15 CHF
Sri Lanka	16 Sept 2014	10	1 CNY = 25.83 LKR
Qatar	3 Nov 2014	35	1 CNY = 0.53 QAR
Canada	8 Nov. 2014	200	1 CNY = 0.20 CAD
Nepal	23 Dec 2014	0.6	1 CNY = 16.38 NPR
Suriname	18 Mar. 2015	1	1 CNY = 1.09 SRD
Chile	25 May 2015	22	1 CNY = 100.24 CLP
Tajikistan	5 Sept 2015	3.2	1 CNY = 1.38 TJS

http://www.pbc.gov.cn/huobizhengceersi/214481/214511/214541/3353326/index.html

Friday, 27 April 2018 (CBN, 2018). The BLCSA is intended for three years and the maximum exchange of 15 Billion CNY for ₦ 720 Billion. The BLCSA between China and African Countries' can be seen in Table 2.

Source: PBC   Database   http://www.pbc.gov.cn/english/130437/index.html

Table 2:
China's BLCSA with African Countries (2015 – 2018)

Countries	Swap Agreement Date	Amount Agreed Upon (000,000,000 CNY)	Exchange rate as of 2019
South Africa	10 April 2015	30	1 CNY = R2.1
Egypt	06 Dec 2016	18	1 CNY = EGP2.51
Nigeria	27 April 2018	15	1 CNY = ₦52.73

Conceptual Definition of Currency Swap

A currency swap is a bilateral agreement to exchange cash flows in different currencies at some predetermined rates for a specified period (CBN, 2016). According to (Jackson et al. 2018), a currency swap agreement entails the process by which two countries make available their respective currencies to one another to facilitate direct trade between them, rather than relying on a third-party currency. It can also be defined as a swap in an equivalent amount in another currency to smoothen bilateral trade settlements and provide liquidity support to financial markets.

These swap deals between countries help facilitate bilateral trade settlements using their national currencies instead of a third-party currency, in this case, the US dollar, the dominant global reserve currency. This agreement between Nigeria and China is designed to "provide naira liquidity to Chinese businesses and provide renminbi liquidity to Nigerian businesses

11

respectively, thereby improving the speed, convenience, and volume of transactions between the two countries," according to the CBN (Ubi, 2018).

More on the Types of Currency Swap and Literature:

Fixed (Plain Vanilla) Currency Swap: A fixed-rate currency swap consists of an exchange between two parties for a fixed interest rate in one currency in return for a fixed interest rate in another currency. It comprises three steps: exchange of principal amount agreed, interest paid at periodic intervals, and re-exchange of principal amount on maturity (Sivakumar & Mathew, 1996). An example would be Nigeria receiving 15 million CNY at a fixed rate of 4.6% while China would receive ₦ 530 million at a fixed interest rate of 3.9% throughout the currency swap deal. Therefore, at maturity, the counterparties exchange the original principal amounts. Nigeria receives 15 million CNY from China and returns ₦ 530 million to China.

    Fixed-Floating Currency Swap (Circus swap): The circus swap is a hybrid of plain vanilla interest rate and currency coupon swap. This type involves the combination of fixed and floating interest rates for a currency swap. It is done in two stages. This consists of the payment of a fixed interest rate on one currency and the receipt of a floating interest rate on another. Considering the earlier illustration, Nigeria receives Chinese Renminbi interest payments from China based on a 4.6% fixed rate on a principal amount of 15 million CNY over the lifespan of the swap. On the other hand, China receives a principal amount of ₦ 530 million from Nigeria at a floating interest rate.

    Floating-Floating Currency Swap (XCCY basis swap): This type requires that the interest rates applied on the two currencies to be swapped are determined by market forces (floating rates). Citing the previous examples, both parties receive interest payments on the principal amounts ₦ 530 million and 15 million CNY. As with other forms of currency swap, irrespective of whether there was an initial exchange, the currency swap parties would re-exchange the agreed amounts initially.

On the relevance of the US dollar sustaining its worldwide position as one of the most used reserve currencies of the world, Van (2014) comments that the effect of China's currency swap agreements with other countries on the US economy will have a significant effect on the dollar. According to him, this will arise due to the international community's reduced dependence on the dollar for foreign trade. Thus, the dollar's reserve currency status will be diminished. Durden (2014) corroborates this, stating that China's currency swap agreement with other countries may threaten the influence of the US dollar as a reserve currency. This he attributed to the imported inflation countries who hold foreign exchange reserves in dollar experience from time to time.

Adhikari (2016) studies the consequence of China's and Indonesia's currency swaps on the US dollar value. The chapter evaluates the effect of China's swap agreements with Indonesia vis the US dollar's exchange rate with the Indonesian rupiah. Variables used in the chapter are natural logs of the Indonesian real Gross Domestic Product (GDP), US real GDP, Indonesian money supply, U.S. money supply, and a dummy variable for the swap deal adopted for the chapter. The outcome of the analysis suggests that China's swap agreement with Indonesia does not affect the exchange rate relations between the US dollar and the Indonesian rupiah. Adhikari stated that a possible reason for this finding is that the amount entered in by the swap agreement might be too insignificant compared to Indonesia's annual trade volume to influence the exchange rate. Looking at the case of Nigeria, with the value of the currency swap agreement at ₦ 720 million for three years, it will not be able to cover 50% of annual trade between Nigeria and China, which stood at ₦ 2 trillion in 2017 (Omotunde, 2018 in Asimiyu, Eze & Ucheaga, 2018). Thus, it might not lead to the appreciation of the Naira against the dollar, as suggested by Idemobi (2018).

Olayiwola and Fasoye (2019) examine the impact of China's currency swap agreements with Nigeria on the US dollar's exchange rate with naira. The chapter employed the Robust Least Squares (RLS) technique spanning 1999 and 2017. The chapter results indicate that the Nigeria-China currency swap agreement will positively affect the exchange rate value of the US dollar and Nigerian naira. That is, the naira will appreciate against the US dollar. However, the period adopted for this chapter might not be sufficient to analyze the impact of Nigeria-China currency swap agreements on the US dollar's exchange rate with naira as the bilateral currency swap deal was introduced and signed on 27th April 2018.

Okwurume and Onuoha (2019) investigate the competitive advantage potential in the currency swap agreement between Nigeria and China and clarify the concept and entrails of currency swap. The chapter employed a historical and descriptive design to establish the advantages and disadvantages of the currency swap deal. The chapter recommends that the government purposefully adopt export-based economic policies and technological transfer between China and Nigeria.

Jackson et al. (2018) examine the bilateral currency swap agreement between Nigeria and China; the chapter focusses on the implications and opportunities inherent in the deal. The chapter expects business operators to exploit the agreement to improve their trading activities maximally.

However, the chapter was unable to ascertain whether the BLCSA will negatively or positively impact building the Nigerian economy.

Oladosu (2018) probes the currency swap's effects on the economies of both Nigeria and China. The chapter opines that the deal will smoothen the bilateral trade relationship between Nigeria and China, which will boost the confidence of the international community to invest in Nigeria. Furthermore, the chapter calls the attention of government agencies to guard against a rampant influx of goods and better manage the country's foreign reserves.

According to Atkins (2016), after analyzing the merits and demerits of Nigeria's swap agreement with China, he opined that increased trade with China benefits Nigeria. However, he believed that political crises might threaten the bilateral currency swap agreement.

The China and Nigeria Currency Swap Agreement:

China is one of Nigeria's largest trading partners. In 2017, the trade value between China and Nigeria was estimated at a record high of ₦ 2.0 trillion, which is 8.7% of total Merchandise trade, making China Nigeria's third-biggest trading partner after India with 12.5%, and the US 10.8% (National Bureau of Statistics in Gbadeyanka, 2018). With US dollars being the world's reserve currency, it is needed for international trade. In other words, if Nigeria wants to import from China, Nigeria would have to convert the Naira to Dollars, which would later be converted to Renminbi to pay China. Nigeria and China's round-tripping of the dollar makes the trade process more tedious. Due to the rise of trade value and volume between Nigeria and China, the continuous use of the US dollar to complete their trade transactions becomes somewhat needless, stressful, and time-wasting. The discontinuation of the US dollar for trade between Nigeria and China would relieve the pressure off Nigeria's foreign reserve in US dollars. Thus, the currency swap agreement also diversifies the Nigerian foreign reserve, which is majorly in US dollars (Moghalu, 2014). The BLCSA between the CBN and PBC for ₦ 720 billion/15 billion CNY would smoothen and make readily available liquidity to business owners from countries interested in doing business together. Thus, the rigors of accessing dollars for trade between these countries are eliminated.

Pros of the Nigeria – China BLCSA:

Access to Naira and Renminbi by businesses of both countries: The BLCSA will grant Nigerian businesses direct access to the Renminbi. At the same time, Chinese companies will also enjoy direct access to the Naira without converting to US dollars. International transactions that require invoices in US dollars for their completion can quickly be issued using the naira or the renminbi.

Ease in doing Business between both countries: Sequel to the above, completing business deals becomes easier. Completion of transactions becomes more manageable because the hassle of obtaining US dollars has been eliminated. The BLCSA will also effectively aid the convenience, speed, and volume of trade transactions between Nigeria and China.

Combating the adverse effects of the dollar-naira exchange rate: During Nigeria's recession (2016q2 – 2017q2), the dollar-naira exchange rate was volatile. Since many Nigerian businesses needed US dollars for importation, the high demand for the dollar led to a scarcity. The shortages, in turn, led to the naira's losses against the dollar. The BLCSA between CBN and PBC will, to no small extent, tackle the adverse effects of dollar volatility and shield the naira from its vulnerability to the dollar. The BLCSA permits the CBN and PBC to acquire each other's currency at a pre-determined exchange rate that would not be subject to fluctuations of the currencies against the dollar.

Better Foreign Reserves Management: According to Anaeto (2018), Nigeria's infrastructure is deplorable, adversely affecting the economy's industrial sector. Due to the unconscious state of the industrial sector, the economy is import-dependent. The import-dependent nature of the economy brings into play the high demand for dollars to complete international trade. This practice has weighed heavily on the country's foreign currency earnings and reserves. With the commencement of the BLCSA, there will be reduced demand on the dollar for international trade, thereby leading to more dollar earnings retained in the Country's foreign reserve. Furthermore, it will also assist both countries in their foreign exchange reserves management and enhance financial stability. Also, the BLCSA will minimize currency losses emanating from the prior conversion of Naira to dollars and back to the renminbi.

Improve trade and investment flow between China and Nigeria: According to Tubel (2018), China is the biggest financial ally to Africa, undertaking several projects within about thirty-five countries continent, especially in Kenya, Ethiopia, Angola, Djibouti, Nigeria, Egypt, Zimbabwe, and others. Little or no surprise that after the 2018 Forum for China-Africa Cooperation (FOCAC) in Beijing, China earmarked 415 billion CNY/$ 60 billion for Africa's development. In Nigeria alone, China's projects and commitments have amounted to about $ 5.4 billion since 2002 (Ide-Jetro, n.d). Evidence of Chinese projects is found throughout the Nigerian economy, from agriculture to manufacturing, telecommunication to construction. The more accessible the Naira is to Chinese companies handling projects, the higher the Foreign Direct and Portfolio Investment rate into Nigeria. Also, another interesting point to consider is the ease at which Chinese investors can repatriate the renminbi back to China.

Alternative Foreign Reserve Currency to the dollar: Due to the signing of the BLCSA, China, and Nigeria will no longer need a dollar while sealing a business deal involving both countries; this could also be a positive between Nigeria and other countries who have signed a BLCSA with China. Therefore, the renminbi can power international trade between Nigeria and other countries. Thus, this, yet again, will shield the naira from its volatile relationship with the dollar. However, the challenge with such an arrangement is that Nigeria does not have enough renminbi to attempt international trade with other countries.

Concerns of the Nigeria – China BLCSA:

Possible Dumping Ground: According to Ogwo and Okpara (2015) and Okechuku and Onyemah (1999), Nigerians prefer foreign goods over domestically made goods. This trend could make the BLCSA deal unfavorable to the Nigerian economy, which could become a dumping ground for Chinese products. Thus, the ease of doing business would lead to an influx of more Chinese products into Nigeria.

Unfavorable Conditions for Nigerian Industries to Compete: Considering Chinese products' cheaper nature and quality compared to domestically made products in Nigeria, it might become impossible for our industrial sector to compete. When this happens, the competition between locally produced and imported goods will likely be impossible to sustain. Invariably, this will lead to the folding up or halting of Nigeria's industrial sector growth.

Nigeria's growing trade deficit with China: Another cause for concern is Nigeria's rising unfavorable trade balance with China. For instance, Nigeria's trade deficit with China was about $ 16.9 billion between 2013 and 2016. While in 2017, it was approximately ₦ 1.6 trillion (National Bureau of Statistics, 2018). Thus, the BLCSA may further weaken Nigeria's trade position with China.

Assessing the Nigeria – China BLCSA (April 2018 – May 2019):

Though the BLCSA came into effect on 27th April 2018, there have been divergent views on the performance of the agreement so far. According to Billy Gillis-Harry, the president of the Coalition of South-South Chamber of Commerce, Industry, Mines, and Agriculture, the BLCSA between Nigeria and China is just on paper and not reality as the US dollars is still used in consummating trade. This statement was corroborated by Ruwase Babatunde, the president of the Lagos Chamber of Commerce and Industry (Nwaoguji, 2019).

On the other hand, in an interview, Ojosipe Ayodele, the head of Enterprise Banking and Trade Finance at Stanbic IBTC, stated that the BLCSA has brought about more accessibility to the CNY by Nigerian businesses. Also, the BLCSA has brought about better terms of trade, further stating that the banks, in collaboration with the Africa – China agent proposition, are working tirelessly on linking Nigerian customers to off-takers or businesses in China. (CNBC Africa, 2019).

The different views are on accessibility to the CNY by Nigeria businesses as of May 2019. At this time, it is impossible to examine whether the BLCSA has impacted the stability of the Naira and its exchange relations with the US dollar.

Policy Implication of the BLCSA on the Nigerian Economy:

China has been Nigeria's biggest import partner over the last five years (OEC, 2019). Thus, the currency swap deal is a strategic attempt by the CBN to achieve Foreign exchange stability of the naira. However, what cost will the currency swap have on the Nigerian economy? Though the deal will reduce the pressure on the dollar demand by Nigerian businesses and translate into a tool for ensuring the stability of the Naira, this might be a temporary fix when what is indeed needed is a robust and lasting solution. Therefore, there is a need to be careful of over-dependence on interim measures to handle the volatile nature of the naira in meeting our import volumes.

Recommendations:

An effective way to bring about the stability of the Naira is the development of the Nigerian industrial sector to produce products that would meet consumer demand globally. Therefore, when Nigerian products are patronized globally, the demand for the naira will increase and lead to stability in the naira. Because Nigeria's topmost import originates from China, steps can be taken by the Nigerian government to sign a Public-Private Partnership (PPP) with those companies or ventures that sell their products to Nigeria to cite factories in Nigeria. This will benefit all parties involved as the Chinese companies will have easier access to the Nigerian market. On the part of Nigeria, these companies will create job opportunities and lead to the development of the economy and technological advancement. Furthermore, citing Chinese industries in Nigeria will reduce the burden on the renminbi available for trade. After all, the BLCSA ₦ 720 billion value is only 30% of the nation's ₦ 2 trillion volume of trade between Nigeria and China in 2017 (National Bureau of Statistics, 2018).

Assessing the Nigeria – China BLCSA (April 2018 – May 2019):

Though the BLCSA came into effect on 27th April 2018, there have been divergent views on the performance of the agreement so far. According to Billy Gillis-Harry, the president of the Coalition of South-South Chamber of Commerce, Industry, Mines, and Agriculture, the BLCSA between Nigeria and China is just on paper and not reality as the US dollars is still used in consummating trade. This statement was corroborated by Ruwase Babatunde, the president of the Lagos Chamber of Commerce and Industry (Nwaoguji, 2019).

On the other hand, in an interview, Ojosipe Ayodele, the head of Enterprise Banking and Trade Finance at Stanbic IBTC, stated that the BLCSA has brought about more accessibility to the CNY by Nigerian businesses. Also, the BLCSA has brought about better terms of trade, further stating that the banks, in collaboration with the Africa – China agent proposition, are working tirelessly on linking Nigerian customers to off-takers or businesses in China. (CNBC Africa, 2019).

The different views are on accessibility to the CNY by Nigerian businesses as of May 2019. At this time, it is impossible to examine whether the BLCSA has impacted the stability of the Naira and its exchange relations with the US dollar.

Policy Implication of the BLCSA on the Nigerian Economy:

China has been Nigeria's biggest import partner over the last five years (OEC, 2019). Thus, the currency swap deal is a strategic attempt by the CBN to achieve Foreign exchange stability of the naira. However, what cost will the currency swap have on the Nigerian economy? Though the deal will reduce the pressure on the dollar demand by Nigerian businesses and translate into a tool for ensuring the stability of the Naira, this might be a temporary fix when what is indeed needed is a robust and lasting solution. Therefore, there is a need to be careful of over-dependence on interim measures to handle the volatile nature of the naira in meeting our import volumes.

Recommendations:

An effective way to bring about the stability of the Naira is the development of the Nigerian industrial sector to produce products that would meet consumer demand globally. Therefore, when Nigerian products are patronized globally, the demand for the naira will increase and lead to stability in the naira. Because Nigeria's topmost import originates from China, steps can be taken by the Nigerian government to sign a Public-Private Partnership (PPP) with those companies or ventures that sell their products to Nigeria to cite factories in Nigeria. This will benefit all parties involved as the Chinese companies will have easier access to the Nigerian market. On the part of Nigeria, these companies will create job opportunities and lead to the development of the economy and technological advancement. Furthermore, citing Chinese industries in Nigeria will reduce the burden on the renminbi available for trade. After all, the BLCSA ₦ 720 billion value is only 30% of the nation's ₦ 2 trillion volume of trade between Nigeria and China in 2017 (National Bureau of Statistics, 2018).

Conclusion:

The currency swap agreement is a deliberate attempt by the CBN to ensure the stability of the naira in the foreign exchange market. However, there is a need to be wary of dependence on short-term measures to handle the volatile nature of the naira in meeting our import volumes. As discussed earlier, a realistic approach to bring about the stability of the naira is the development of the Nigerian industrial sector to produce products that would meet consumer demand globally. Furthermore, if the Nigerian manufacturing industry significantly improves, it would help curb the balance of trade deficit that Nigeria currently experiences. A favorable trade balance would mean an increase in the demand for Nigerian goods globally, which would lead to the appreciation of the naira.

Appendix:

Table 3:

Abbreviation	Meaning
CBN	Central Bank of Nigeria
PBC	Peoples Bank of China
BLCSA	Bilateral Currency Swap Agreement
US	United States of America
PPP	Public-Private Partnership
CNY	Chinese Yuan Renminbi
GDP	Gross Domestic Product
RLS	Robust Least Squares
FOCAC	Forum for China-Africa Cooperation
OEC	Observatory of Economic Complexity

REFERENCE

Adhikari, D.R. (2016), "Effect of China's New Trade Settlement Policy on the Value of Dollar." *Journal of Applied Business and Economics,* 18(7), 23 – 31.

Adu, D. & Ahmed, O. (2018). The CBN Nigeria /PBOC China bilateral currency swap agreement (BCSA).

Anaeto, E., (2018, October 1). Infrastructure Deficit: Challenges and Opportunities. Vanguard Newspaper. Retrieved from:
https://www.vanguardngr.com/2018/10/infrastructure-deficit-challenges-and-opportunities/

Atkins, D. (2016, April 27), "Benefits and Dangers of the Currency Swap Agreement Nigeria had with China," The Voltage Post.

CNBC Africa (2019, April 29). Nigeria, China Currency Swap Deal: Progress Made so far (Video File). Retrieved from
https://www.cnbcafrica.com/videos/2019/04/29/nigeria-china-currency-swap-deal-progress-made-so-far/

Central Bank of Nigeria (2017). Swap Transactions. Education in Economics Series No 7. Retrieved from
https://www.cbn.gov.ng/Out/2017/RSD/SWAP%20TRANSACTIONS.pdf

Central Bank of Nigeria (2018). "Foreign Exchange Rate, Research Department," Education in Economic Series, No.4, Abuja, Nigeria.

Durden, T., (2014). The March of Global Dedollarization Continues. Political Vel Craft, November, 13.

Gbadeyanka, M., (2018, July 23). Gains of Bilateral Currency Swap Deal between Nigeria, China. Business Post, Nigeria. Retrieved from
https://www.businesspost.ng/2018/05/07/gains-of-bilateral-currency-swap-deal-between-nigeria-china/ 1/11

Ide-Jetro (n.d). China Infrastructural Footprint in Africa. Retrieved from https://www.ide.go.jp/English/Data/Africa_file/Manualreport/cia_10.html

Jackson, Etti & Edu (2018). Overview of the bilateral currency swap agreement: implications and opportunities.

Nwaoguji, C. (2019, April 29). 'Currency Swap Agreement: Stakeholders Express Divergent Views on Policy Outcomes.' Sun News

OEC (2019). Nigeria (NGA) Exports, Imports, and Trade Partners. Retrieved from https://atlas.media.mit.edu/en/profile/country/nga/#Imports

Okechuku, C. & Onyemah, V. (1999). Nigerian Consumer Attitudes toward Foreign and Domestic Products. *Journal of International Business Studies 30*(3) 611-62.

Okwurume, C.N. & Onuoha, B.C. (2019). Currency Swap and Competitive Advantage: A Case Study of Nigeria and China. *International Journal of Advanced Academic Research 5*(3), 33-45.

Olayiwola, A.S., & Fasoye, K. (2019). Does China's Currency Swap Agreements have Impact on the U.S dollar's Exchange Rate in Nigeria? *Global Journal of Human-Social Science, 19*(3), 31-38

Tubel, G. (2018, September 25). 10 Massive Projects the Chinese are Funding in Africa, Including railways and a brand-new city. Business Insider SA. Retrieved from
https://www.businessinsider.co.za/here-are-150-million-rand-projects-in-africa-funded-by-china-2018-9

Van N.A. (2014, November 18). Russia, China Preparing to Eliminate Our Reserve Currency Status", The Washington Times.

ECONOMIC IMPACT OF AGRICULTURE

INTRODUCTION

The chapter uses the economic impact model IMPLAN to estimate the economic impact(s) of a Cassava and Fish farm development in Gwagwalada, Nigeria. The project-specific impact is estimated at the aggregate level of the Nigerian economy (i.e., the impact(s) of Ane Osiobe Altruism Farm on the Nigerian economy as a whole). This chapter addresses the primary economic policy question of how Cassava and Fish farm production in Gwagwalada, Nigeria, affects the nation's economy. During the starting phase of the farm, it is estimated that the farm will employ approximately two full-time farmers and five part-time workers for both the Cassava and Fish farms, giving a total of roughly ten to thirteen new jobs that will be created in the city of Gwagwalada. In the running phase of the project, it is expected that Ane Osiobe Altruism Farm will employ approximately thirteen workers on the farm site (both full and part-time). The total economic activity to the nation would be substantial, equating to approximately ₦ 4,122,761.90k as the net impact in the first year and ₦

6,159,243.10k as the net impact in the subsequent years. Given the current level of impact(s) observed by other farms in Nigeria and the potential for increased impact(s) due to optimal utilization of mechanized farming equipment and trained industry-specific labor, Gwagwalada appears to be well-positioned and equipped to see the increasing effect (s) from the Ane Osiobe Altruism Farm. Agriculture is recognized as an essential sector of the Nigerian economy, accounting for 21.18% of Nigeria's gross domestic product (GDP) (Central Bank of Nigeria, 2016). On average, the GDP from the agricultural sector is ₦ 3,771,185.70k, with a high of ₦ 5,189,365.99k and a low of ₦ 2,594,759.86k.

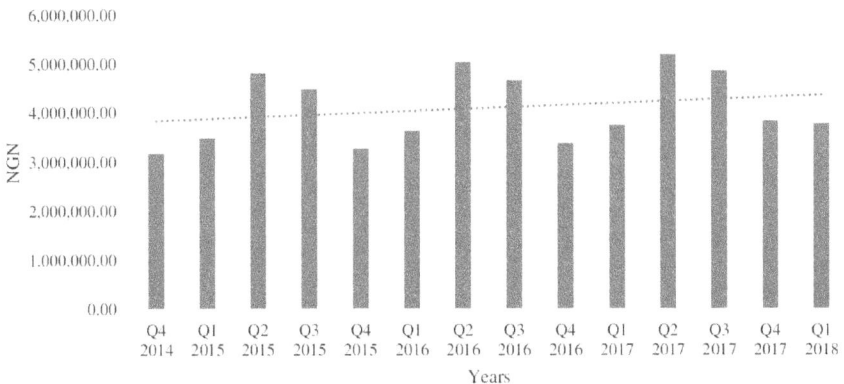

Figure 1
Nigerian GDP from Agriculture
Q4 2014 - Q1 2018

Source: Trading-Economic | National Bureau of Statistic, Nigeria.

Social and political support for agriculture has been growing more robust, as some states in Nigeria (Adamawa, Borno, and Yobe) were declared to be in famine as of Feb. 2017 by the United Nations (UN) (The Guardian News Paper, 2017). Agricultural farms are part of the social and political environment and movement that influences how agricultural farms operate, and supply produce to different parts of Nigeria. If food production in Nigeria is to be sustainable, it is critical to understand the net contribution of the agriculture sector to the total GDP of the economy. Figure 2 shows the agricultural sector's participation in Nigeria's entire GDP.

Figure 2
Agriculture Sector as a Percentage of GDP
2006 - 2016

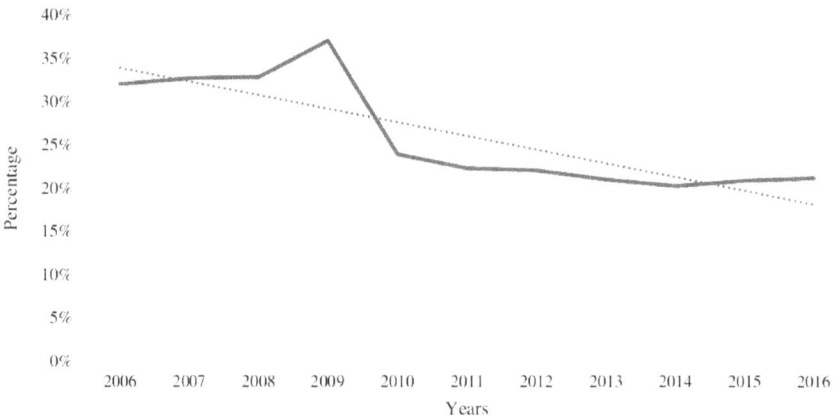

Source: National Bureau of Statistic, Nigeria.

Many of the impact(s) from agriculture are recognized as predominantly local (e.g., rural to urban farm production transitions). While in Nigeria, the public supports the agriculture industry, starting a new farm in any community, especially by non-indigenes, is a trend that has frequently raised concerns in local rural communities. Among these concerns are question(s) about community reinvestment, as most of the farms don't reinvest in the local communities they operate in. Advocates often argue that these agricultural operations (s) are beneficial to most rural small towns and have zero social or private cost to the communities. On the other hand, critics in these communities have asserted that the agricultural project(s) have little lasting local economic impact in their communities. Economic development today emphasizes a favorable and sustainable economic climate, where job creation is paramount, and such questions carry greater weight. In the past, studies of the economic impact of starting and running a Cassava and Fish farm in Nigeria suggest that the economic implications to the local government area, state, and country are substantial. However, few studies have sought to quantify these impacts.

This chapter uses the data from (Enyinnaya and Osiobe, 2017) and the optimization results from (Enyinnaya, 2018) to analyze the economic impact(s) of starting and running the Ane Osiobe Altruism Farm in Gwagwalada, Nigeria. The IMPLAN model was used to assess and analyze the farm's economic impact(s). The project-specific impacts are estimated at the national level. The primary economic policy question addressed in this chapter is how this investment affects the Nigerian economy and where the Cassava and Fish farm will be located (Gwagwalada). The results presented in the chapter will include total jobs created, labor income, value-added, benefits, overall economic output (activity) in the community, direct, indirect, induced, and total effect. This analysis also discusses agriculture trends likely to influence the economic impacts of continued farming in Gwagwalada and the nation.

About Ane Osiobe Altruism Farm:

Ane Osiobe Altruism Farm will be located at Gwagwalada, CKC district, FCT, Nigeria. Gwagwalada is one of the six local government area councils of the Federal Capital Territory of Nigeria. Gwagwalada's land mass is about 1,043 km2, and its population was 157,770 at the 2006 census. The Federal Capital Territory is one of the fastest-growing areas in Nigeria due to its political status as the nation's capital city and geographical location (Enyinnaya and Osiobe, 2017). The FCT grand-master plan (2000) illustrates the location of FCT. The chapter shows that the FCT lies between latitude 8° 25' and 9° 25' North of the equator and longitude 6° 45' and 7° 45' East of the Greenwich meridian (Aondoakaa, 2012). The FCT is located in an area known as the middle belt region of Nigeria. The size of the capital is about point eight percent (0.008) of Nigeria. FCT shares borders with four states: Kaduna in the North; Nassarawa in the West; Kogi in the South; and Niger in the East. The capital has a land mass of 8,000 square kilometers (Km2). The Ane Osiobe Altruism Farm was established to support feeding students at the Special Needs School (Abuja School for the Blind) in Jabi, FCT, Nigeria.

Why Impact Analysis is Important:

Recently, policymakers have placed a significant amount of attention on fiscal and economic policies at the federal, state, and local levels; however, many urban and rural communities have faced various economic challenges over the past few decades, varying from the great depression of the 1930s to the great recession of 2007 – 2010.

The scaling of agricultural produce led to the creation of more jobs, leases for landlords, better opportunities, construction, manufacturing, and maintenance, and increases in tax revenues for the government. The economic impact is multi-faceted, or, to put it another way, a chicken and egg dilemma. A project's overall impact(s) depends on the availability of resources and the ability of local businesses to participate in agricultural production in the city of Gwagwalada, as well as the preference and participation of individual independent contractors. In most extreme cases in Nigeria, agricultural production can begin with little capital, resulting in little or zero economic impact or value for the locality or host community where the project or farm is sited. Tracing the distribution of effects within the federal, state, and local economy is essential to understanding the value of agriculture for the localities where the project(s) are sited. The information from an impact study can help guide policymakers when creating new policies to ensure that the federal, state, and local communities capture the impact they desire or wish to see in their communities. The Crompton (2001) study presented a generalized model for understanding how to write, analyze, and interpret an economic impact study. The chapter offered a conceptual rationale for undertaking an impact study regardless of the software one is using, either IMPLAN, JEDI, RIMS II, REMI, or a Dynamic System Model (DSM). The author presented four principles to guide our research process and how to interpret the input-output result(s) carefully.

Cassava Production:

The cassava plant is Yuca, Manihot esculenta, Manico, Mandioca, or the Brazilian arrowroot. It is a perennial shrub from the family Euphorbiaceae. This crop is grown in the world's tropical areas—such as Nigeria, Ghana, Brazil, and Paraguay—and some other countries, such as Thailand and Indonesia, because of its starchy tuberous root, consumed by man and fed to animals. Cassava is a famous staple food crop in West-Africa and a significant source of income for rural communities. As a ground-rooted crop, Cassava has excellent resistance to many pests and diseases, making it an essential food crop to enhance food security; this is why most rural communities support its growth. Cassava value-added products include but are not limited to gari and fufu, as they are easy to prepare. Cassava is an industrial raw material to produce alcohol, gums, pharmaceuticals, and

31

confectionaries. Nigeria is among the most significant cassava producers in the world, with an annual production of 38.6 million tons. This is because of the development of high-yielding cultivars and improved production technologies. (Toluwase S.O et al. 2013).

Fish Production:

Fish production makes up a high percentage of the total world supply of animal protein. In West-Africa, fish production has helped significantly reduce the epidemic of anemia, kwashiorkor, and other ailments resulting from protein deficiency (Enyinnaya and Osiobe, 2017). There are several economic importance of fish production, including but not limited to improvement in nutrition, job creation, agro-industrial development, foreign exchange/trade, and overall development of rural areas (Toulwase S.O et al., 2013).

Figure 3
World Capture Fisheries VS Aquacture (Farmed Fish) production
1960 - 2014

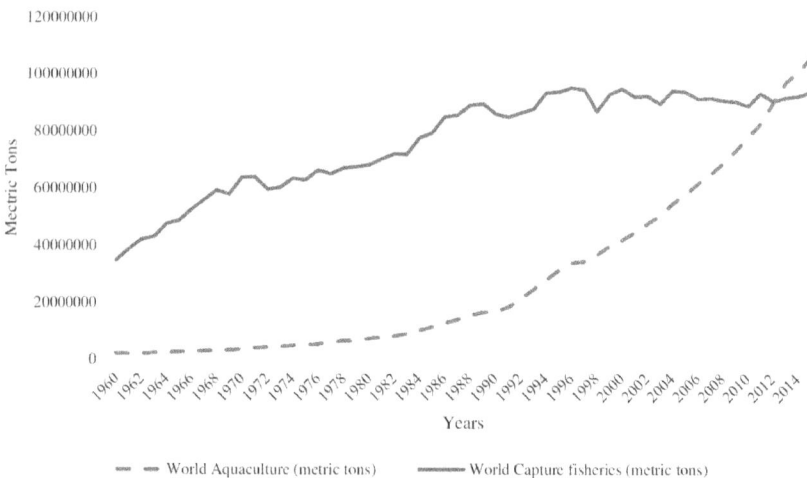

32

The annual seafood production from wild-catch fisheries and aquaculture (farmed seafood) practices are measured in metric tons per year. Figures 3 and 4 show the yearly statistics of fish caught, as the UN Food and Agricultural Organization (FAO) reported.

Figure 4
Nigeria Capture Fisheries VS Aquaculture (Farmed Fish)
Production
1960 - 2014

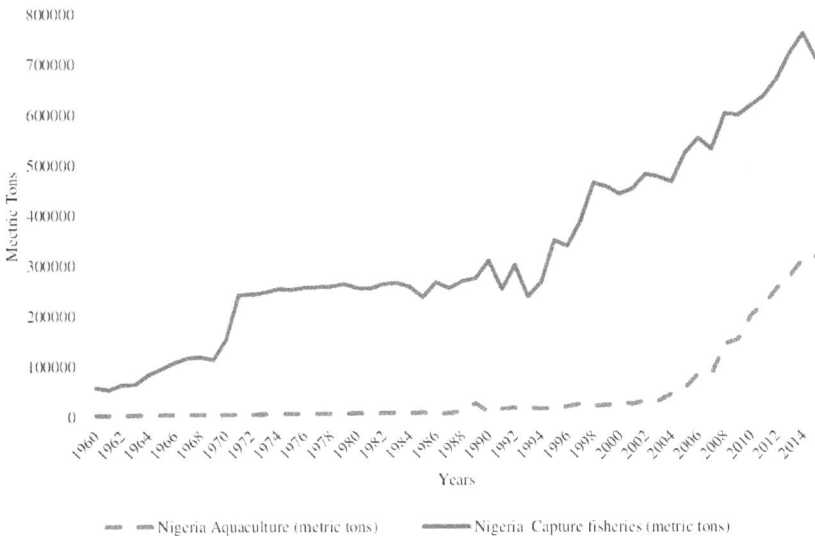

Source: World Bank – World Development Indicators

Figures 3 and 4 show the total production from wild fisheries and aquaculture (fish farming) across all seafood types (including fish, crustaceans, and sea plants). Figure 3 shows that global catch from wild fisheries has had little or no change, while that of Nigeria in Figure 4 has been increasing. While aquaculture worldwide has increased, particularly over the last 20 years, that of Nigeria has only begun to grow over the previous 10 years. Global aquaculture production is greater than the wild fishery caught, but not so for Nigeria.

Figure 5

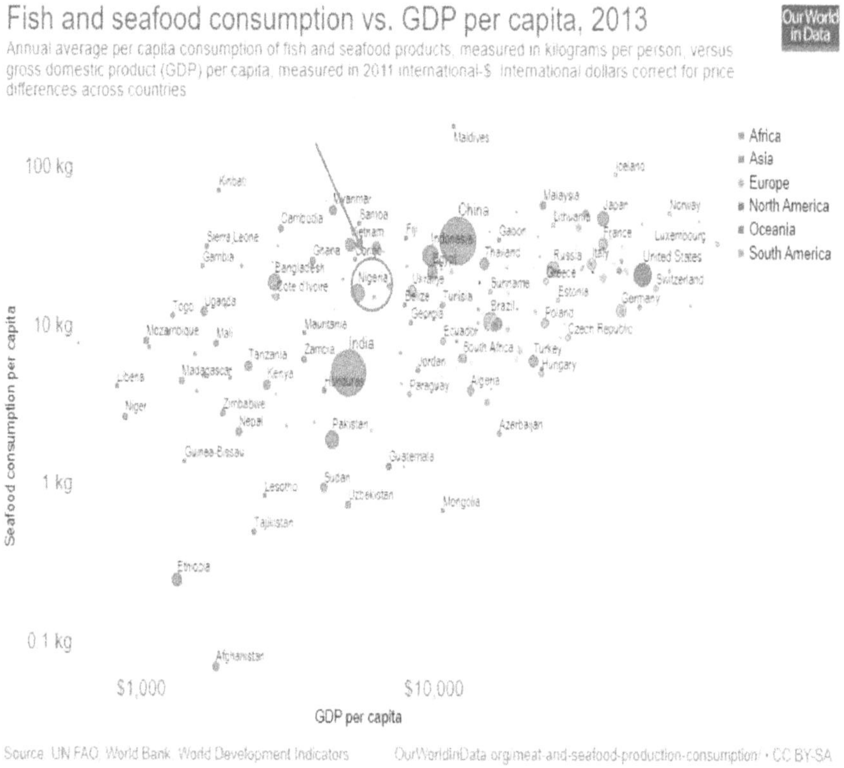
Fish and seafood consumption vs. GDP per capita, 2013
Annual average per capita consumption of fish and seafood products, measured in kilograms per person, versus gross domestic product (GDP) per capita, measured in 2011 international-$. International dollars correct for price differences across countries
Our World in Data
Africa
Asia
Europe
North America
Oceania
South America
100 kg
10 kg
1 kg
0.1 kg
Seafood consumption per capita
$1,000
$10,000
GDP per capita
China
India
Nigeria
Source: UN FAO, World Bank: World Development Indicators
OurWorldinData.org/meat-and-seafood-production-consumption/ • CC BY-SA

Methodology:

To analyze the economic impact of the farm project in Gwagwalada, Nigeria, this chapter utilized the IMPLAN software. The appropriateness of this model for this chapter was determined because IMPLAN is the only Input-Output data company with aggregate labor force data for Nigeria.

About IMPLAN Software:

IMPLAN is wholly an input-output model. It is non-survey based, and its structure typifies that of input-output models found in the regional science literature. Like REMI, IMPLAN assumes a uniform national production technology and uses the regional purchase coefficient approach to regionalize the technical coefficients (Lynch 2000). The IMPLAN model generates two types of multipliers: Type I and Type III. The difference between the two IMPLAN multipliers is as follows:

1. Type I and Type III multipliers have an induced consumption effect. IMPLAN's Type III multiplier differs from the standard Type I multiplier in the following ways:
    1. The consumption function is nonlinear; the marginal propensity to consume is not constant, decreasing as income in the region rises.
    2. The population thoroughly responds to employment changes and drives consumer spending. Multipliers are generated for employment, output, value-added, personal, and total income.

The IMPLAN Input-Output Model

The IMPLAN model software is a regional input-output modeling system created by the Minnesota IMPLAN Group. The modeling system is an interactive, computer-based modeling system capable of producing input-output accounts and models for any region(s) in the United States as small as a single county and the national level for other countries across the globe.

The system consists of regional databases and software that allows users to develop these models to describe the structure of local economies and predictive analyses, especially those associated with estimating the economic impacts of a quantifiable change in regional production. The data regarding inter-sector relationships used for this analysis are from 2011.

National Industry Data

The IMPLAN model uses national production functions for nearly 500 industries to estimate how an industry spends its operating receipts to produce its goods and services. The model also uses a national matrix to determine the byproducts that each sector generates. To analyze the impacts of household spending, the model treats households as an "industry" to determine their expenditure patterns. IMPLAN couples the national production functions with a variety of National-level (in the case of Nigeria) economic data to assess the impacts of every case analyzed with the software.

County-Level Economic Data

IMPLAN combines national industry production functions with state and local government areas economic data to estimate the national-level impacts. IMPLAN collects data from economic, industrial, and financial sources to generate average output, employment, and productivity for each industry. IMPLAN also receives data on average prices for all the goods and services sold in the local, state, and national economy.

Multipliers:

The IMPLAN software integrates the data collected from various sources to create a variety of Type I and III multipliers for Nigeria's national economy.

The multiplier analyzes the total economic activity that results from industry (or household) spending an additional dollar in the local, state, and national economy. Based on these multipliers, IMPLAN generates a series of tables to show the economic effects: the direct, indirect, and induced impacts.

The Direct Effect (DE):

The DE refers to the dollar value of economic activity instigated in the economy due to the start of that project. In the case of a farm in Gwagwalada, the direct impacts are equal to the original farm equipment and tools needed to start, that is, the farm and the farmer's discretionary spending. The DE does not include household savings and payments to federal, state, and local taxes, as these payments do not circulate through the economy (Richmond, 2018). The direct effect is the immediate consequences of a change in economic activity or policy.

Indirect Effect (IE):

The IE refers to the inter-industry impacts of the input-output analysis. In the case of the new farm in Gwagwalada, indirect impacts result from spending by the local and regional companies from the new farm, and farmers buy their tools and equipment. More examples include but are not limited to retail establishments, farm service providers, and other firms that use the payments they receive from new farms and farmers to purchase equipment and supplies, rent space, pay their employees, etc. The indirect effect is the second-round consequence of a change in economic activity or policy. It occurs when one industry purchases input-materials from another sector.

Induced Effect (INE):

The INE refers to the impacts of household spending by the employees generated by the DE and ID. In other words, INE results from the farm spending of employees of business establishments that the new farm and farmers patronize (directly) and their suppliers (indirectly). The IMPLAN model accounts for local commute patterns in the geography. The INE results from the employees of the new farm project (farmers) spending their wages in the local economy of Gwagwalada.

Other terms used in the chapter include employment, which is the amount of labor required for the job; labor income, which consists of the employees' wages; value-added, which refers to the change in the values of a good or service during each stage of production; total effect, or the total of the direct, indirect, and induced effects; and output, which refers to the gross industry expenditure.

Results:

The economic impact results are reported for full-time job(s) equivalent, earnings, total value added, and total output. The results are divided into two main groups: the starting and operating phases. The Enyinnaya (2018) optimization study on Ane Osiobe Altruism Farm provides our study with the base, first, and second iteration assumptions used to carry out our impact analysis. A summary of the optimization result can be seen in the appendix section of the chapter, Table 11 – 12, and Figure 10.

Table 1: Analytical Categories

Table 1 Analytical Categories	
Meaning	**Acronym**
Starting the Cassava Farm	SCF
Starting the Fish Farm	SFF
Base Iteration Operating both the Cassava and Fish Farm	BOCFF
First Iteration Operating both the Cassava and Fish Farm	FOCFF
Initial Farmer Operating a Mazie farm	OMF
Base Iteration Net Operating Impact (BOCFF – OMF)	BNOI
First Iteration Net Operating Impact (FOCFF – OMF)	FNOI
Nigerian Naira	NGN

The estimated annual impact of Ane Osiobe Altruism Farm to the city of Gwagwalada from starting and operating the Cassava and Fish Farm project is shown in Figures 6 – 9. Specific numbers can be seen in the appendix section or the report. See Tables 2 – 10.

Figure 6
Employment

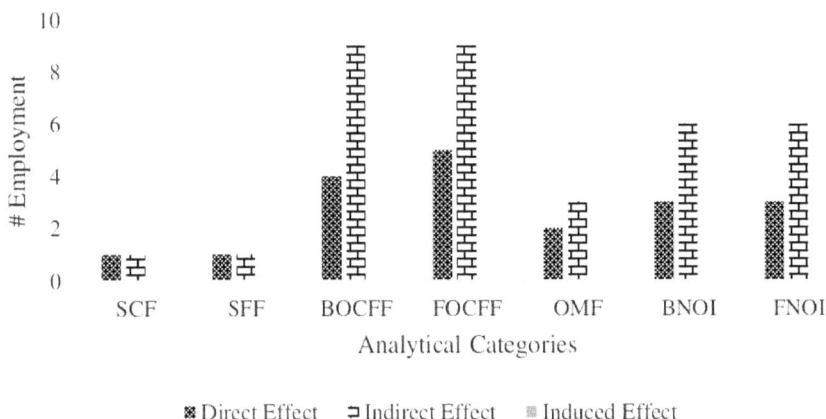

Figure 6 shows the total employment per capita of each analytical category.

Figure 7
Labor Income

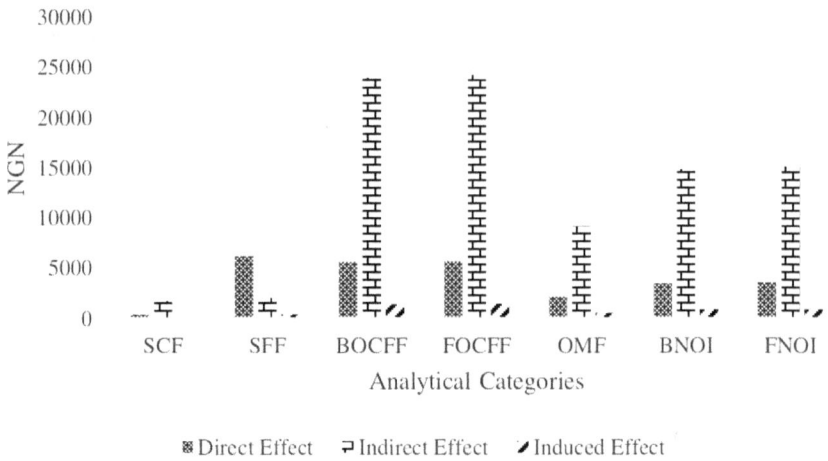

Figure 7 shows the labor income per capita of each category.

Figure 8
Total Value Added

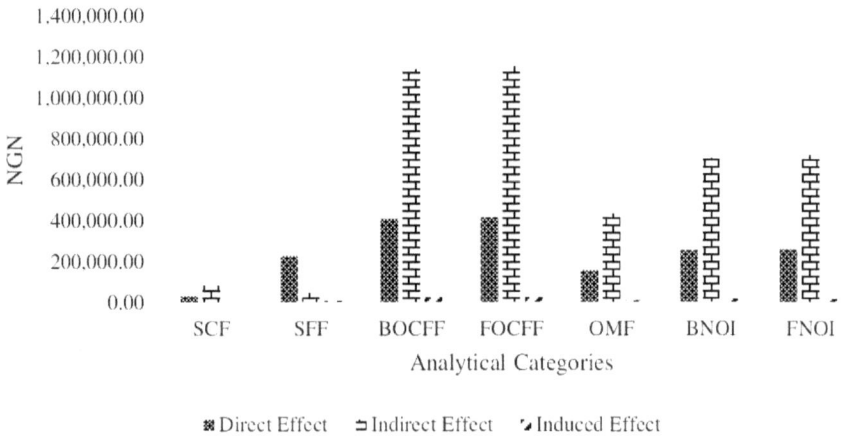

Figure 8 shows the total value added for each category.

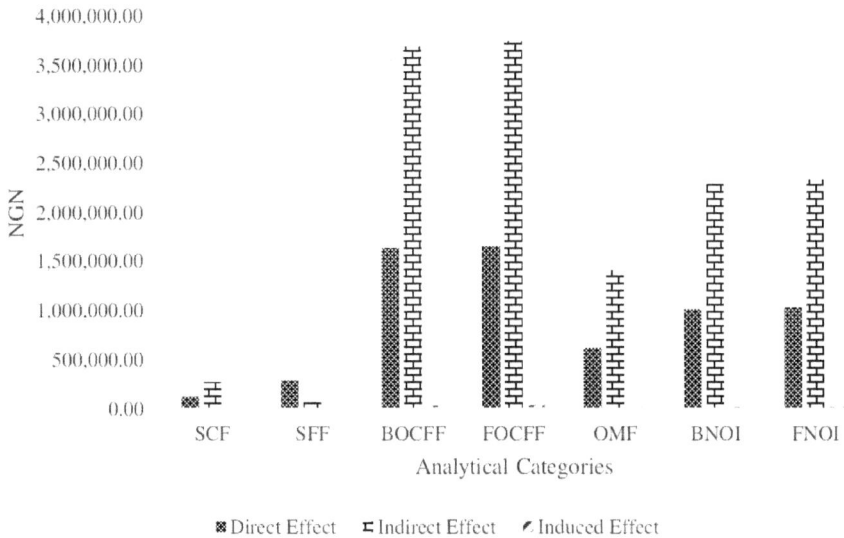

Figure 9
Output

Figure 9 shows the total value added for each category.

Discussion and Policy Implication:

Economic development considerations in studies of agricultural produce impacts typically focus on the state and local level jobs because of the low capital cost of starting a small farm in a rural community. Starting and operating a Cassava and Fish Farm can present a long-term, significant infusion of money into the local economy of Gwagwalada.

Ultimately, the level of impacts and their distribution depends on how much the local economy can directly participate in the construction, starting phases, operating phase, and project ownership. Because community farm projects are common in Gwagwalada, and they constitute about 70% of total farm capacity in FCT, the impacts are more often a function of the ability of the local societies to supply goods and services, labor force both for the construction and operations phase. Likewise, the ability of local businesses to participate in a project is a function of local economic development, developer preferences, and whether or not the industries affected by farm projects are situated in the community.

The Gwagwalada focus of this chapter provides a unique perspective on the question(s) of the economic impact of agricultural produce. Over time, various factors are likely to influence the total economic development activities captured by the nation of Nigeria as a whole as the distribution of those economic impacts within a given country. Workforce development and technical training programs may increase the number of skilled agricultural workers in Gwagwalada and specific localities where larger ongoing aggie organizations are sited. On the other hand, if such programs are not accessible to individuals living in localities where agricultural projects are sited, the development and training of skilled construction and operating workers may not boost economic growth and development at the level of the project host community.

Economic development impacts the nation, state, and a few specific localities (Gwagwalada); the labor force will grow where there is a skilled agricultural industry. Impacts on rural communities and local government may not grow and may even be reduced because other highly trained and specialized workers are available in neighboring local government areas or regions. In today's agricultural industry, workers often live in the communities where the project is sited; however, developing remote monitoring and operations capabilities could reduce the demand for local skilled labor.

Conclusion:

This chapter shows the economic impact of constructing and running the Ane Osiobe Altruism Farm at Gwagwalada, Nigeria. The project has a positive effect on Gwagwalada and the Nigerian economy. Our results were generated from the IMPLAN software, and the chapter observed the direct, indirect, and induced impact of starting and operating the Cassava and Fish Farm. Other results provided by IMPLAN include the top ten industries affected (see appendix). Based on our results, it is agreeable to say it will be in Gwagwalda's best interest if the project is carried out.

REFERENCES

Abdu-Raheem, S.O. Toluwase and K.A. "Cost and Returns Analysis of Cassava Production in Ekiti State." *Scholarly Journal of Agricultural Science*, 2013: Vol. 3 (10) pp. 454 - 457.

David W. Archer, Julie Dawson, Urs P. Kreuter, Mary Hendrickson, and John M. Halloran. "Social and Political Influences on Agriculture Systems." *Renewable Agriculture and Food System*, 2008: 23(4); 272-284.

Eninnaya, Joy C. "Economic Optimization of Agricultural Production in Abuja." 2018.

Enyinnaya, Joy and Ejiro Osiobe. "Cost-Benefit Analysis: The Ane Osiobe Altruism Farm of the Edison 3.0 Project 2017 Price Value." 2017.

Guide, IMPLAN Pro User's. *IMPLAN*. 2000.
http://www.ci.richmond.ca.us/DocumentCenter/View/6474/Appendix_E (accessed May 12, 2018).

John L. Crompton, Seokho Lee, and Thomas J. Shuster. "A Guide for Understanding Economic Impact Studies: The Springfest Example." *Journal of Travel Research*, 2001: Vol. 40, 79 – 87.

Lynch, Dr. Tim. "Analyzing the Economic Impact of Transportation Projects Using RIMS II, IMPLAN, and REMI." 2000.

Richmond. "An Overview of IMPLAN." 2018.

S.C., Aondoakaa. "Effects of Climate Change on Agricultural Productivity in the Federal Capital Territory (FCT), Abuja, Nigeria." *Ethiopian Journal of Environmental Studies and Management*, 2012: EJESM Vol.5 no.4.

APPENDIX

Table 2
Impact Summary
SCF

Impact Type	Employment	Labor Income N	Total Value-Added N	Output N
Direct Effect	0.3	404.0	29,571.3	117,640.0
Indirect Effect	0.6	1,728.8	82,145.8	266,516.0
Induced Effect	0.0	100.6	1,811.6	2,249.8
Total Effect	1.0	2,233.4	113,528.7	386,405.9

Table 3
Impact Summary
SFF

Impact Type	Employment	Labor Income N	Total Value-Added N	Output N
Direct Effect	0.4	6,191.2	227,678.7	284,073.0
Indirect Effect	0.1	2,026.7	47,739.3	60,838.6
Induced Effect	0.0	387.6	6,980.3	8,668.9
Total Effect	0.5	8,605.5	282,398.3	353,580.5

Table 4
Impact Summary
BOCFF

Impact Type	Employment	Labor Income N	Total Value-Added N	Output N
Direct Effect	4.2	5,593.9	409,470.8	1,628,947.9
Indirect Effect	8.9	23,938.8	1,137,463.4	3,690,417.6
Induced Effect	0.0	1,392.7	25,085.0	31,153.3
Total Effect	13.2	30,925.4	1,572,019.1	5,350,518.9

Table 6
Impact Summary
FOCFF

Impact Type	Employment	Labor Income N	Total Value-Added N	Output N
Direct Effect	4.3	5,665.7	414,731.2	1,649,874.9
Indirect Effect	9.0	24,246.4	1,152,076.3	3,737,828.2
Induced Effect	0.0	1,410.6	25,407.2	31,553.6
Total Effect	13.4	31,322.7	1,592,214.8	5,419,256.7

Table 7
Impact Summary
OMF

Impact Type	Employment	Labor Income N	Total Value-Added N	Output N
Direct Effect	1.6	2,129.1	155,850.2	620,000.0
Indirect Effect	3.4	9,111.4	432,934.2	1,404,623.7
Induced Effect	0.0	530.1	9,547.7	11,857.3
Total Effect	5.0	11,770.6	598,332.1	2,036,481.1

Table 7
Impact Summary
OMF

Impact Type	Employment	Labor Income ₦	Total Value-Added ₦	Output ₦
Direct Effect	1.6	2,129.1	155,850.2	620,000.0
Indirect Effect	3.4	9,111.4	432,934.2	1,404,623.7
Induced Effect	0.0	530.1	9,547.7	11,857.3
Total Effect	5.0	11,770.6	598,332.1	2,036,481.1

Table 8
Impact Summary
BNOI

Impact Type	Employment	Labor Income ₦	Total Value-Added ₦	Output ₦
Direct Effect	2.6	3,464.8	253,620.6	1,008,947.9
Indirect Effect	5.5	14,827.4	704,529.2	2,285,793.9
Induced Effect	0.0	862.6	15,537.2	19,295.9
Total Effect	8.2	19,154.8	973,687.0	3,314,037.7

Table 9
Impact Summary
FNOI

Impact Type	Employment	Labor Income ₦	Total Value-Added ₦	Output ₦
Direct Effect	2.7	3,536.6	258,881.0	1,029,874.9
Indirect Effect	5.6	15,134.9	719,142.1	2,333,204.4
Induced Effect	0.0	880.5	15,859.5	19,696.1
Total Effect	8.3	19,552.1	993,882.6	3,382,775.5

Table 10
Top Ten Industries for Employment

#	Sector	Description	Total Employment	Total Labor-Income ₦	Total Value-Added ₦	Total Output ₦
1	1	Agriculture	8.2	10,826.7	792,519.2	3,152,783.1
2	21	Financial intermediation and business services	0.0	3,062.8	112,384.9	116,627.1
3	16	Wholesale Trade	0.0	1,517.4	18,617.2	22,591.7
4	13	Electricity, gas and water	0.0	245.0	4,643.9	5,596.0
5	7	Petroleum, Chemical and Non-metal mfg.	0.0	986.5	23,770.7	28,373.6
6	6	Wood and paper	0.0	447.5	7,096.4	8,328.6
7	4	Food and beverages	0.0	353.7	10,467.9	15,654.3
8	17	Retail Trade	0.0	149.0	1,624.1	2,589.8
9	9	Electrical and machinery	0.0	215.9	2,758.7	3,537.3
10	8	Metal products	0.0	185.8	2,170.2	2,650.1

Table 11
Comparison of First and Second Iteration:

	First Iteration	Second Iteration
Total Gross Profit	₦ 1,649,874.92	₦ 1,667,893.73
Additional Cost	₦ 11,250	₦ 37,369.82
The difference from Base Iteration	₦ 20,926.99	₦ 38,945.82
Actual Benefit	₦ 9,676.99	₦ 1,575.98
Percentage Increase of Benefit compared to Base Iteration	↑ 46%	↑ 4%

Table 12	
Break-Down Structure of Ane Osiobe Altruism Farm:	
Base Iteration	
Total Land Size	4 Hectares
{Office Space}	{0.9} Hectares
[Cassava]	[1.9] Hectares
(Fish)	(1.2) Hectares
Total Labor Hours	100 Hours
Total Cost	₦ 1, 462, 630.18
(Per-Hour)	₦ 500
First Iteration	
Total Land Size	5.11 Hectares
{Office Space}	{0.9} Hectares
[Cassava]	[2.14] Hectares
(Fish)	(1.8) Hectares
"Cost Per – 0.5 Hectare"	"₦ 1, 250"
Total Labor Hours	100 Hours
Total Cost	₦ 1, 462, 630.18
(Per-Hour)	₦ 500
Second Iteration	
Total Land Size	4 Hectares
{Office Space}	{0.9} Hectares
[Cassava]	[1.9] Hectares
(Fish)	(1.2) Hectares
Total Labor Hours	120 Hours
Total Cost	₦ 1, 500, 000.00
(Per-Hour)	₦ 500

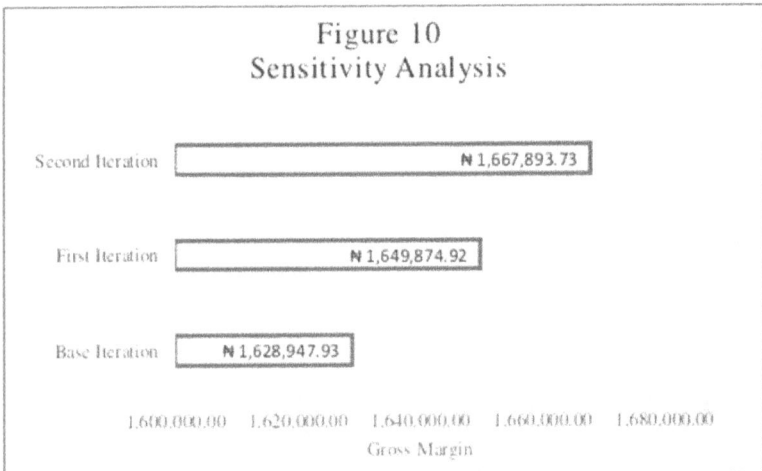

Figure 10
Sensitivity Analysis

Second Iteration: ₦ 1,667,893.73

First Iteration: ₦ 1,649,874.92

Base Iteration: ₦ 1,628,947.93

1,600,000.00   1,620,000.00   1,640,000.00   1,660,000.00   1,680,000.00
Gross Margin

COST AND RETURN ESTIMATES OF CASSAVA, GROUNDNUT, MAIZE, AND FISH PRODUCTION

Introduction

The cost and return estimate was made for cassava, groundnut, maize, and fish production in Abuja, Federal Capital Territory (FCT), Nigeria. The chapter of the climate in the FCT and our interaction with producers in the area guided our recommendation for all four enterprises. The data was generated from existing budgets in different states of the country. To forecast each enterprise's expected cost and returns, we used the results from the selected budgets and adjusted the price to 2017. We did this by using the average of 12 months' inflation rates between June 2016 – May 2017 and the last available month of 2017, May 2017. The result shows that all four enterprises are very likely to be profitable. The total cost needed to generate from the sum of the total cost per enterprise was estimated to be ₦

295,569.39. The total revenue was projected to be ₦ 551,374.69, leaving the farm with a gross profit of about ₦ 255 805.30 per cycle.

This Chapter will analyze the cost, benefit, and profitability of cassava, groundnut, maize, and fish production on the Ane Osiobe Altruism Farm, Gwagwalada, Abuja, FCT. The Federal Capital Territory is one of the fastest growing areas in Nigeria due to its political status as the nation's capital city and geographical location. As a result, this has led to a large and steady influx of people from all over the country (Aondoakaa et al. 2012). This would explain the increase in settlements and, consequently, the shortage in food production. Based on this need, the Edison 3.0 project seeks to bridge the gap between the students at the special needs school Jabi and the food production in the area by engaging them and locals in agricultural practices. The goal is to produce healthy, nutritious food for their consumption and raise some money from selling their produce to meet their numerous needs.

METHODOLOGY

Study Area

According to the Abuja master plan (2000), the chapter area, Federal Capital Territory (FCT), lies between latitude 8° 25' and 9° 25' North of the equator and longitude 6° 45' and 7° 45' East of the Greenwich meridian. It is located in the middle belt of Nigeria. Its size is equivalent to 0.8% of Nigeria. It is bordered by four states: Kaduna in the North, Nassarawa in the West, Kogi in the South and Niger in the East. It covers a land mass of 8,000 square kilometers (Km2). The FCT is predominantly underlain by Precambrian magmatites, gneisses, quartz, geamites, and schist of crystalline basement complex rocks, and the terrain is generally undulating, which controls the weather condition of the city. It has an extrusive schist belt occurring along the south-western margin of Gwagwalada—the high-grade metamorphic and igneous rocks formed in the Precambrian age. The older granites produce the rugged terrain. The Usuma River, Gurara, and other smaller tributaries drain the city.

Recommended Agricultural Enterprises

Four enterprises were recommended for production on the Ane Osiobe Altruism farm. They include cassava, maize, groundnut, and fish enterprises. Two factors guided our recommendation. First is the climate study in the FCT area. The location of FCT in the middle belt region of Nigeria rids it of the extreme characteristics of North and Southern Nigeria climates. The Federal Capital Territory experiences two major seasons: rainy and dry (Balogun, 2001). Change in temperature of as much as 17°C has been recorded between the highest and lowest temperature in a single day. The maximum temperature is lower during the rainy season due to dense cloud cover. The diurnal annual range is also much lower, sometimes not more than 7°C in July and August. Its temperature ranges from 30.4°C and 35.1°C. During the dry season, relative humidity falls in the afternoons (Abuja master plan, 2000). The terrain's undulating nature also affects the FCT's temperature patterns. The rainy season usually begins in March and ends in the middle of October in the North and early November in the South. Mean annual rainfall is about 1400mm (Abuja master plan, 2000), resulting from its location on the windward side of the Jos Plateau, leading to frequent rainfall and a noticeable increase in the mean annual total from the South to the North. The season's beginning and end are characterized by frequent wind storms accompanied by thunderstorms and lightning, followed by strong wind and high-intensity rainfall, which may last for just 30 minutes and then be replaced by drizzles for hours. This condition is replaced by a few days of bright, clear skies (Abuja master plan, 2000).

The second factor that guided our recommendation was our interaction with agricultural producers in the area. Cassava, maize, groundnut, and fish thrived in the FCT and were in high demand in the area.

COST AND RETURN ESTIMATES

To forecast the expected cost and returns of each enterprise, we used results from previous studies and adjusted the price to 2017. We did this by using the average of 12 months' inflation rates, June 2016 – May 2017, and the last available month of 2017, May 2017. According to Trading Economics, 2017, Nigeria's consumer prices increased 16.25% year-on-year in May of 2017, easing from a 17.24% rise in the previous month. The inflation rate fell for the fourth month to the lowest in 11 months, led by a general price slowdown.

Table 1: Price adjustment index

Months/Year	Inflation Rate (%)	Inflation Change (%)
Jun-16	16.5	
Jul-16	17.1	3.64%
Aug-16	17.6	2.92%
Sep-16	17.9	1.70%
Oct-16	18.3	2.23%
Nov-16	18.5	1.09%
Dec-16	18.55	0.27%
Jan-17	18.7	0.81%
Feb-17	17.78	-4.92%
Mar-17	17.26	-2.92%
Apr-17	17.24	-0.12%
May-17	16.25	-5.74%
Sum	**211.68**	
Average	**17.64**	

Cassava production:

Cassava (Manihot esculenta) is a perennial shrub from the family Euphorbiaceae. It is commonly grown in the tropics for its starchy tuberous root, mainly consumed by humans and fed to animals. Cassava is one of Nigeria's major staple food crops and, as such, a major source of income for rural food crop farmers in Gwagwalada, FCT. Cassava has a fair resistance against many pests and diseases, thus making it an important food crop to enhance food security. Cassava value-added products such as garri and fufu are easy to prepare and more filling because they take longer to digest than other food. Cassava can also be used as an industrial raw material to produce alcohol, gums, pharmaceuticals, and confectionaries. Presently, Nigeria is the world's largest cassava producer, with an annual production of 38.6 million tons. This was because of the development of high-yielding cultivars and improved production technologies. (Toluwase S.O et al 2013).

Table 2: Cassava production budget for one hectare

Item	Unit	Quantity	Prize per unit(₦)	Cost value for 2010(₦)	2017 Avg Price(₦)	2017 Price(₦)
Gross revenue yield	Tons	40.00	2,500.00	100,000.00	117,640.00	116,250.00
Variable cost Stem cutting	Bundles	2.50	500.00	1,250.00	1,470.50	1,453.13
Fertilizer	Kg	3.00	2,000.00	6,000.00	7,058.40	6,975.00
Labour	Man/day	40.00	500.00	20,000.00	23,528.00	23,250.00
Interest on variable cost				27,250.00	32,056.90	31,678.13
cost of 150% for 6 months				4,087.50	4,808.54	4,751.72
Total variable cost				31,337.50	36,865.44	36,429.84
margin				68,662.50	80,774.57	79,820.16
Benefits-cost ratio				2.19	2.58	2.55

Source: Costs and returns analysis of cassava production in Ekiti State, Nigeria, 2013.

The result of a cost and return estimate of the cassava production in the chapter area shows that the total revenue for 2017 (using real prices) is projected to be ₦116,250.00k per cycle. In contrast, the total cost is estimated to be ₦36,429.84k per cycle. This implies that cassava production is very likely to be profitable. The rate of Return on Investment is projected at 2.55. This means that for every ₦1 invested, there should be a return of ₦255.00k.

Groundnut production

Groundnut (Arachis hypogaea L.) seeds contain high-quality edible oil (50%), easily digestible protein (25%), and carbohydrates (20%). According to the Food and Agriculture Organization, It is grown on 26.4 million ha worldwide with a total production of 36.1 million metric tons and an average productivity of 1.4 metric tons/ha (FAO 2009). Groundnuts are an essential component of the Nigerian diet because groundnuts contribute to about 58.9g of crude protein available per head per day. The value-added products from groundnuts include Kuli-Kuli, which is a snack made from deep-frying or drying groundnuts. The haulms from groundnuts are also beneficial as they can be used for livestock feed. Groundnuts are grown in nearly 100 countries, with China, India, Nigeria, the U.S.A, Indonesia, and Sudanbeings significant producers. Developing countries accounted for 96 percent of the global groundnut area and 92 percent of the worldwide production. This implies that groundnuts are not just a local crop but are ideal for international trade (A. A. Girei et al., 2013).

54

Table 3: Groundnut production budget for one hectare

Variables	Value (₦)	2017 Avg Price	2017 Price
Variable cost	59,480.00	69,972.27	69,145.50
Fixed cost	2,360.00	2,776.30	2,743.50
Total cost of production	61,840.00	72,748.58	71,889.00
Total output Price/kg	95.00	111.76	110.44
Total revenue	90,843.75	106,868.59	105,605.86
Gross margin (TR-TVC)	31,363.75	36,896.32	36,460.36
NFI (GM-TFC)	29,003.75	34,120.01	33,716.86
Return to naira	0.47	0.55	0.55

Source: An economic analysis of groundnut (Arachis hypogea) in Hong Local Government Area of Adamawa State, Nigeria, 2013.

The result of a cost and return estimate of the groundnut production in the chapter area shows that the total revenue 2017 (using accurate prices) is projected to be ₦105,605.86k per cycle. In contrast, the total cost is estimated to be ₦71,889.00k per cycle. This implies that groundnut production is also likely to be profitable. The rate of Return on Investment is projected at 0.55. This means that for every ₦1 invested, there should be a return of ₦55.00k.

Maize production

Maize (Zea mays) is a significant food source in Nigeria, and its production is rising. This is because maize is a staple for an estimated 50% of the population. It is a vital source of carbohydrates, protein, iron, vitamin B, and minerals. Maize is the main ingredient in several well-known national dishes. Examples are tuwon, masara and akamu in northern Nigeria. Maize is also used as animal feed and raw material for brewing beer and starch production (IITA 2008). In developed countries, maize produces high-fructose corn syrup, a liquid sweetener alternative to sucrose (table sugar), and ethanol used in gasoline production. The profitability potential for maize is projected to increase in Nigeria for several reasons, including the development of hybrid varieties, the emergence of maize as a significant substitute industrial material, enhanced adoption of maize growing technologies through extension services, and the relative ease of transporting and storing maize grains (Zalkuwi J. et al., 2014).

Table 4: Maize production budget for one hectare

Production Variables	Value (₦)	2017 Avg Price	2017 Price
Hired Labour	11,154.67	13,122.35	12,967.30
Family Labour	5,089.72	5,987.55	5,916.80
Seed	2,075.25	2,441.32	2,412.48
Fertilizer	3,472.89	4,085.51	4,037.23
Herbicide	2,375.91	2,795.02	2,762.00
Pesticide	857.98	1,009.33	997.4
Ploughing	4,664.15	5,486.91	5,422.07
Transportation	1,880.64	2,212.38	2,186.24
Storage	127.59	150.1	148.32
Total Variable Cost	**31,698.80**	**37,290.47**	**36,849.86**
Returns		-	-
Average output of Maize (kg)/ha	1,148.46	1,351.05	1,335.08
Average price of Maize (N/kg)	53.73	63.21	62.46
Total Revenue	**39,092.76**	**45,988.72**	**45,445.33**
Gross Marigin (TR-TVC)	7,393.96	8,698.25	8,595.48
Gross Ratio (GR)	0.813	0.9564132	0.9451125
Operating Ratio	0.815	0.958766	0.9474375

Source: Analysis of Cost and Return of Maize Production in Numan Local Government Area of Adamawa State, Nigeria, 2013.

The result of a cost and return estimate of the maize farming in the chapter area shows that the total revenue for 2017 (using actual prices) is projected to be ₦45,445.33k per cycle, whereas the total cost should be ₦36,849.86k per cycle. This implies that maize production is also likely to be profitable. The rate of Return on Investment is projected at 0.947. This means that for every ₦1 invested, there should be a return of ₦95.00k.

Fish production

Fish makes up a high percentage of the world's total supply of animal protein. In Nigeria, fish production has helped significantly reduce the epidemic of anemia, kwashiorkor, and other ailments resulting from protein deficiency. This is because fish allows for protein-improved nutrition due to its biological value, which leads to high protein retention. Factors such as

Table 5: Fish production budget for one hectare

Item	Value (₦)	2017 Avg Price	2017 Price
Total Revenue	244,364.30	287,470.16	284,073.50
Fixed Cost	-	-	
Land	26,656.25	31,358.41	30,987.89
Drag Net	1,740.08	2,047.03	2,022.84
Water Pump	2,147.86	2,526.74	2,496.89
Weighing Scale	1,576.42	1,854.50	1,832.59
Knives/Cutlasses	638.89	751.59	742.71
Other Fixed Input	7,014.29	8,251.61	8,154.11
Total Fixed Cost (TFC)	**39,773.79**	**46,789.89**	**46,237.03**
Variable Cost	-	-	
Labor	19,335.02	22,745.72	22,476.96
Fingerlings (Catfish)	32,503.40	38,237.00	37,785.20
Fingerlings (Tilapia)	1,144.34	1,346.20	1,330.30
Poultry Dung (kg)	9,905.71	11,653.08	11,515.39
Maggot (kg)	1,050.11	1,235.35	1,220.75
Concentration Diet (kg)	10,445.95	12,288.62	12,143.42
Other Feeds (kg)	2,801.11	3,295.23	3,256.29
Limes	12,420.09	14,610.99	14,438.35
Total Variable Cost (TVC)	**89,605.73**	**105,412.18**	**104,166.66**
Total Cost	**129,379.52**	**152,202.07**	**150,403.69**
Net Profit	**114,984.78**	**135,268.10**	**133,669.81**
Benefit-Cost Ratio (BCR)	1.9	2.24	2.21
Return on investment (ROI)	0.889	1.05	1.03

Source: Economic Analysis of Costs and Return of Fish Farming in Saki-East Local Government Area of Oyo State, Nigeria, 2015.

drought, virus diseases, and the high cost of animal feed have made livestock production fall short of meeting the protein needs of the increasing population. Several economic importance of fish production includes improvement in nutrition, job creation, agro-industrial development, foreign exchange/trade, and overall development of rural areas (S.O Toulwase et al., 2013).

The result of a cost and return estimate of fish production in the chapter area showed that the total revenue for 2017 (using actual prices) is projected to be ₦284,073.50 per cycle. In contrast, the total cost is estimated to be ₦150,403.69k per cycle. This implies that fish farming is also very likely to be profitable. The rate of Return on Investment is projected at 1.03. This means that for every ₦1 invested, there will be a return of ₦103.00k.

CONCLUSION

The results of all four enterprise budgets show they are likely to be profitable. The total cost needed, generated from the sum of the total cost per enterprise, is estimated to be ₦295,569.39. From our results, the total revenue is projected to be ₦551,374.69, leaving the farm with a gross profit of about ₦255,805.30 per cycle.

REFERENCES

A. A. Girei et al (2013) An economic analysis of groundnut (Arachis hypogea) production in Hong Local Government Area of Adamawa State, Nigeria

Adeniyi B. T, Kuton M. P, Ayegbokiki A. O and Lawal H. O (2015) Economic Analysis of Costs and Return of Fish Farming in Saki-East Local Government Area of Oyo State, Nigeria, 2015

An Assessment of Land Suitability for Rice Cultivation in Dobi, Gwagwalada Area Council, FCT

Balogun, O. (2001), The Federal Capital of Nigeria. A geography of its development. University of Ibadan Press Ltd.

IITA (2008). Increasing maize production in West Africa.
http://www.iita.org/cms/details/newssummary.aspx

Master plan for Abuja the New Federal Capital of igeria (2000), Canadian International development agency

S. O. Toluwase and K. A. Abdu-raheem (2013) Costs and returns analysis of cassava production in Ekiti State, Nigeria Ekiti State University, Ado – Ekiti, Nigeria

Zalkuwi J., Ibrahim A. and Kwakanapwa E. (2014) Analysis of Cost and Return of Maize Production in Numan Local Government Area of Adamawa State, Nigeria

THE ECONOMIC IMPACT OF LOCAL NON-GOVERNMENTAL DIRECT INVESTMENT(S)

INTRODUCTION

This chapter uses IMPLAN to estimate the economic impact of Non-Governmental Direct Investment (NDI) from Non-Governmental Organizations' (NGO) activities in central Nigeria. The estimation of NDI project-specific impact(s) would be carried out at the local level in the city of Lugbe, Federal Capital Territory (FCT); that is, the effect (s) of Ane Osiobe International Foundation's business activities and outreach donations on the Nigerian economy. The main economic policy question addressed in this chapter is how NDI affects the Lugbe community and the local government areas where NGOs operate. Results presented in this chapter include economic development impacts such as job creation, salaries, and benefits and their effect(s) on the whole economy. The total economic activity of

Lugbe FCT is approximately ₦13,302,418.65k as the net impact from NDI (2015 – 2018). Our observation covers the foundation's activities in Lugbe, FCT. Increasing the foundation's economic Impact(s) can be optimized by effectively utilizing public and private resources, training industry-specific labor, and linking the goal(s) of the NGO, the government, and the beneficiaries together to achieve a synchronized objective in Lugbe, FCT. The community appears well positioned and equipped to see the increasing incidence(s) from the Ane Osiobe International Foundation's outreaches.

NDI human and financial capital have been a crucial catalyst for fostering economic growth and development in countries that experience economic growth and development gap(s) and lag(s). In Nigeria, NDIs managed by NGOs undertake projects that support services that, directly and indirectly, affect the lives of people in a local community, such as, but not limited to, campaigns and policy advocacy in the healthcare, education, human rights, and agricultural industries. Between 2014 – 2017, the Nigerian economy experienced a sharp decline in GDP per capita, ranging from 17 percent to 18 percent percentage decline (see Figure 1-A; shows the GDP per capita in (2018 current USD ($)) while Figure 1-B shows the percentage change in GDP per capita). As a result, the interest in community development and poverty alleviation has grown substantially in Nigeria. According to Yusuf, I.D. et al. (2017), It could be inferred that the most significant achievement towards poverty alleviation in small communities has been supported by NGOs directly or indirectly.

Figure 1-A displays the absolute monetary value of GDP per capita change from 1960 – 2017 (2018 current USD ($)), while Figure 1-B shows the percentage change of Figure 1-A, which exhibits an oscillation pattern contrary to that of a stable, growing economy. Figure 1-A and 1-B have a positive relationship; hence, as Figure 1-A increases, Figure 1-B shows a positive change in economic growth, and as Figure 1-A decreases, Figure 1-B shows an adverse shift in economic development.

Figure 1-A: Nigeria's GDP Per Capita Income (2018 current USD ($)) (1960 – 2017)

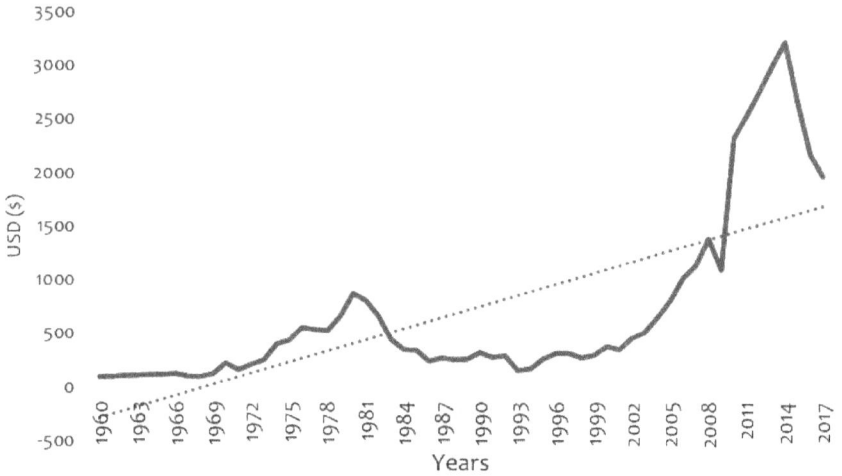

Figure 1-B

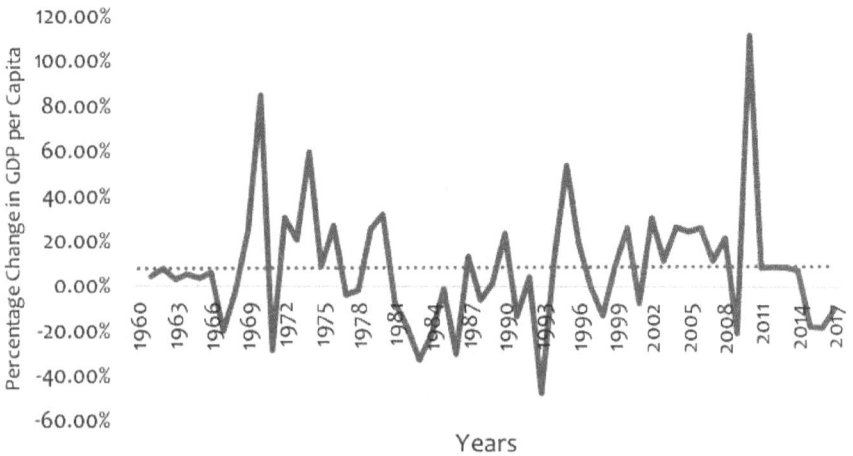

Source: World Bank national accounts data and OECD National Accounts date files

Since the 80s, local and international NGOs, economists, sociologists, and political scientists have routinely discussed the impact of NDIs by working together to ensure the effective and efficient use of NDI to promote progressive change. The chapter analyzed Ane Osiobe International Foundation NDI impact on the Nigerian economy from 2015 to 2018.

Endowed with abundant natural capital, Nigeria seems plagued with the Dutch disease. It is ranked among the poorest countries when comparing GDP per capita with the rest of the world (see Table 1), consumption standard, provision of basic human – rights needs, shelter, and overall economic performance. NDIs have attracted the attention of economists, sociologists, political scientists (academics and practitioners), and policymakers worldwide. NGOs in Nigeria focus on a spectrum of poverty alleviation strategies to promote rural and community development specific to their targeted area(s)1. This phenomenon has led to the search for sustainable economic growth and development practices to boost community development and alleviate poverty.

Table 1: Top Ten Countries with the highest GDP per capita (2017)
(2018 current USD ($))

Ranking	Country Name	GDP per capita (current USD ($))
1	Luxembourg	$ 104,103.04
2	Macao SAR, China	$ 80,892.82
3	Switzerland	$ 80,189.70
4	Norway	$ 75,504.57
5	Iceland	$ 70,056.87
6	Ireland	$ 69,330.69
7	Qatar	$ 63,505.81
8	United States	$ 59,531.66
9	North America	$ 58,070.07
10	Singapore	$ 57,714.30
174	Nigeria	$ 1,968.56
	World Average	$ 13,265.17

Source: World Bank national accounts data and OECD National Accounts data files

63

The chapter aims to estimate the direct, indirect and induced NDI from Ane Osiobe International Foundation on the Nigerian economy from 2015 to 2018. This chapter uses the IMPLAN model to assess the economic impact of NDIs in Lugbe, FCT. The primary economic policy question addressed in this chapter is how NDI affects the community of Lugbe, FCT, and the local government jurisdiction where NGOs operate. Results presented in this chapter include economic development impacts such as job creation, salaries, benefits, and the top ten industries that benefited from the NGOs' NDIs and their effect(s) on the whole economy.

Location

Lugbe is a small suburban community located along the airport road and divided into five districts: Lugbe South, Lugbe North, Lugbe Central, Lugbe West, and Lugbe East. The latitude of Abuja, Nigeria, is 9.072264, and the longitude is 7.491302. Meanwhile, the town of Lugbe, FCT, has a longitude and latitude of 8.9868° N and 7.3626° E. Other settlements close to Luge are Chika, Kuchigworo, Pyakassa, Dei-Dei, Mpape, Karimu, and Gwagwa; FCT shares boundaries with Kaduna, Source: created by Aaron Adams3 using the GIS 10.6.1 software and Google maps Nassarawa, Kogi, and Niger, while Nigeria shares its border with Chad, Niger, Benin, and Cameroon.

Figure 2

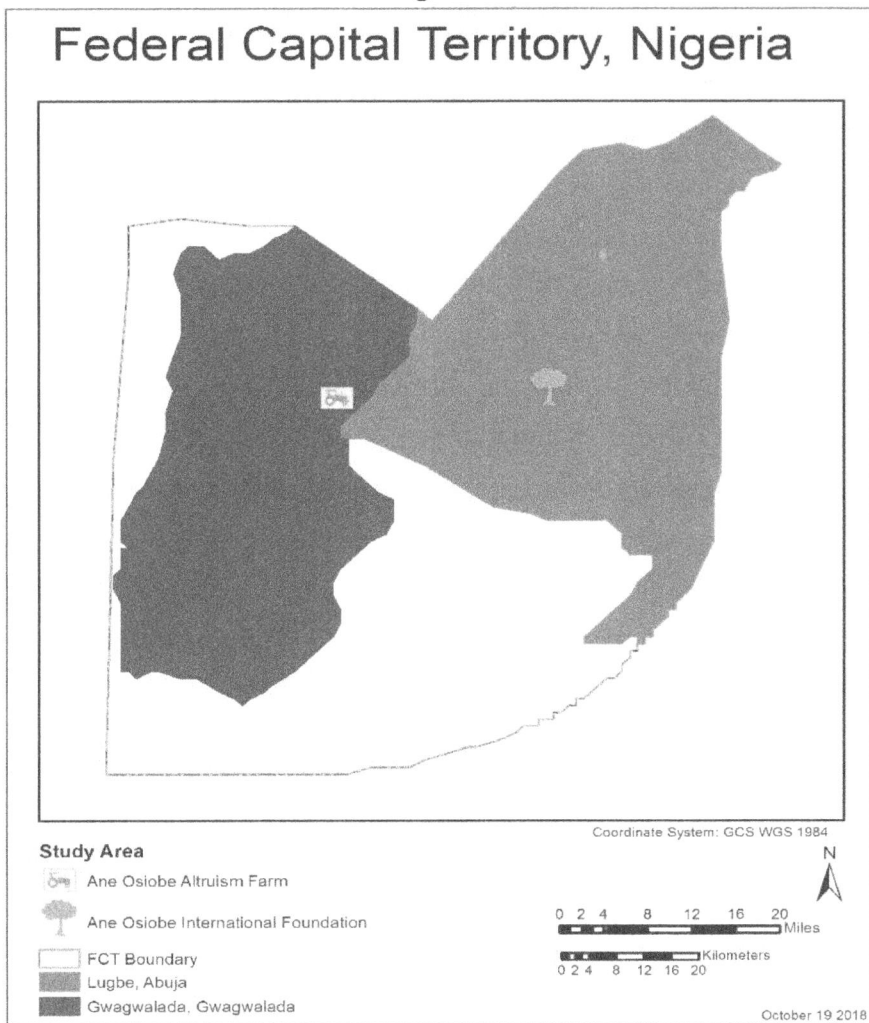

Federal Capital Territory, Nigeria

Coordinate System: GCS WGS 1984

Study Area

Ane Osiobe Altruism Farm

Ane Osiobe International Foundation

FCT Boundary

Lugbe, Abuja

Gwagwalada, Gwagwalada

N

0 2 4   8   12   16   20
Miles

Kilometers
0 2 4   8   12   16   20

October 19 2018

Source: created by Aaron Adams3 using the GIS 10.6.1 software and Google maps

REVIEWS

Community development dates to the discovery of stone and the knowledge to create and control fire. Economic development improves the welfare state of affairs in the community. Udensi et al. (2012) explored how community leaders contribute towards community development by managing incentive projects that benefit its stakeholders in the Bola Local government area, Cross River State, Nigeria. The authors analyzed 150 community leaders using a qualitative questionnaire multi-stage sampling methodology. They discovered that leadership position was not an exclusive preserve of sex, age group, marital status, or educational status. Udensi et al. (2012) showed that residential community leaders are a significant factor in the community's success. The Crompton (2001) paper offered a conceptual rationale for undertaking an impact study, regardless of the software one uses: IMPLAN, JEDI, RIMS II, REMI, or a Dynamic System Model(DSM). The author provided a generalized model for understanding how to write, analyze, and interpret an economic impact study. Crompton's paper also presented four principles to guide our research process and how to explain the input-output result(s) carefully. Osiobe, E. (2018) offered more insight into the direct, indirect, and induced effects and how impact studies could be used by NGOs in Africa when carrying out outreaches, projects, and research. The chapter showed the extent of its multiplier effect. The assertion that the government alone can provide the facilities and services to its citizens blurs the net impacts of NGOs' direct investment in poverty alleviation and community development.

WHY IMPACT ANALYSIS IS IMPORTANT

Academics, researchers, and policymakers have placed a significant amount of attention on fiscal and economic policies at all levels of the government; however, local communities have faced various economic challenges over the past few decades, varying from the great depression of the 1930s, the Asian financial crisis of 1997, to the great recession of 2007. NGOs provide local support in their regions, although the governing administration has overlooked the scaling of their NDIs effect(s). These operations/outreach led to new jobs, forward and backward linkages, and alternative opportunities for locals. NDIs' overall impact(s) in any community depends on the ability of a community to exploit its built, political, and human capital in a manner that puts the needs and welfare of locals as its primary objective. Tracing the net-impact(s) of NDIs is essential to understanding the value of local NGOs in any community where they operate. The information from this impact study would provide some insights into our study's primary query.

METHODOLOGY

The author used the IMPLAN software to estimate the direct, indirect, and induced economic impact(s) of NDIs in Lugbe, FCT. The appropriateness of this model for this chapter was justified as IMPLAN is the only Input-Output data company that has the aggregate labor force data for Nigeria (Osiobe, 2018).

DATA

The chapter used publicly available data from the foundations' audited financial reports from 2015 – 2018.

Table 2: NDI and Donations Report (2018 current NGN (₦))
(2015 – 2018)

Year	Balance Sheet Report (₦)	Donations Report (₦)
2015	₦ 791,350.00k	₦ 0.00k
2016	₦ 2,029,300.00k	₦ 250,000.00k
2017	₦ 2,430,603.00k	₦ 650,000.00k
2018	₦ 4,410,327.00k	₦ 914,000.00k

RESULTS

The economic impact statement shows full-time job(s) equivalent, earnings, total value added, and overall output of the NDI. Table 3 shows the impact summary of NDI in Lugbe, FCT, from 2015 – 2018. The highlighted soft-grey color shows the total economic effect of the NDI in a year. Column 3 – row 20 shows the aggregate amount of new jobs created directly associated with the foundation's NDI. for every ₦11,784,893.61k invested in the community, 2.63 full-time new jobs are created; the total value-added is ₦10,443,456.98k; and labor income ₦1,068,174.55k excluding outreach donations. If outreach donations are analyzed, a total of 3.65 full-time new jobs would be created in the economy for every ₦13,302,418.65k investment into the community. The sum effect of NDIs and outreach activities in the city would translate to ₦11,673,523.99k total value-added and ₦1,097,054.31k as labor income. Table 4 shows the top ten industry gainers associated with the foundation's NDI. Our findings show education, health, and other services; financial intermediation and business services; and others as the top three sequentially, with a total of 2.8 new jobs created in the Lugbe FCT community.

DISCUSSION AND POLICY IMPLICATION

As a branch of Economic Development, NDI is a unique source of capital injection into any economy. NGOs generate these investments through different means, including, but not limited to, friends, family, and fundraising. Ultimately, the impact NDIs can bring to a community depends on the effectiveness, painstakingness, and tenacity of the NGO managing its

Table 3: NDI Impact Summary (2015 – 2018)

Year	Impact Type	Employment	Labor Income	Total Value-Added	Output
	Direct Effect	0.12	₦ 80,592.30k	₦ 707,858.65k	₦ 791,350.00k
2015	Indirect Effect	0.04	₦ 2,958.36k	₦ 76,564.77k	₦ 85,778.43k
	Induced Effect	0.05	₦ 3,940.20k	₦ 70,967.70k	₦ 88,135.59k
	Total Effect	**0.22**	**₦ 87,490.86k**	**₦ 855,391.11k**	**₦ 965,264.02k**
	Direct Effect	0.31	₦ 206,667.03k	₦ 1,815,198.78k	₦ 2,029,300.01k
2016	Indirect Effect	0.11	₦ 7,586.27k	₦ 196,339.02k	₦ 219,966.09k
	Induced Effect	0.14	₦ 10,104.06k	₦ 181,986.16k	₦ 226,010.68k
	Total Effect	**0.55**	**₦ 224,357.36k**	**₦2,193,523.96k**	**₦ 2,475,276.78k**
	Direct Effect	0.37	₦ 247,536.34	₦ 2,174,162.32k	₦ 2,430,603.01k
2017	Indirect Effect	0.13	₦ 9,086.49k	₦ 235,165.93k	₦ 263,465.35k
	Induced Effect	0.16	₦ 12,102.19k	₦ 217,974.73k	₦ 270,705.28k
	Total Effect	**0.66**	**₦ 268,725.02k**	**₦ 2,627,302.97k**	**₦ 2,964,773.65k**
	Direct Effect	0.66	₦ 449,154.48k	₦ 3,945,015.62k	₦ 4,410,327.02k
2018	Indirect Effect	0.24	₦ 16,487.43k	₦ 426,708.36k	₦ 478,057.65k
	Induced Effect	0.30	₦ 21,959.40k	₦ 395,514.95k	₦ 491,194.50k
	Total Effect	**1.20**	**₦ 487,601.31k**	**4,767,238.93k**	**₦ 5,379,579.16k**
Aggregate Impact Excluding Donations (2015 - 2018)	Direct Effect	1.45	₦ 983,950.15k	₦ 8,642,235.37k	₦ 9,661,580.05k
	Indirect Effect	0.52	₦ 36,118.55k	₦ 934,778.08k	₦ 1,047,267.52k
	Induced Effect	0.65	₦ 48,105.85k	₦ 866,443.54k	₦ 1,076,046.04k
	Total Effect	**2.63**	**₦ 1,068,174.55k**	**₦ 10,443,456.98k**	**₦ 11,784,893.61k**
Aggregate Impact (2015 - 2018)	Direct Effect	2.35	₦ 1,001,933.89k	₦ 9,613,416.93k	₦ 10,890,580.06k
	Indirect Effect	0.63	₦ 45,713.96k	₦ 1,170,237.97k	₦ 1,306,700.08k
	Induced Effect	0.67	₦ 49,406.46k	₦ 889,869.10k	₦ 1,105,138.51k
	Total Effect	**3.65**	**₦ 1,097,054.31k**	**₦ 11,673,523.99k**	**₦ 13,302,418.65k**

Author's calculation using the IMPLAN model software

resources. This chapter provides a unique perspective on the economic impact of NDIs in Nigeria. Over time, various factors are likely to influence the total economic development activities captured by NDIs in Nigeria as globalization and innovation continue to increase exponentially. Improved regulatory policies, workforce development, and technological advancements would significantly shape the nation.

CONCLUSION

The chapter shows the economic impact of NDI coming from Ane Osiobe International Foundation from 2015 – 2018 in Lugbe, Abuja, FCT. The human and financial investment made by the foundation has a positive social impact on the Lugbe community and the Nigerian economy.

Table 4:
Top Ten Industry Gainers from NDIs and NGOs Donations (2015 – 2018)

Table 4
Top Ten Industry Gainers from NDIs and NGOs Donations (2015 – 2018)

IMPLAN's Industry Sector Code	Description	Total Employment	Total Labor Income	Ranking #	Total Value-Added	Ranking #	Total Output	Ranking #
23	Education, Health and other services	1.50	₦997,424.50k	1	₦8,760,583.80k	1	₦9,793,887.50k	1
25	Others	0.90	₦18,091.80k	3	₦977,015.60k	3	₦1,236,382.80k	3
21	Financial intermediation and business services	0.40	₦33,271.10k	2	₦1,220,833.70k	2	₦1,266,916.10k	2
13	Electricity, gas and water	0.20	₦2,319.20k	9	₦43,968.20k	8	₦52,981.90k	10
1	Agriculture	0.20	₦331.40k	10	₦24,259.50k	10	₦96,508.60k	7
16	Wholesale Trade	0.10	₦7,350.80k	4	₦90,189.80k	6	₦109,444.10k	6
17	Retail Trade	0.10	₦5,466.90k	6	₦59,591.20k	7	₦95,023.80k	8
20	Post and telecommunications	-	₦6,171.70k	5	₦113,983.10k	4	₦131,854.50k	4
7	Petroleum, Chemical and Non-metal mfg.	-	₦3,836.60k	7	₦92,443.50k	5	₦110,344.10k	5
9	Electrical and machinery	-	₦3,435.90k	8	₦43,903.80k	9	₦56,294.90k	9

Author's calculation using the IMPLAN model software

Author's calculation using the IMPLAN model software

The results observed the direct, indirect, and induced effects of Ane Osiobe International Foundations NDI. Other results provided by IMPLAN include the top ten industries affected by NDI and NGO donations (see Table 4). Based on our findings, it is agreeable to say it will be in the best interest of policymakers to create an environment that encourages, attracts, and retains NDI from international and local NGOs.

REFERENCE

Guide, IMPLAN Pro Users. IMPLAN. 2000.
http://www.ci.richmond.ca.us/DocumentCenter/View/6474/Appendix_E (accessed May 12, 2018).

John L. Crompton, Seokho Lee, and Thomas J. Shuster. "A Guide for Understanding Economic Impact Studies: The Springfest Example." *Journal of Travel Research*, 2001: Vol. 40, 79 – 87.

Oke, J.T.O and R. Adeyemo. *Impact of Non-governmental Organizations (NGOs) on Rural Poverty Alleviation in Southwestern Nigeria.* International Journal of Applied Agricultural and Apicultural Research, 2007.

Osiobe, E. U. *The National Economic Impact from Agriculture.* May 2018.

Richmond. "An Overview of IMPLAN." 2018.

Udensi, L.O., Udoh, O.S., Daasi, G.L.K and Igbara, F.N. *Community Leadership and the Challenges of Community Development in Nigeria: The case of Boki-Local-Government Area, Cross River State, Nigeria.* International Journal of Research and Sustainable Development. Vol. 1 (3). Pp. 912 - 923, 2012.

Yusuf, I.D. *Prospects and Problem of Non-Governmental Organization (NGOs) in Community Development and Poverty Alleviation in Gombe State.* 2015.

Yusuf, I.D., Abbas, B., Husain, M.A., and Mohammed, R.I. *Appraisal of the Contributions of Non-governmental organizations (NGOs) to Poverty Alleviation and Community Development in Gombe State, Nigeria.* American Journal of Engineering Research (AJER), 2017.

FORECASTING HOW CRUDE OIL EXPORT IS CHANGING THE DYNAMICS OF NIGERIA'S ECONOMY 1970 – 2030

INTRODUCTION

The chapter investigates the contribution of crude oil exportation on the future gross domestic product (GDP) and its impact on the economic performance of Nigeria from 1970 to 2013. International trade has been a significant source of revenue for Nigeria; the chapter reveals that crude oil export has contributed to improving the Nigerian economy. This chapter employs the Multiple Linear regression model (MLRM) and the Autoregressive Integrated Moving Average (ARIMA) model to test the structural relationship between oil exports and the GDP of the Nigerian economy. Our results show that using the MLRM, most of our explanatory variables are significant, and the model explains a large part of the behavior of the Nigerian economy and its performance. This chapter has been organized into the following sections, with subsections in each part. The introduction gives the purpose of the chapter; the body will consist of the historical background of crude oil in Nigeria, the performances of the oil sector, the impacts of crude oil on the Nigerian economy, and the overall GDP performance of Nigeria. The last section of the chapter comprises the conclusion based on the findings, insight into the economic question posed in the chapter, and some recommendations.

The Nigerian economy has faced many challenges that have significantly impacted its economic activities. Over the years, crude oil production in the south-south region has been less than expected due to security challenges and global warming (floods) occurring over the last few years. The floods and weaker consumer demand affected the non-oil sector (Agriculture, wholesale and retail trade). According to the NNPC, oil production was estimated at 2.37 Mbps in 2012, as opposed to 2.48 Mbps in 2011. The 4.4% decline in crude oil production is due to cases of oil theft and vandalization in the oil-producing areas.

According to the Banknote World Education, [and if we fail to factor in per capita oil production], Nigeria is an Oil-rich nation that has been hobbled by political instability, corruption, inadequate infrastructure, and poor macroeconomic management. In 2008, it began pursuing economic reforms. Nigeria's former military rulers, who ruled in the 60s through the late 90s, failed to diversify the economy away from overdependence on the capital-intensive oil sector, which provides 95% of foreign exchange earnings and about 80% of budgetary revenues or is the mainstream [1]. Following the signing of an IMF agreement in late August 2000, Nigeria received a debt-restructuring deal from Paris and a $1 billion credit from the IMF contingent on economic reforms. Nigeria pulled out of its IMF program in 2002 after failing to meet spending and exchange rate targets over the set period, which made Nigeria ineligible for additional debt forgiveness from the Paris Club [1]. In November 2005, Abuja won the Paris Club approval for a debt-relief deal that eliminated $18 billion of debt in exchange for $12 billion in payments--a package worth $30 billion of Nigeria's total $37 billion external debt [1].

Since 2008, the Nigerian government has begun to show political zeal to implement the open market policy recommended by the IM, including modernizing the banking system, removing oil subsidies, and resolving regional disputes over the oil industry's earnings distribution. The Nigerian GDP rose sharply in 2007-2012 because of growth in non-oil sectors and robust global crude oil prices. According to Yahoo News, written by Ambassador Adebowale Adefuye and Stephen Hayes, the government is also working toward developing stronger public-private partnerships for all sectors of the economy.

The chapter aims to investigate the impact of crude oil export on the Nigerian economy by examining the factors that affect crude oil production, price, and export and to generate a model to estimate a 17-year GDP forecast. Statistically, the direction and magnitude of the interdependence among the variables is of significant interest to the chapter and forms the basis for understanding the interaction between crude oil exports and Nigeria's economic performance. Such findings can illuminate why crude oil exports have, in the past and presently, played a crucial and essential role in driving Nigeria's economic performance.

ECONOMIC OVERVIEW AND PERFORMANCE

With a population of about 186 million, Nigeria accounts for 47% of West

Africa's population and is also the largest economy. Nigeria is the largest oil exporter and has the largest natural gas reserves on the continent. The country has been on an ambitious reform path over the last 15 years; one of these paths focused on restructuring oil prices and excess crude accounts. Responding to these reforms, the economy grew stronger between 2003 and 2008, averaging 7.6% before the Great Recession 2007. Nigeria is one of the first countries to adopt and implement the Extractive Industries Transparency Initiative (EITI) to improve governance and the oil sector. The country became EITI compliant in 2011, and the power sector reform initiative was launched in 2005-2006, noting that an improved power sector is critical to address some developmental challenges.

Implementing these reforms is the major challenge faced by the Nigerian government. Implementing a more open market system, property rights enforcement, and diversifying the economy will help mitigate weaknesses in the oil sector that could translate into complicated macroeconomic risks. The oil industry accounts for 90% of the nation's exports and roughly 75% of the consolidated budgetary revenues of the Nigerian economy. Any significant decline in oil output, weaker oil prices, and a decline in the agricultural sector of the economy can be associated with a deficit in the nation's balance of payments account and shortfalls in its budgetary revenues. The short-term portfolio capital inflows that reportedly reached more than $17 billion in 2012 have raised concerns, and the short-term inflows of capital have primarily been targeting the government bond market, with interest rates at 12-14%, leading to volatility in the market.

The declining oil revenues have placed increasing pressure on government budgets and expenditures. The total federation revenues available for sharing by the three tiers of government fell short of projections by 20%. The balance of the country's fiscal reserve (Excess Crude Account) declined from over $9 billion in early 2013 to $5 billion by mid-2013. Early indications from the 2014-2016 medium-term expenditure framework point towards a significant fiscal contraction in 2014. Structural reforms in utilities and agriculture appear to pay at least some dividends, and the economy is moving toward its reform goals.

BACKGROUND

The Nigerian oil industry is categorized into three sub-sectors: up-stream, down-stream, and gas. The most problematic is the downstream sector, the distribution arm and connection with final consumers of refined petroleum products in the domestic economy. Oil production by Victor Company of Japan (JVC) accounts for about 95% of Nigeria's crude oil production, of which the NNPC has a 60% stake. The over-dependence on oil has created a less diversified economy and has affected Nigeria's overall GDP.

Nigeria has become more profound since the deregulation of the downstream segment of the Nigerian oil industry in 2003. The contribution is more glaring now with the recent rise in crude oil prices in the global market. The chapter builds on the theoretical relationship between crude oil exports. Nigeria's GDP growth has gained much attention from different authors. It has divided these authors into two groups: those that fail to reject the hypothesis "crude oil export has a positive impact on the economic performance of Nigeria" and those that reject the hypothesis. The Central Bank of Nigeria (CBN) last released the GDP outlook market study in 2016, which provides a thorough report showing the Nigerian economy's performance measured in GDP.

The CBN used these GDP reports and trends of other variables in the coming years and forecasted the future GDP of the Nigerian economy up to 5 years, or even ten years, ahead. Most internet-based forecast reports and other experts predict the Nigerian GDP to be lower in the foreseeable future. The CBN's recent updates identify specific market trends that could render those predictions inaccurate. As economies recover, it is difficult to predict if investors will still hold onto their assets or sell them. The CBN analyzes the Nigerian regional economic and financial trends that may affect investment in the Nigerian economy and GDP. A rising Consumer Price Index (CPI), GINI-index, dollar appreciation to Naira, and decreasing Human Development Index (HDI) have influenced the Nigerian economy's GDP. A higher CPI and a lower saving rate have reduced the Nigerian economy's Real Gross Domestic Product (RGDP) in recent years. A higher output (export of crude oil production), better quality of products, and a growing power industry are likely to lead to an increase in the GDP of the Nigerian economy.

Jung and Marshal (1985) argued that growth in real exports tends to cause growth in RGNP for three reasons. First, increasing exports may reduce the binding foreign exchange constraint and increase productivity. Secondly, export growth may represent an increase in the demand for the country's output and thus serve to increase RGDP; in Nigeria's case, an increase in demand for primary products in the international market will lead to a rise in crude oil export. Thirdly, export growth may result in enhanced efficiency and, thus, might lead to greater output.

Adam Smith (1776), In his book *An Inquiry into the Nature and Causes of the Wealth of a Nation*, said that the main mercantilist proposed the classical theory of international trade based on the "absolute advantage model." According to Smith, the stock of human, human-made, and natural resources, rather than the stock of precious metals, is the true wealth of a nation. He also argued that the wealth of a nation could be expanded if the government would abandon mercantilist control. David Ricardo (1817) Articulated the model of comparative advantage, which states that a country should specialize in the production it has in abundance and export the commodity, that is, the commodity it can produce at the lowest relative cost. Ajayi (1974) Emphasized that in developing economies, in which Nigeria is a typical example, the emphasis is always on fiscal rather than monetary policy. In his work, he estimated the variable of monetary and budgetary policies using OLS techniques and found that monetary influences are much larger and more predictable than fiscal influences. His result was confirmed using the beta coefficient, which showed that monetary action changes were more remarkable than fiscal actions. In essence, greater reliance should be placed on monetary actions regarding the Nigerian economy's general performance.

Betten and Hafer (1983) Discussed the relative effectiveness of the two stabilization policies in some developed countries. Their study found that monetary action rather than fiscal actions had a more significant influence on a country's nominal GDP and GNP. Dr. Kingsley Moghalu (2012), The present Deputy Governor of the CBN, says that the financial system stability has stated that the rebasing of Nigerian Gross Domestic Product is a welcomed idea and is necessary and, at the same time, beneficial to the economy. Expectations from rebasing the GDP are high, with sources citing that it can increase the size of the Nigerian economy by 40%; this increase will see Nigeria's earnings increase from $250 billion to about $350 billion.

METHODOLOGY

For this chapter, yearly data was used from 1970 to 2013. The data used for the empirical analysis was collected from the CBN database and the World Bank database.

TEST OF HYPOTHESIS

H0 = 0

Where: crude oil export significantly contributes to the Nigerian economy's GDP.

H1 ≠ 0

Where: crude oil export has no significant contribution to the GDP of the Nigerian economy.

MODEL

$$lni=0+1lnPopi+2lnT+3lnExpi+4lnC+i$$
$$ln=0+1lnPop+2lnT+3lnExp+4lnCBA+i$$

Where:
i = Real Gross Domestic Product
= Forecasted Real Gross Domestic Product
$Popi$ = Total Population
Pop = Forecasted Total Population
T = Total Reserve (Gold and USD)
T = Forecasted Total Reserve (Gold and USD)
$Expi$ = Total export of goods and services (Non-crude oil)
Exp = Forecasted Total export of good and services (non-crude oil)
$CBAi$ = Crude oil production barrels per day
CBA = Crude oil production barrels per day
i = Error term

Table 1
Model 1-Results

	β	t- stat (P-value)	Std. Error	R^2 (Adj.)
	16.515	4.312 (0.0001)	3.829	.92 (.91)
$lnPop_i$	-0.465	-1.704 (0.096)	0.273	
lnT_{R_i}	0.106	1.066 (0.292)	0.099	
$lnExp_i$	0.847	6.444 (0.000)	0.131	
$\beta_4 lnC_{BA_i}$	-0.719	-2.221 (0.032)	0.323	

			Model 2-Results			AR (1)	AR (2)	AR (3)
	7.03E+10	2 (0.050)	3.51e+10	.99 (.99)		0.623	0.231	0.4088
$lnPop_{f_i}$	-1097.845	-3.007 (0.004)	365.05					
lnT_{Rf_i}	-1.436	-3.982 (0.000)	0.360					
$lnExp_{f_i}$	1.663	9.308 (0.000)	0.178					
lnC_{BAf_i}	9584699.0	0.912 (0.366)	10508528					

Figure 1:
Actual Real Gross Domestic Product and Forecasted Real Gross Domestic Product

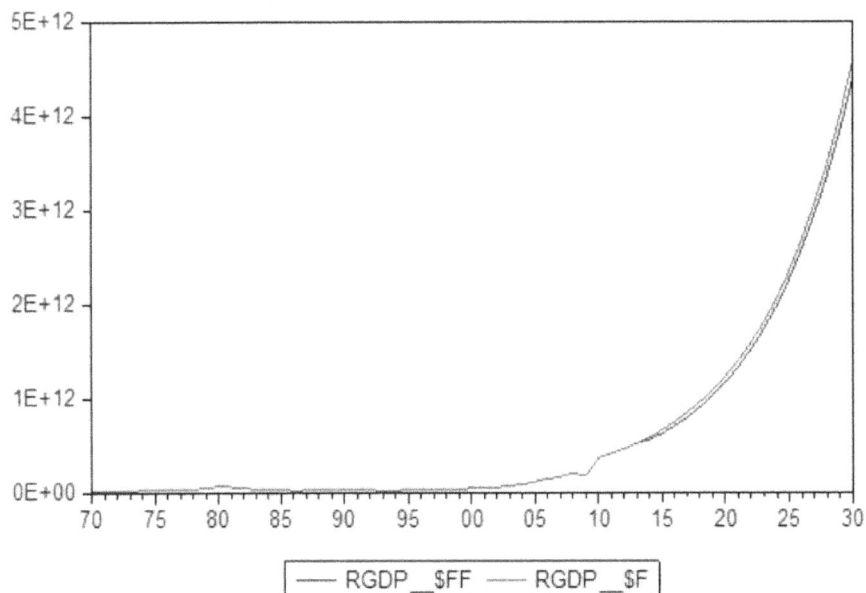

81

FINDINGS

All the variables used in this chapter contained unit roots in their level form, as revealed by the ADF test. This is corrected by using the first differences of the variables while building the model. White's test also reveals heteroscedasticity in the model, which was also corrected for using the HAC filter. Adding more variables into the model, such as demand and supply of money, NNPC excess crude account, and total refined crude oil import, will improve the model and make the forecasts more reliable. Also, the use of monthly data would give better results than the annual data. These are gaps that future researchers can fill.

High fluctuation in the country has made many investors skeptical of investing in Nigeria. Oil prices also affect RGDP as they increase. RGDP increases also show a positive relationship between oil price and RGDP of the Nigeria economy. Also, the performance of the Nigerian stock market affects the RGDP as an investment alternative, which affects the economy.

As the Nigerian economy starts to recover from the recent financial crisis and the dollar depreciates, it can be expected that the RGDP of the Nigerian economy will follow an upward trend in years to come, even though it has had slow growth over the last year. However, this rise in RGDP also depends on how quickly other profitable investment alternatives are available. Money supply should be more regulated, and the level of available liquidity in the general economy should be higher.

In the regression output in Table one, the two significant variables are the Exp_i, and CBA_i. Our R^2 is moderate enough at 92%, and the DW is 0.72. Exp_i, and CBA_i Have a positive impact on the i. This would be expected because productivity will increase when the crisis in an economy

82

goes down. As a result, net foreign assets will also increase, and domestic credit will go up due to business optimism, also known as the animal spirit of the market. On the other hand, a one percent increase in the $\ln Pop_i$ will cause the Nigerian $\ln i$ to decrease by 46.5%, a one percent increase in the $\ln T$ of the Nigerian economy will cause $\ln i$ to increase by 10.6%; a one percent increase in $\ln Exp_i$ in the Nigerian economy will cause the $\ln i$ to increase by 84.7%, a one percent increase in the $\ln CBA_i$ will cause $\ln i$ of the Nigerian economy to reduce by 71.9%.

RECOMMENDATIONS

First, it's recommended that the government increase its investment in the utility and transportation sectors of the economy to facilitate the production and distribution of goods and services. Second, commercial and investment bank activities in the region, supported by private and public investment in STEM education, will help revamp the economy. Third, developing a well-structured economic framework for the distribution of domestic gas-to-power sales and gas improvement project will help significantly increase the nation's gas-based generation capacity. Fourth, more federal grants and loans should be increased to the agricultural sector of the economy. Community-driven development programs will improve the productivity level, income, and welfare of farmers in the nation. Five, an improvement in healthcare services will save more lives in the region and improve the economic development status of the country. Finally, improving the quality of primary, secondary, and post-secondary education will be valuable.

The Strategy reform should focus on the improvement of governance in the nation and maintaining and growing the non-oil sector industry. Governance should cover six areas: transparency, accountability, participation, capacity development, judicial reform, and democratic governance. All these will help strengthen government systems and property rights.

CONCLUSION

The recent volatility in the Nigerian economy has shown a need for accurate RGDP forecasts for investors, producers, and the public, which is why some firms worldwide are involved. RGDP is mainly used to measure the overall performance of a country and how it grows. As the RGDP of the Nigerian economy has been increasing in value over the years, Nigeria has been an alternative place for investors. Without any dynamics out of the sample, forecasting is not feasible in the current model. Hence, further development of the model, including demand and supply factors, would have better value as it can better forecast out of the sample, which is one of the most critical pieces of information required for all stakeholders affected by the overall performance of the Nigerian economy. Though widely tracked, GDP may not be the most relevant summary of the economic performance of all economies, primarily when production occurs at the expense of consuming capital stock. While GDP estimates based on the production approach are more reliable than estimates compiled from the income or expenditure side, various countries use different definitions, methods, and reporting standards for GDP. World Bank staff review the quality of national accounts data and sometimes adjust to improve consistency with international guidelines.

Nevertheless, significant discrepancies remain between international standards and actual practice. Many statistical offices, especially those in third-world countries, face severe limitations in the resources, time, training, and budgets required to produce reliable and comprehensive series of national accounts statistics and accurate statistical data for research. Among the difficulties these nations face, unreported economic activity also occurs in the secondary economy. In emerging markets, a large share of agricultural output is either not exchanged because it is consumed by households or traded using the barter exchange method.

REFERENCES

Adedokun, Adeniyi Jimmy. "Oil export and economic growth." *Pakistan journal of social sciences*, 2012: pp. 46 - 58.

Ajakaiye, O. "Economic Development in Nigeria: Issues and Experience, in Proceedings of the First CBN annual monetary policy conference titled, growing the Nigerian economy." 2001: pp. 12 - 36.

B., Gambo. "An Evaluation of Nigerian Shipping Policy; A research work conducted in 1999." 1999.

C., Odularu G.O., and Okonkwo. "Does energy consumption contribute to the economic performance? Empirical evidence from Nigeria." 2009.

Diebold, Aruoba and. "Real-time macroeconomic monitoring: Real activity, inflation, and interaction." 2010.

F.A., Olalokun. "Structure of the Nigerian economy." 1979.

Hafer, Betten and. "Monetary Reforms and Economic Growth in Cemac Zone." 1983.

Khadijat, Afolabi. "Impact of oil export on economic growth in Nigeria from 1970 - 2005." 2011.

Mahler, Annegret. "Nigeria: A prime example of the resource curse? revisiting the oil-violence link in the Niger Delta." *German Institute of global and area studies*, 2010: GIGA WP 120.

Olusegun, Gbadebo Odularu. "Crude oil and the Nigerian economic performance." 2008.

Priewe, Jan. "Dutch Disease, Resource Curse and Development." 2011.

Smith, Adams. "An Inquiry into the nation and causes of the wealth of the nation." 1776.

AGRICULTURAL AND MARKETING AND HOW THE SHAFFER-STAR IS UTILIZED

This chapter examines the application of Shaffer's – Star model in the distribution of agricultural produce. As a case study, the chapter analyzes the Ane Osiobe Altruism Farm in Gwagwalada, Federal Capital Territory (FCT). The analysis aims to define the marketing concept and its application to grow the farm's revenue. Furthermore, the chapter seeks to review previous research on the farm and apply Shaffer's – Star in the distribution of the farm output to consumers. The reviewed literature (Osiobe E.U. 2018), and (Enyinnaya J.C. and Osiobe E.U. 2017) shows that the farm may likely earn ₦255.00k for every ₦1.00k invested. However, it depends on efficiently utilizing resources such as land, labor, and capital (Eninnaya J.C. and Osiobe E.U. 2017). In the analysis, marketing will be delved into because it is an essential strategy in raising more revenue for the Altruism farm, and the distance between the Altruism farm and nearby market(s) will be analyzed using the gravity model. Our results show that market N would be the best place to sell the farm's products as it's ranked number one, followed by markets G and A. The rankings are based on the number of commuters moving in and out of the market, which reflects the volume of transactions that occur within the market.

Nigeria has practiced non-mechanized agriculture since its independence in 1960. The arable land for agricultural production can be attributed to the nation's climate conditions. The agriculture sector has employed more than 80% of the Nigerian population, and the famous groundnut pyramids of Kano showed the strength of the agricultural sector's capacity in the 1960s. It was estimated that the remaining 20% of the population was involved in small businesses such as pottery, weaving, carving, and tool-making to support and supplement their livelihood from farming (Adebola and Oguzor, 2009).

An agricultural business enterprise is an economic unit that makes independent decisions to optimize the use of its resources for production and profit maximization. In Nigeria, average small business enterprises make zero economic profit; at best, they break even after every fiscal year. In setting up a farm, it is necessary to look at the following factors: proximity to labor, land, market availability, resources, and ease of transportation. The Ane Osiobe Altruism Farms, located in Gwagwalada, FCT, specializes in producing cassava, groundnut, and fishery. The main goal of the farm is to produce healthy food for the residents of Gwagawlada, FCT, and to raise money from the sale of the products to meet some of the foundation's stated needs:

- To bridge the gap between the students at the special needs school Jabi and the food production in the area by engaging locals in agricultural practices (Eninnaya J.C. and Osiobe E.U. 2017, p 3).
- To produce healthy, nutritious food for students at the Special Needs

School, Jabi, FCT, and raise some money from the sale of the surplus produce to meet their diverse needs (Eninnaya J.C. and Osiobe E.U. 2017, p 3).

- To support and grow the local economy of Nigeria. (Osiobe E.U. Sunday's Leadership News Paper, pp13 April 29, 2018).
- To create local economic growth and development in the Gwagwalada area by creating jobs and employing the host and neighboring communities. (Osiobe E.U. 2018, pp 5).

To achieve Ane Osiobe's Altruism Farm's goals, it is necessary to adopt Shaffer's – Star strategy and implement the findings from the gravity model.

THE SHAFFER–STAR CONCEPT

Ron Shaffer developed the Shaffer–Star to help solve community economic development problems, practitioners' concern(s), and cooperative issues. The star focuses on economic and non-economic actors in community economic development. The star comprises six components, which include:

Markets: This part of the star deals with economic forces that drive the allocation of economic resources; it refers to the demand and supply of goods and services. It takes into consideration the concept of a business location. The idea of inter-industry linkages, the return to scale, and the agglomeration ideology come into play.

Decision Making: This part of the star involves setting and implementing policies that affect economic growth, development, and stability. The decision-making capacity is the ability to distinguish between the economic problem(s) and symptom(s). Effective decision-making depends on the leader drawing from all available resources; in other words, effective leadership depends on learning from mistakes and making productive decisions to manage available resources.

Resources: This part of the star involves the labor, capital, and technology used by the farm in producing output. Labor refers to human capital; capital can be grouped into physical capital, including but not limited to building and machines, and natural capital, including but not limited to water and land.

Rules: This is an essential part of the star because it governs what is done within the market environment/space. The laws that govern a community stand as gatekeepers into the market. Hence, two major things must be considered when making new laws and amending old ones. First, does the community influence these rules, and second, do these rules hinder economic growth, development, and stability?

Society: This is part of the star that many community economic development practitioners agree on a certain level of social infrastructure that must be in place before any commercial development efforts can occur. The Shaffer's star focuses on how societies can cooperate to promote favorable changes, deal with diverse cultural dynamics, and encourage economic growth, development, and stability.

Space: This is the part of the star that measures the firm's distance to the nearest local market. The concept builds on the idea that communities are defined within spatial parameters and communication networks.

The chapter aims to analyze how the Shaffer's – Star concept can optimize the distribution of the Ane Osiobe's Altruism Farm's production of cassava and fish in Gwagwalada, FCT, NG.

CONCEPT OF AGRICULTURAL MARKETING

Marketing and marketing are related but not the same. The market is any place or setting that allows buyers and sellers to exchange ownership of goods, services, and information to satisfy customer's needs. According to (Olukosi J.O. and Isitor A. 1990), Agricultural marketing refers to all activities that direct the ins and outflow of goods and services to the consumer from the producers. In agriculture, there are two types of markets: output and input. The input market supplies various inputs from the manufacturing firms to the farms. In contrast, the output market deals with multiple activities of the crops and livestock products in their marketing channels.

Agricultural marketing involves all business activities participating in the flow of goods and services from the point of production to the final consumer (Kohls. R.L. 1985). (Olukosi J.O. et al., 2005) asserts that an efficient marketing system finds surpluses of agricultural products and brings them to where there are shortages. For communities whose products are mostly export-based, payment plans are used in their economic development programs; marketing is essential for such communities to foster economic growth, development, and stability. Agricultural marketing faces challenges, including many intermediaries, poor handling, packaging, lack of standardization, storage facilities, market information, and multiplicity of market charges.

REVIEWS ON AGRICULTURAL MARKETING

Asoguwa B.C and Okwoche V.A.'s (2012) study on Sorghum marketing in Benue, Nigeria, analyzed the market structure, market channel, socioeconomic characteristics of respondents, marketing margin, and marketing problem of Sorghum. The chapter used primary data samples from 100 randomly selected Sorghum Benue, Nigeria, commuters. The results from the survey showed that for every ₦1:00k spent in the Sorghum market, the market margin was ₦0:34k. The chapter failed to identify efficient marketing strategies to maximize its market margins, but to improve on this margin, the authors recommended that an access feeder road should be constructed to reduce the cost associated with marketing and adequate security should be provided to minimize the theft problem in the market. Lawal A.M. et al. (2013) study on cassava processing in Kwara, Nigeria, identified marketing and production constraints, various products that can be produced from cassava, and estimated the cost and benefit analysis in producing cassava in Kwara, Nigeria.

The author used a four-stage random sampling technique to obtain primary data from 118 respondents for the chapter. Their results showed that 88.1% of their sample were female farmers; within the female farmers, 60.20% had formal education, and the average age within the group was 32 years. The author's analysis revealed that four main cassava products were produced in Kwara, Nigeria, due to the high-profit margins. These products include Garri, flour (lafun), fufu, and starch. The costs and returns analysis revealed that processing cassava to Garri gave the highest gross margin even though processing cassava to all four products was profitable.

THE ANE OSIOBE INTERNATIONAL FOUNDATION'S PAST RESEARCH ON THE ALTRUISM FARM

Previous research works have been carried out on the Ane Osiobe Altruism Farm located at Gwagwalada, FCT, Nigeria, and used an optimization model to estimate cost and returns on the farm-selected products, which included cassava, corn, groundnut, and fish. These products were selected based on (Eninnaya J.C. and Osiobe E.U., 2017) cost and benefit analysis on the farm. The overall goal of the two studies was to maximize the farm's profit. The studies showed that the farm would maximize profit by producing Cassava and fish. The authors' analysis revealed the second iteration of the constraint's variables was more profitable, with a 46% increase from the base model.

In comparison, the first iteration had a 4% increase from the base model. Osiobe E.U. (2018) analyzed the economic impact of the farm on the Nigerian economy. The author used an input-output model (IMPLAN) to run his model. The chapter results showed that the farm would have a net positive impact on the Nigerian economy. The author's findings also revealed that the net effect on the first year would be ₦ 4,122,761, and the subsequent year is ₦6,159,243.10k if resources are managed well.

REVIEW OF THE SHAFFER'S – STAR MODEL

Deller S., in his community development rule mini-article, reflects on community economic development using a system approach to arrange one's thinking. At the same time, Ron Shaffer offers a six-step program known as the Shaffer–Star. Another study by the University of Wisconsin on community development paradigm tilted "the Shaffer star and community capitals." Analyzed new approaches in addressing a community complex system. Shaffer, R.E. et al. (2006) argued that the interdisciplinary approach to the community economic paradigm, which involves six Shaffer Star elements and integrates economic and non-economic factors in community development, is essential to foster economic growth and development.

DATA ANALYSIS

For this chapter, the gravity model is employed. The gravity model uses Newton's law to analyze and estimate the relationship between trading in two distinct marketplaces. Using Newton's law as the idea's bedrock, instead of gravitational pull, the model uses the degree of interaction between cities, towns, or regions. Newton's law of gravity predicts that larger and closer bodies will exert more force. The variables for the gravity model are the size of the market and the distance to the market. For our study, length is measured in population, and the distance is measured in kilometers. The idea in the gravity model is similar to that of Newton's law: the more significant and closer two places are, the more friction and interaction/motion they will have on one another.

The gravity model's interaction(s) is proportional to the market size. Hence, there is a positive relationship between the market size and the interaction in the market. Ceteris paribus, as the population in a market increases, the interaction(s) in that same market also increases. Based on the positive relationship preposition, the interactions in the market are inversely proportional to the distance between them. As the distance gets larger, the expected interaction in a market decreases.

According to the gravity model, the interaction between places is directly proportional to the size of the market and is inversely proportional to the distance to the market.

Figure 1: The Distance between the Ane Osiobe Altruism Farm
and Local Markets in FCT, Nigeria
Source: Google Maps

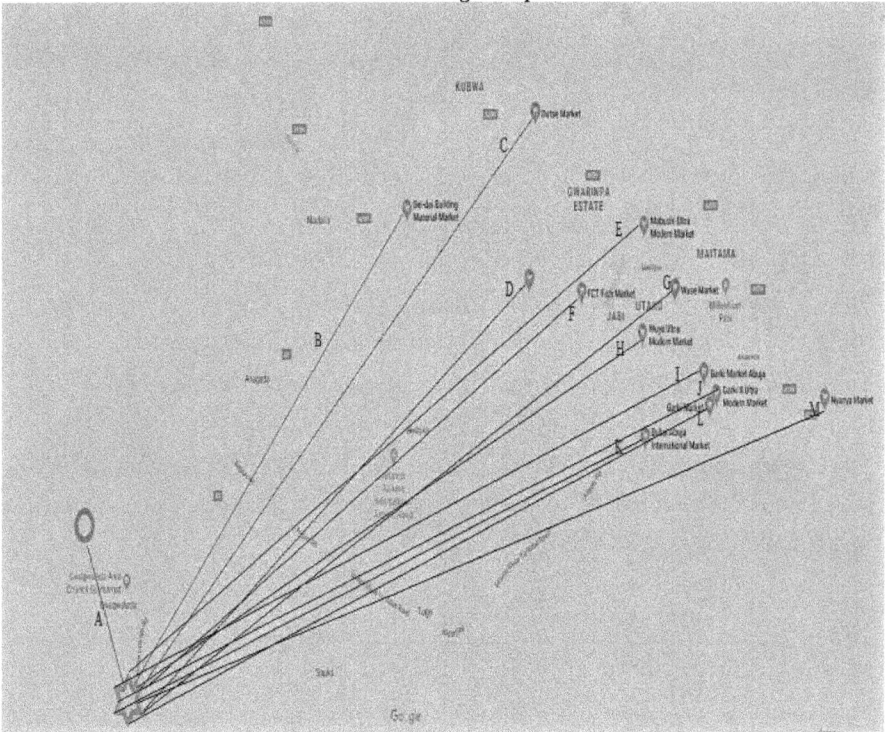

Table 1: Map Key

#	Kilometer (km)	Market Info
✸	0 km	Ane Osiobe Altruism Farm a product of Ane Osiobe International Foundation.
A	5.0 km	Gwagwalada Market, Gwagwalada, Nigeria.
B	32.5 km	Dei-dei Building Material Market, 102 Inner Northern Road, Abuja, Nigeria.
C	43.7 km	Dutse Market, 1 Bwari Express Rd, Abuja, Nigeria.
D	42.8 km, 42.4 km, and 42. 1 km (Average 42.4 km)	Karmo Market 1, Idogwari, Abuja, Nigeria; Market 2Idogwari, Abuja, Nigeria; and Market 3Idogwari, Abuja, Nigeria.
E	56.1 km	Mabushi Ultra-Modern Market, Kado, Abuja, Nigeria.
F	56.8 km	FCT Fish Market, 194/199 ZubaGarki Rd, Gwarinpa, Abuja, Nigeria.
G	56.5 km	Wuse Market, 24 Wuse Market Rd, Wuse, Abuja, Nigeria.
H	58.5 km	Wuye Ultra-Modern Market, 697, 697 Idris Gidado St, Utako, Abuja, Nigeria.
I	57.4 km	Garki Market Abuja, 7 Awka St, Garki, Abuja, Nigeria.
J	57.0 km	Garki II Ultra-Modern Market, 1 Triumph Bank Street, Garki, Abuja, Nigeria.
K	50.5 km	Dubai Abuja International Market, Kaura, Abuja, Nigeria.
L	56.3 km	Garki Market, 22 Samuel Ladoke Akintola Boulevard, Garki, Abuja, Nigeria.
M	70.0 km	Nyanya Market, Urban Mass Nyanya Market, Nigeria.
N	41.4 km	Lugbe Fruit Market, Lugbe, FCT, Nigeria.

Source: Google Maps

95

Formula:

$$A = \frac{a \cdot Pop_{M_i} \cdot Pop_{M_j}}{D^2}$$

Where
A = then in and outflow of trade
a = constant
Pop_{Mi} = Market size at base market (Gwagwalada)
Pop_{Mj} = Market size at the alternative market (B – M) see figure 1
D^2 = distance between the market size of M_i and the market size of M_j

The chapter implements a Market Population Proxy/Multiple Visit (MPP_{MV}) to estimate the number of customer visits to each market—the formula for the MPP_{MV}.

$$MPP_{MV} = \frac{Number\ of\ Google\ Reviews_{M_{i,j}}}{Sum\ Number\ of\ Google\ Reviews_{M_{i,j}}} \cdot FCT\ Total\ Population_{2019}$$

Where: *FCT Total Population*$_{2018}$ = 3.095.118

RESULTS

The results show that market N would be the best place to sell the farm's products as it's ranked number one, followed by markets G and A. The rankings are based on the number of commuters moving in and out of the market, which reflects the volume of transactions that occur within the market.

Table 2: Results
Source: Authors' calculation

| Table 2 Results | | | | | |
Market	$Pop_{M_{i,j}}$	MPP_{MV}	D^2	A	Ranking
A	81	13341.03	25	7119319	3
B	1086	179642.9	1056.25	2268990	8
C	2269	398458	1909.69	2783613	7
D	198	39908.4	1797.76	296156.9	13
E	298	60848.74	3147.21	257937.9	14
F	1010	210368	3226.24	869906	10
G	7929	1771927	3192.25	7405224	2
H	339	177207.4	3422.25	690811.2	11
I	1358	752986.4	3294.76	3048966	6
J	596	436716.5	3249	1793243	9
K	144	122849.2	2550.25	642656.5	12
L	1058	939906.7	3169.69	3956008	5
M	1794	2288805	4900	6231635	4
N	632	3095118	1713.96	24091606	1

Source: Authors' calculation

CONCLUSION

This chapter examines the Shaffer's – Star model and how it can be applied in the distribution of agricultural produce. The chapter uses the Ane Osiobe Altruism Farm in Gwagwalada, FCT, Nigeria, as a case study. The chapter aims to define the concept of marketing as a section of the Shaffer's - Star and its application to grow the Ane Osiobe Altruism Farm's revenue. Furthermore, the chapter seeks to review previous research by the foundation on the Altruism Farm, namely, "Cost-benefit analysis, optimization, and economic impact study." The chapter also aims to apply the Shaffer's – Star in distributing the farm's output to the final consumers. The foundation's peer-reviewed literature (Osiobe E.U., 2018), and (Enyinnaya J.C and Osiobe E.U., 2017) shows that the farm may likely earn ₦255.00k for every ₦1.00k invested. However, it depends on efficiently utilizing resources such as land, labor, and capital (Eninnaya J.C. and Osiobe E.U., 2017).

The chapter delved into agriculture marketing because it is an essential strategy in raising more revenue for the Altruism farm, and the distance between the Altruism farm and nearby market(s) was analyzed using the gravity model. Our results show that market N would be the best place to sell the farm's products as it's ranked number one, followed by markets G and A.

REFERENCES

Adebola, H.E, and Oguzor, N.S (2009). *Gender, Development, and Society*. Granada: Afro Euro Centre for Development Studies.

Asoguwa B.C. and Okwoche V.A. (2012). Marketing of agricultural produce among rural farm households in Nigeria: the case of sorghum marketing in Benue state. International Journal of Business and Social Science (vol.3 No.13)

Deller S. University of Wisconsin-madison department of agricultural and applied economics

Ekpa D., Adeola S., Mukhtar U.,and Ekpa M.,(2016). Analysis of processing methods, marketing channels, and profitability determinants of selected cassava products in Kogi state. International Journal of agricultural science, research, and technology in extension and education system. ISSN:2251-7596

Eninnaya J.C and Osiobe E.U. (2017). Cost and return estimates of cassava, groundnut, maize and fish production on the Ane Osiobe altruism farm for the Edison 3.0 project in Gwagwalada, FCT.

Kohls, R. L. (1985). Marketing of Agriculture Products. Macmillan Publishing Company, 866 Third Avenue New 10022

Lawal A.M, Omotesho O.A., and Oyedemi F.A.,(2013). *An Assessment of the Economics of Cassava Processing in Kwara State, Nigeria*. 4th International conference of the African Association of Agricultural Economics.

Olukosi J.O. and Isitor, A. (1990). Introducing to Agricultural Marketing and Prices: Principles and Application. Abuja: G.U. Publication, pp. 1-3

Osiobe E.U. (2018). The national economic impact from Agriculture: Gwagwalada case study.

Shaffer, R.E., Deller S.C., and Marcouiller D.W. (2006). "Rethinking Community Economic Development." Economic Development Quarterly. 20(1):59-74

THE ROLE OF NON-GOVERNMENTAL ORGANIZATIONS IN COMMUNITY ECONOMIC DEVELOPMENT

INTRODUCTION

Non-governmental organizations (NGOs) are essential institutional players in mobilizing regional economic growth and development, community growth and development, motivating people, and implementing social welfare program(s) to support government effort(s) at the grassroots level. This chapter explores the impact of NGOs on rural community development while referencing the case study of the community of Lugbe in the city of Abuja, Federal Capital Territory (FCT), Nigeria. This chapter utilizes the NGO-Donation-system dynamics model ($NGO_D - DEM$) to explore, visualize, and analyze the following dilemmas of NGO donations' responsiveness to Nigeria's per capita income, returns on foreign capital, and the returns on local capital. It analyzes two sensitivity scenarios from the base $NGO_D -$

DEM (see Figure 1). The findings show how NGO activities foster economic growth and development in the community. Our results show that if Local Returns on Capital (L_{RK}) are more significant than Foreign Returns on Capital (R_{FI}), there will be a higher inflow of Foreign Direct Investment (*FDI*) into the nation and vice versa. Hence, if the latter statement holds, the cost-effectiveness for individuals and businesses to donate or invest in the country will decrease (see Figure 3). But, if the former statement is true, there will be zero donations to NGOs as long as individual per capita income is below the Income Threshold to Donate (Y_{donate}) and companies make zero economic profits in their businesses. The Y_{donate} is between $0 - $ 13,000. But, when the individual per capita income or a business's net economic profit is between $ 14,000 - $ 80,000, which is above Y_{donate}, donations and investments will increase until the point when it peaks and starts to decrease (see Figure 4). Further result(s) show that the involvement of NGOs in societies where citizens are underserved by the financial, educational, entrepreneurial, political, and health industries have a normal distribution relationship shaped curve for the labor force per capita income threshold, an inverse relationship on returns on L_{RK}, and a positive returns on R_{FI}. The participation of NGOs in communities, *ceteris paribus*, has had a significant positive effect on the Nigerian economy, but the research does not overlook mistakes made by these NGOs in trying to solve wicked problems in an economy.

Emerging markets, as they try to restructure their communities, and social services have become paramount with the full participation of its members (United Nations Department of Economic and Social Affairs, 2008). Economic community development is the process by which people partner with their government to improve their society's economic, social, political, and cultural welfare (United Nations (UN), 1956). This phenomenon can be categorized as trying to solve a wicked problem in a community. A wicked problem is a complicated and challenging social issue that requires analysis to address changing dynamics and blind spots. In general, wicked problems usually involve an interdisciplinary approach to be resolved. The UN's definition of economic community development posits that the people in a community must utilize their political, built, cultural, and financial capital with the government (public sector – private sector – NGOs) in a partnership to foster long-term sustainable economic growth and development.

The altruistic desire for people to participate in community growth and development in Nigeria led to the establishment of the NGO industry. In 1945, the term NGO came into use because of the need for the UN to differentiate between participation rights for specialized intergovernmental agencies and those for international private organizations. These international private organizations are civil society organizations, citizen associations, and private voluntary organizations. Today, they are called NGOs. The UN employs this term to differentiate between representatives of these agencies from those of governments (Ime, 2014).

The establishment of NGOs in Nigeria dates to the pre-independence period (Elumilade et al., 2006). When the successive post-colonial governments found it difficult to manage the developmental needs of Nigerians, people began to see the importance and impacts of NGOs on the public. An NGO is a company that has the following characteristics:

- They are not created to generate personal profit: Although they may engage in revenue-generating businesses, they are distributed to the public per their goals and objectives.
- They are voluntary: This means that they are formed voluntarily and

that there is usually an element of voluntary participation in the organization.

- They are subject to their fiduciary duty: They are accountable to their members, donors, and stakeholders under the fiduciary law.
- They are independent of the government, public authorities, political parties, or commercial organizations. NGOs' independence is crucial to their operations because this empowers them to play supervisory and advocacy roles effectively. Their autonomy from government, political parties, and religious institutions position them to earn the public trust. This characteristic makes NGOs highly reputable and very influential.

REVIEW

The stoic belief that people can work together to shape their destiny when allowed to participate in a free, open, and non-threatening environment formed the basis of community development. Community development has been one of the most significant social forces in the process of planned and effective change. A community is a recognized social unit, such as a group or association of individuals with everyday needs, values, interests, and functions.

Community growth, development, and stability can be viewed as a continuous process through which community stakeholders come together to take collective actions and generate solutions to their everyday problems. Community development can range from a small initiative within a small group of people to greater actions that involve a broader environment. The concept of community development has evolved over the years from the primitive period, pre-industrial, post-industrial, to the modern-day. In the primitive period, community development aimed at protecting communities from enemies or other cities. The highest priority was establishing a robust defense strategy for community protection. Customs, traditions, and taboos were the guiding principles in that era.

In the pre-industrial period, community development transcended into the mobilization of resources. Societies plundered the resources of other communities for their growth, development, and sustainability. The focus of community development during this period was workforce development and self-defense, which was achieved by resource mobilization. During the industrial period, community development was seen in a new light. During this period, infrastructure development and resource mobilization for industrial growth were the two driving forces of community development. In modern times, community development has witnessed a drastic shift in focus. The social well-being of people is the focus of community growth and development. These activities are spread across all the positive elements required to enhance the individual's and society's social welfare.

The planning and implementation of community development programs involve more people in the modern-day than all other periods. Today, it is more of an interdisciplinary affair aimed at solving the wicked problem of society and making judicious use of our scarce resources (United Nations Department of Economic and Social Affairs, 2008). This has become a necessary skill required for effective community growth and development. The development of community needs has become enormous, and efforts made by local organizations and the government to cater to all the ramifications of individual and societal needs are insufficient. Hence, there is a need for NGO interventions to address these gaps.

The term NGO was first used after World War II by the UN to refer to the private organizations that helped heal the victims of the war who were displaced and the millions of children who were made orphans. The term NGO encompasses a broad range of organizations, which vary according to their purpose, philosophy, sectorial expertise, and scope of activities.

Study Area:

FCT is the capital city of Nigeria. Located around the middle belt region, it shares its borders with the Niger, Kaduna, Nasarawa, and Kogi states. The FCT lies within latitude 8o25 and 9o20 North of the Equator and longitude 6o45 and 7o39 East of the Greenwich meridian. These coordinates position Abuja in the center of Nigeria. The FCT has a landmass of 7,315 km2. Based on the most recent population projection in 2016, the FCT had a population of 2,679,200.

FCT was created on February 3rd,1976, from parts of the Nasarawa, Niger and Kogi states. Abuja is the Central Business District (CBD) of FCT, and the name Abuja is used interchangeably as both the capital FCT within the nation and the CBD within FCT. Abuja officially became the capital of Nigeria on December 12, 1991, replacing Lagos as the nation's capital. Abuja was chosen as the capital because it is centrally located in Nigeria, thus making it easily accessible to other states. It has a low population density because of the availability of landmass for future expansion and its favorable climate.

Table 1: Area Councils in the Federal Capital Territory
with their respective Headquarters and population densities.

#	Area Council	Head Quarters	Population
1	Abuja Municipal Area Council	Garki	1,967,500
2	Abaji Area Council	Abaji	148,600
3	Gwagwalada Area Council	Gwagwalada	402,000
4	Kuje Area Council	Kuje	246,400
5	Bwari Area Council	Bwari	581,100
6	Kwali Area Council	Kwali	218,400

Source: City Population

A significant monument that brands Abuja is Aso-rock, a 400-meter monolith left by a series of water erosions. Another city monument is the Zuma Rock, situated West of Abuja with an elevation of 1125m. The Zuma rock is very famous for having natural contours that project the face of a human with visible eyes, nose, and mouth. Owing to its location, the FCT is classified under the moderate climatic zone as it is situated in the savannah region. As a result, the FCT experiences three seasons every year: a warm, humid rainy season, a blistering dry season, and a brief harmattan in between, which is a result of the northeast trade wind. Minerals found in abundance in this region are marble, tin, mica, clay, wolframite, tantalite, and talc.

Six administrative units divide the FCT. These units are also known as area councils and are the equivalent of local government areas in other states; thus, they are headed by a chair (see Table 1). These chairs are elected the same way local government chairs are elected in other states in the country.

Figure 1: Map of the FCT, Nigeria

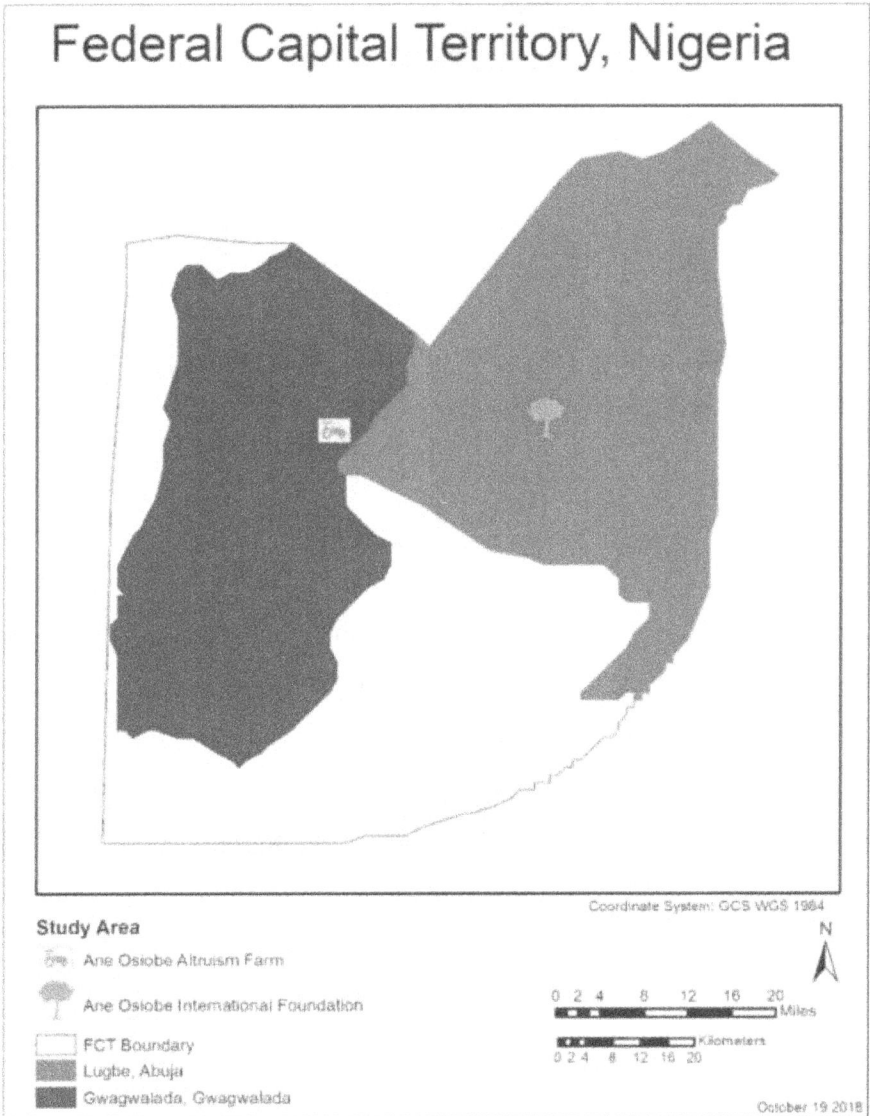

NGOs AND RURAL DEVELOPMENT

364 NGOs in the FCT area alone are recognized by the Nigerian Network of NGOs carrying out various forms of programs and projects in Abuja. Even though these NGOs differ in their focus, they are united by the same purpose: to improve the socio-economic condition of people in FCT. Some of the various facets of community development that are of interest to these NGOs include but are not limited to anti-corruption, war against human trafficking, children's rights advocacy, girls' education advocacy, economic empowerment, rural infrastructure development, community health, education for all, women empowerment, and capacity building. This chapter will analyze how donations flow into NGOs for them to carry out their set goals and objectives.

METHODOLOGY

Developed in 1956 by the Massachusetts Institute of Technology (MIT), the System Dynamics (SD) model is a methodology used to simulate the dynamic movement of a scenario. The SD field grew out of cybernetics, control theory, and cognate research into nonlinear dynamics. The idea of SD originated in physics, mathematics, and engineering (Forrester, 1968, 1973; Sterman, 2002). The equations for the overall model are in the Appendix, while Table 2 shows the work breakdown structure and the Simulation Parameters of the stocks, flows, and variables in the $NGO_D - DEM$.

Data

The data used for the $NGO_D - DEM$ (Figure 2) was generated from the information in Table 2.

Table 2: Simulation Parameters, Data, and Sources

Variables	Parameter	Most Recent Value	Sources	URL/Meaning	Most Recent Year	Last Updated
Growth Rate	POP_R	2.6	WDI	https://data.worldbank.org/indicato r/SP.POP.GROW?locations=NG	2017	2019
Population	POP	190 M	WDI	https://data.worldbank.org/indicato r/SP.POP.TOTL?locations=NG	2017	2019
Population Growth	POP_g			$POP_R * POP$		
Labor Market Participation	LM_P	55.21%	WDI	https://data.worldbank.org/indicato r/SL.TLF.ACTI.ZS?locations=NG	2018	2019
GDP	GDP	$375 B	WDI	https://data.worldbank.org/indicato r/NY.GDP.MKTP.CD/locations=N G	2017	2019
Capital Stock	CO	$ 1.87 T	FRED	https://fred.stlouisfed.org/series/RK NANPNGA666NRUG	2014	May 2018
	LO	1.90886e + 08	WDI	https://data.worldbank.org/indicato r/SP.POP.TOTL?locations=NG	2017	2019
Foreign Direct Investment	FDI			$max\,(\gamma * (L_{RK} - FDI),0)$		
Investment	I	$Y * S_R$				
Labor	L			$POP * LM_P$		
Local Return on Capital	L_{RK}			$A * (1 - a) * (L^a) * (K^{-a})$		
Depreciation	δ	10%	T. Piketty, 2014	Capital in the Twenty-First Century	N/A	N/A
Depreciation Rate	δ_R	10%	T. Piketty, 2014	Capital in the Twenty-First Century	N/A	N/A
Foreign Return on Capital (Risk-free investment)	R_{FI}	2.53 (monthly)	FRED	https://fred.stlouisfed.org/series/GS 10	2019	May 2019
Cobb-Douglas Parameter	$AL^a K^{1-a}$	a = .2 A = 9.46	Adetunji et al. (2012)	On Restricted Least Squares: The Cobb-Douglas Production Function for the Nigerian Economy	N/A	N/A
Alpha	a					
Savings Rate	S_R	18.2%	WDI	https://data.worldbank.org/indicato r/NY.GNS.ICTR.ZS?locations=NG	2017	2019
Income Threshold to Donate	Y_{donate}	Anything greater than $14,000	A_{SA}	A_{SA}	N/A	N/A
Lambda	λ	A_{SA}	A_{SA}	The responsiveness of NGOs donations to the difference between the Nigerian income threshold and per capita income at time(t)	N/A	N/A
Capital	K			$Integ\,(FDI + I + NGO_{Donation} - \delta, CO)$		
Sigma	Σ	A_{SA}	A_{SA}	The responsiveness of investment to the rate of foreign retune on capital to local retune on capital at time(t)	N/A	N/A
Income Per Capita	$Y_{per-cap}$			Y/POP		
Output	Y			$A * (L^a) * (K^{1-a})$		
Gamma	γ	A_{SA}	A_{SA}	The responsiveness of FDI retunes to local retunes on capital at time(t)	N/A	N/A
NGO – Donations	$NGO_{Donation}$			$max\,(\lambda * (Y_{donate} - Y_{per-cap}),0) + \,If\,then\,else\,(Y_{per-cap} < Y_{donate}, max\,(\Sigma * (R_{FI} - L_{RK}),0),0)$		

Where:
ASA = Authors' sensitivity analysis

109

System Dynamics Model

The *NGO$_D$ − DEM* was built based on the information from Table 2, and three simulations were analyzed to estimate the sensitivity of an individual's per capita income and NGO donations.

Figure 2: *NGO$_D$ − DEM*

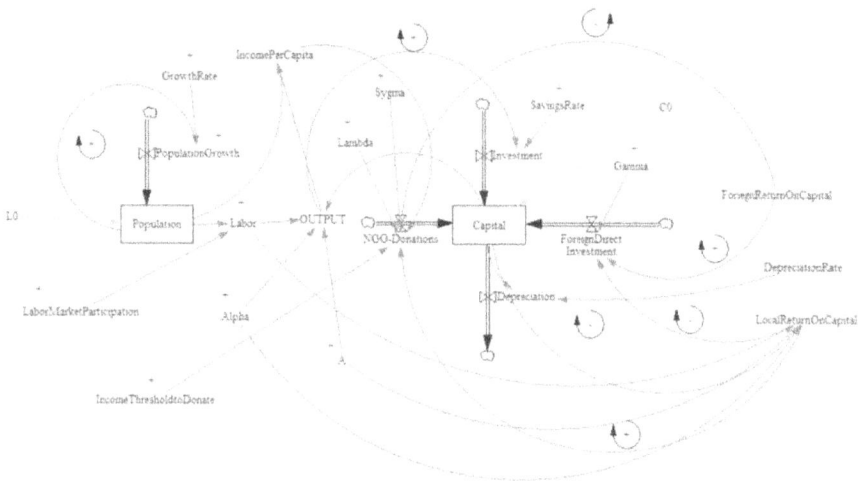

This methodology is ideal for exploring NGO donations, but one limitation of the chapter is the lack of data on the NGO industry in the country. The discrepancies between the *Y$_{donate}$* results in stakeholders' variations in donating to the causes of NGOs. This uncertainty includes the *nation's RFI, LRK, SR, and FDIs.* Our results reveal the sensitivity of *Y$_{donate}$* as it relates to *Y$_{per-capita}$*.

Results

The stock and flow diagram of *NGOdonation* can be seen in (Figure 2). Figure 3 shows the sensitivity analysis of *FDI* in the country. The results

Figure 3: Foreign Direct Investment

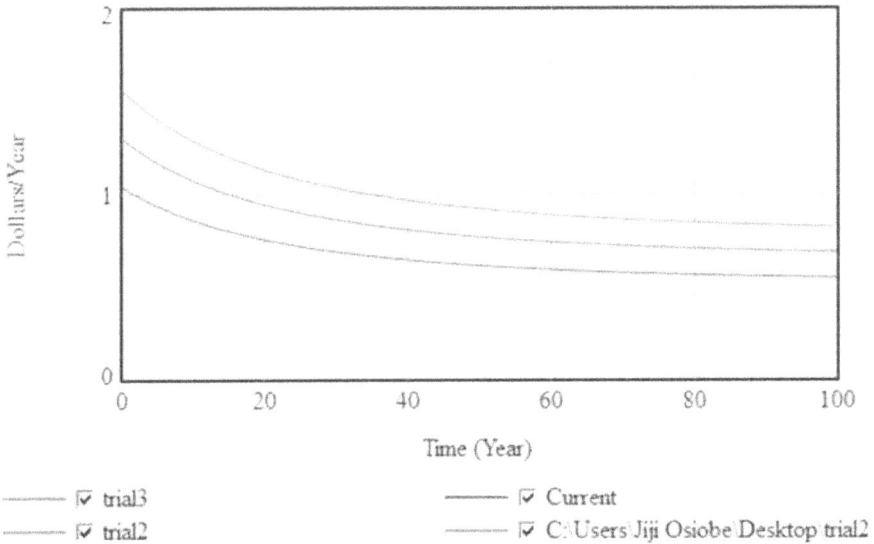

ForeignDirectInvestment

- ☑ trial3
- ☑ trial2
- ☑ Current
- ☑ C:\Users\Jiji Osiobe\Desktop\trial2

indicate that if L_{RK} is greater than R_{FI}, there would be a high inflow of *FDIs* into the nation and vice versa. If the latter holds to be accurate, it is more cost-effective for individuals and businesses to donate to the country than to invest in it. But if the former holds to be true, it would be more profitable for a business or individual to invest in the nation than to donate, as investing would create more jobs and opportunities, increasing the multiplier effect (direct, indirect, and induced effect) of every dollar spent in the nation.

Figure 4: NGO-Donation

NGO-Donations

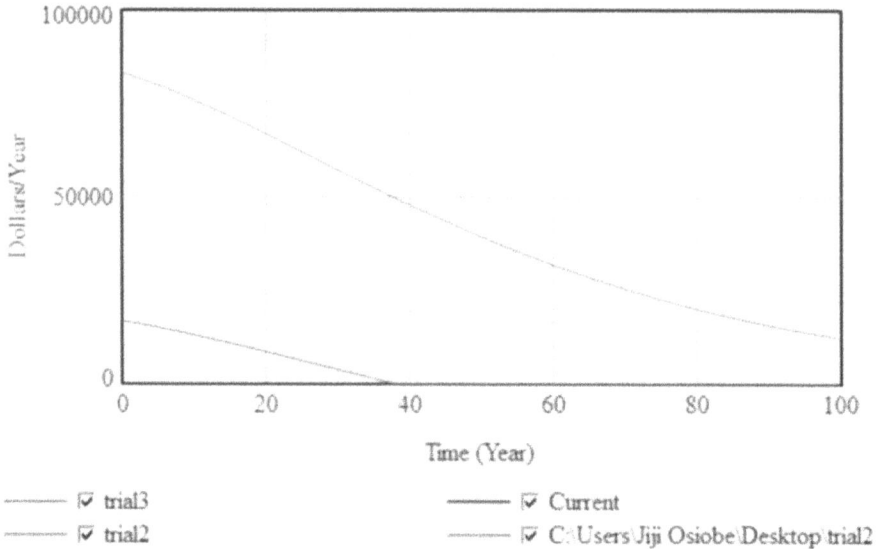

Ceteris paribus, if the former statement in Figure 2 holds, Figure 4 shows the sensitivity analysis of donations by individuals and businesses nationwide. Hence, there would be zero donations to NGOs if the annual income of an individual or net economic profit made by a corporation is between $0 - $13,000. But with a yearly salary of $14,000 - $80,000, holding the same figures projections, for companies' net economic profits, donations would increase until they hit a peak; then, it starts to decrease. The diminishing return trend/phenomena in Figure 4 can be explained as an overall economic boost, revealing that NGOs would be self-sufficient. Hence, residents in the community would not need their services, as the general standard of living in that economy would increase, and everyone would be better off. The green line in Figures 3 and 4 shows the initial simulation of the $NGO_D - DEM$; the red line is the second simulation of the $NGO_D - DEM$; and the blue line is the third and final simulation of the

$NGO_D - DEM$, where the L_{RK}, S_R, and $Y_{per\text{-}capita}$ were adjected to see how sensitive they are to the $NGO_D - DEM$.

RECOMMENDATION

The UN Sustainable Development Goals (SDGs) are based on the normative ideology that measurements create metrics; metrics create set targets, and set targets to create economic growth and development programs of intervention. The UN SDGs have been successful in creating global awareness of developmental issues around the world. The SDGs have been widely embraced and are now the guiding principle for most economic growth, development, and sustainability plans. Despite the acceptance and support for the UN SDGs, which were first the millennium goals by the joint efforts of presidents and prime ministers, public and private sectors, and local and international development organizations, over the past years, have been somewhat successful. Based on an idea that has been gaining a lot of attention, with little action to support the movement, the following are some recommendations that will foster economic growth, development, and stability in the region:

The Nigerian government should be more diligent in enforcing the nation's rule of law. This will attract more FDIs into the country and promote local growth and development.

- The Nigerian government should ensure that property rights laws effectively protect foreign investment in properties in Nigeria.
- A diversified economy will attract more FDIs, creating new avenues for people to invest.
- Local return on investments should be more attractive than

competing markets worldwide. This will spur investors to take a risk, as the rewards will be greater.

- NGOs and other agencies involved with economic growth, development, and stability need to be more proactive in their policies and decision-making strategies rather than being reactive, which has been the norm.
- The partnership between the public, private, and NGOs should have an agreed-upon, unified goal(s) where all parties involved are heard, their values are respected in the execution of the project, and particular agenda(s) are met without infringing on anyone's right or harming the environment.
- The NGOs should create and maintain an accurate database to help scholars and researchers study the industry.

Overarching Findings

Our results (Figures 3 and 4) illustrate essential principles that will inform policymakers and management in the public, private, and NGO sectors. When the per capita income, net economic profit made by companies, and return on local investment drop, the demand for NGO donations will increase as the living standard in the society starts to decrease (not shown in the chapter).

For the data (Table 2) and $NGO_D - DEM$ (Figure 2) structure used, our findings will spark policy debates over various NGO programs, donations, funding, and the measures we considered. While the detailed numerical results are valid only for the city of Lugbe, FCT, Nigeria, other NGOs around the world can use the approach to create sustainable economic development plans, projections, and recommendations.

Discussion

We have confidence that the analytical evidence presented in this chapter will contribute to informing debates over the best way to handle the ongoing donation challenges that face the managerial staff of NGOs and policymakers for controlling the economic burden placed on some NGOs in rural areas. A similar approach as described in this chapter could be used to discover financial and economically viable measures to address local return on investment related to foreign return on investment. The same approach can also guide local saving rates pertaining to foreign and domestic direct investments.

Takeaways

This chapter has addressed the challenges NGOs face regarding donations, for which ongoing debates of why donation keeps decreasing and how NGO management can persuade the public to increase contributions. It is more defensible to design a donation projection plan with information on the total and marginal inflow and outflow of cash by NGOs, information typically missing in the NGO industry worldwide. This chapter has presented an original approach (with the model in the Appendix) to address widespread information gaps on how local returns on investment, foreign returns on investment, and income per capita threshold affect donations. While the $NGO_D - DEM$ developed and documented investigations much more than donation patterns in the NGO industry, those donations are the focus of the chapter. Our approach can be used to provide valuable information to guide future researchers interested in this topic.

Further Study

Although our findings show a positive economic impact on the Nigerian economy if $Y_{donation}$ is achieved, the economy shows a steady growth pattern. Further research is necessary for analyzing how Y_{donate} can be accomplished while ensuring that the $Y_{per\ cap}$ increases $\geq$ to the nation's inflation rate, the L_{RK} is as attractive as other competing countries, S_R is at a healthy level, and I continue to grow.

CONCLUSION

The issues discussed in this chapter are not exhaustive. Considering the NGO_D–DEM and its subset of factors, local communities' challenges in pursuing economic growth, development, and stability are immense. The impact of L_{RK}, R_{FI}, S_R, and $FDIs$ on the local economic growth, development, and stability process appears to become more pressing. There are circular dilemmas and a cumulative relationship between the stocks, flows, and variables in the NGO_D – DEM discussed above in trying to simulate the issues of a regional economy, in some cases resulting in a vicious cycle that requires a clear understanding of the wicked problem to generate virtuous cycle sets of factors to interrupt adverse outcomes.

This chapter utilizes the NGO_D–DEM to explore, visualize, and analyze the following dilemmas of NGO donations' responsiveness to Nigeria's per capita income, returns on foreign capital, and the returns on local capital. This chapter also analyzed two sensitivity scenarios from the base $NGO_D - DEM$ (see Figure 1). The findings show how responsive NGO activities are in fostering economic growth and development in the community. Our results show that if L_{RK} is greater than R_{FI}, there will be a higher inflow of *FDI* into the nation and vice versa. Hence, if the latter statement holds to be accurate, the cost-effectiveness for individuals and businesses to donate or invest in the country will decrease (see Figure 2). But, if the former statement is true, there will be zero donations to NGOs as long as individuals' per capita income is below Y_{donate} and companies make zero economic profits in their businesses.

The Y_{donate} is between \$0 - \$ 13,000. But, when the individual per capita income or a business's net economic profit is between \$ 14,000 - \$ 80,000, which is above Y_{donate}, donations, and investment will increase until a certain point when it peaks and starts to decrease (see Figure 3). Further result(s) show that the involvement of NGOs in societies where citizens are underserved by the financial, educational, entrepreneurial, political, and health industries had a normal distribution relationship-shaped curve for the labor force per capita income threshold, an inverse relationship on returns on L_{RK} and a positive return on R_{FI}.

In Nigeria, we need to have a normative standard focusing on the economy's wicked problems and evaluate the threats in our society to take advantage of the available opportunities. It is essential to restore consumer confidence for a peaceful and fair environment where local businesses and individuals can flourish.

REFERENCES

Binder-Aviles, H. (2012). *The NGO Handbook* (The Handbook Series Edition ed.). United States of America: Bureau of International Information Programs, United States Department of State. Retrieved May 12, 2019

Chattopadhyay, S. (2014, August 4). *The World Bank*. Retrieved from Redefining the Roles of NGOs: http://blogs.worldbank.org/publicsphere/redefining-roles-ngos

City Population. (2017, November 7). *Federal Capital Territory, Nigeria*. Retrieved from City Population:

Etuk, I. O. (2014, May-June). The Role of Non-Governmental Organizations In Participatory and Sustainable Rural Economic Development in Nigeria. *IOSR Journal of Economics and Finance*, IV(1), 22-30. Retrieved April 28, 2019, from www.iosrjournals.org

Forrester, J. (1973). Confidence in models of Social Behavior with Emphasis on System Dynamics Model. *System Dynamics Group Working Paper*.

Forrester, J. W. (1968). Industrial Dynamics.

Forrester, J. W. (1989). The Begining of System Dynamics

Grantspace. (2015, May 11). *What is an NGO? What role does it play in civil society?* Retrieved April 28, 2019, from Grantspace: https://grantspace.org/resources/knowledge-base/ngo-definition-and-role/

Launi, S. (2016). Zaria, Kaduna, Nigeria: A.B.U Zaria.

Launi, S. (2016, February). *Assessing The Contribution of Non-Governmental Organizations in Human Development in Bauchi and Gombe States, Nigeria*. Zaria, Kaduna, Nigeria: Kubanni.

Launi, S. (2016). *Assessing the Contribution of Non-Governmental Organizations on Human Developments in Bauchi and Gombe States, Nigeria*. Zaria: A.B.U Press.

Launi, S. (2016). *Assessing the Contribution of Non-Governmental Organizations on Human Developments in Bauchi and Gombe States, Nigeria*. Zaria: A.B.U Press.

Law Nigeria. (2011, November 29). *Federal Capital Territory*. Retrieved from Law Nigeria: http://lawnigeria.com/Abuja/Abuja.html

Louisiana Community Network. (2008). *Introduction to Community Development*. Louisiana: Louisiana Community Network.

New World Encyclopedia. (2019, January 29). *Abuja*. Retrieved from New World Encyclopedia: https://www.newworldencyclopedia.org/entry/Abuja

Omofonmwan, S. I., & Odia, L. (2009). The Role of Non-Governmental Organisations in Community Development: Focus on Edo State–Nigeria. *The Anthropologist*, XI(4), 247-245. Retrieved April 28, 2019

State Resource Centre Kerala. (2015). *Community Development*. Kerala: Commonwealth of Learning.

The United Nations Department of Economic and Social Affairs. (2008). Achieving Sustainable Development and Promoting Development Cooperation. New York, NY: United Nations Publications.

USING A PRIORITIZATION-BASED MODEL IN DECISION-MAKING

INTRODUCTION

The world's socio-economic issues are all equally essential, but we can't prioritize them simultaneously because economics studies optimizing scarce resources to satisfy human needs. In August 2017, according to a survey given to millennials by the World Economic Forum (WEF), the ten most critical problems in the world were (see Table 1).

The questionnaire was completed by more than 31,000 participants aged 18 and 35 across 186 countries. While global warming, conflict resolution, and peacekeeping continue to be among the most visible efforts of the United Nations (UN), they and their specialized agencies have, over the years, been engaged in a wide range of activities to improve the lives and living standards of people around the world. These activities range from education, disaster relief and the advancement of women's rights.

Rank	Table 1: Most concerning world issues.		Converted to 100%
1	Climate change / destruction of nature	48.8%	19.17%
2	Large scale conflict / wars	38.9%	15.28%
3	Inequality (income, discrimination)	30.8%	12.10%
4	Poverty	29.2%	11.47%
5	Religious conflicts	23.9%	9.39%
6	Government accountability and transparency	22.7%	8.92%
7	Food and Water Security	18.2%	7.15%
8	Lack of Education	15.9%	6.25%
9	Safety / security / well being	14.1%	5.54%
10	Lack of economic opportunity and unemployment	12.1%	4.75%

Source: Business Insider | https://www.businessinsider.com/world-economic-forum-world-biggest-problems-concerning-millennials-2016-8

OTHER RELATED CHALLENGES

- About 2.1 Billion (B) people lack access to safe-managed drinking water (WHO/UNICEF 2017).

- About 4.5 B people lack essential sanitation services. (WHO/UNICEF 2017).

- 1 in 9 people around the world experiences chronic hunger, which is equivalent to 821 Million (M) people worldwide out of 7.53 B (World Bank (WB)) (FAOUN Report 2019).

- About 2 M people in 16 "non-self-governing territories" live under virtual colonial rule (UN University[1]).

- Since 1991, the UN has provided various forms of electoral assistance to more than 100 countries, including advisory services, logistics, training, civic education, computer applications, and short-term observation (UN[2]).

In an ideal world, we could solve all these problems and more, but we can't, so the question is, which issues do we prioritize? With the limited resources we have in this world and our homes, where should we spend it? One of our biggest obstacles is that all men and women die, and we don't have the technology to solve that yet. So, our goal should be prioritizing solutions to the world's problems, or at least the issues we can address.

Why has the Prioritization Based Model (PBM) never been done before? Because using the PBM based on the contents in Table 1 will mean ignoring some problems (think opportunity cost), and the PBM is widely unpopular and uncomfortable for policymakers to execute. People and agencies that tackle the issues in Table 1 would love to be on top of the prioritized list, and nobody will allow themselves to be at the bottom of that list.

To prioritize the solutions to these problem more efficiently, the third Global Copenhagen Consensus (GCC) was held in May 2012 to provide an answer to the question: If you had 75 B USD for a worthwhile cause(s)— such as de-escalating armed conflict, sustaining and protecting the biodiversity system, treating and controlling chronic diseases, tackling climate change, improving the human capital (education), mitigating and fighting hunger and malnutrition, better preparing for natural disaster, ensuring a sustainable population growth, ensuring clean drinking water supply for everyone, and promoting sanitation; which of the following will you tackle first, that will have the most significant impact, in an emerging community. A panel comprised five Nobel Economists: Robert Mundell*, Nancy Stokey, Thomas Schelling*, Vernon Smith*, and Finn Kydland*. The deliberation was informed by 30 new economic research papers written just for the project by scholars from around the world.

Before the 2012 summit, in 2008, economists like Jagdish Bhagwati, Francois Bourguignon, Robert Mundell*, Douglass North*, Vernon L. Smith*, Finn E. Kydland*, Thomas Schelling*, and Nancy Stokey—and in

2004, economist like Jagdish Bhagwati, Robert Fogel*, Thomas Schelling*, Vernon L. Smith*, Bruno Frey, Justin Yifu Lin, Douglass North*, and Nancy Stokey— all worked on ten different world challenges, ranging from infectious diseases, conflicts, education, financial instability, global warming, government and corruption, malnutrition and hunger, population growth and migration, sanitation and water, and subsidies and trade barriers3. Given the budget restraints, these economists found the following problems worthy of investment (see Table 2).

Table 2		
2012 Priority Solutions	2008 Priority Solutions	2004 Priority Solutions
The introduction of national programs such as a micronutrient intervention program, food program to fight hunger, the improvement of the educational systems, deworming treatment and prevention programs, expanding the subsidy for malaria treatment, expanding childhood immunization coverage, expanding TB treatment, and increasing hepatitis B immunization. Strengthening the operational capacity, using low-cost drugs in situations of acute heart attacks in poorer nations (these are already available in developed countries), Accelerated HIV vaccine.	The introduction of a health supply program that will distribute micronutrient—supplements to children such as vitamin A, zinc, iron, iodized salt, deworming, expanding immunization coverage for children, community-based nutrition promotion programs, malaria prevention, and treatment programs, tuberculosis (TB) and HIV finding, prevention, and treatment programs, improving surgical capacity at the district hospital level	The introduction and implementation of new measures to prevent the spread of the Human Immunodeficiency Virus (HIV) and Acquired Immunodeficiency Syndrome (Aids). The economists' estimated that an investment of 27 B USD could avert nearly 30 M new infections by 2010; The introduction of policies to reduce malnutrition and hunger in nations; and the control and treatment of malaria. The economists' estimated that it will cost about 13 B USD.
Increase investments in R & D to improve the total output of the nation, decrease hunger, fight biodiversity destruction, construction of boreholes, water systems, and Increase the investment in geoengineering R & D into the feasibility of solar radiation management, lessen the effects of climate change. Investing and creating an effective early warning system to protect the population against natural disasters and salt reduction campaign to reduce chronic disease and the benefits of education.	The implementation of the 2001 Doha Development Agenda (DDA)4, investment in R & D for low-carbon energy technologies, biofortification, Microfinancing for small businesses, bio-sand filters for household water treatment, rural water supply, larger multipurpose dams, sanitation campaign, and the introduction of a tobacco and carbon dioxide tax. Increase and improve girls' access to education, provide support for women's reproductive role, lowering the price of tuition.	The introduction of trade liberalization policies that will; yield substantial benefits to emerging nations and the world, lowering barriers to migration for skilled workers, and the introduction of a migration program for the (un/semi)-skilled workers and a program that will address global warming. The introduction of a national spending budget that will encourage investment in Research and Development (R & D) in new agricultural technologies, sanitation, and water quality.
	Peacekeeping in post-conflict situations and Conditional cash transfer	

Source: Copenhagen Consensus Final Results (2004) | https://www.copenhagenconsensus.com/sites/default/files/2004copenhagen_consensus_result_final.pdf
Copenhagen Consensus Final Results (2008)
https://www.copenhagenconsensus.com/sites/default/files/cc08_results_final_0.pdf
Copenhagen Consensus Final Results (2012)
https://www.copenhagenconsensus.com/sites/default/files/outcome_document_updated_1105.pdf

At this point, people may ask, why should an economist lead this optimization process? The answer to this is found in the first seven principles of economics (excluding economic—principle five): resources are scarce, opportunity cost, marginal analysis, exploiting opportunities, the economy eventually moves to the equilibrium, and division of labor and specialization leads to efficient use of principle one, that leads to a society achieving its goals. Think of this: if you want to know about malaria, you ask a malaria expert; if you're interested in the climate, you ask a climatologist; if you're curious about tax accounting, you seek a tax accountant, hence, if you want to optimize, you ask an economist.

PBM makes us think about our priorities. One of the things to observe from Table 3 and Figure 1 is that climate change didn't make the top three priorities. Still, a lot of people see it as a top priority (excluding first-world nations), and they believe we should engage in climate change activities and practices if for no other reason but because Earth is the only planet we have. However, we can't solve all of the problems; we can only prioritize, and if we must prioritize, we must focus on the right ones, where we can do a lot of positives rather than a bit of good.

According to Thomas Shelling*, an elite economist who explained the PBM much better, people forget that 100 years from now, when the future generation is talking about the impact of climate change, people around the world will be much wealthier and well-off (using the current trends and the differences between the 1st century AD or BC and the 21st century). Even the UN's most pessimistic impact scenario of chaos estimates that the average person in an emerging market in 2100 will be as wealthy as the average person in the Western world today. This forecast can be supported using or based on the bet between Julian Simon5 (pro-Adam Smith theory) and Paul Ehrlich6 (pro-Malthusian theory) in 1980. Following J. Simon's 1980 ideology, it is much more likely the average person will be two to four times richer.

Bringing it back to the PBM, the real question becomes: do you want to help a rich man in an emerging economy in 2100 (having present-day Western world living conditions), or do we want the lives of residents to improve in these same emerging economies right now (2020)? Who needs help, and who we can help with the least amount of money? Because, based on J. M. Keynes's words, in the long run, we're all dead. This means we need to use our money in a way that can create the most impact now.

This ideology tells us why we should get our priorities straightened by using the PBM, even when it doesn't accord with the trending topics of today and the way we see the world's problems. In solving the world's problems, we need to realize it's not about making us feel good or tackling the issues that can attract the most media attention. It's about taking action in areas that do the most good. Don't get me wrong: in an ideal world, if possible, we should and will solve all the world's problems. But it's not that simple.

In the '70s, western nations agreed to spend twice as much on emerging markets as we are in the 21st century. Since then, aid to those economies has fallen, so it doesn't look like the world economy is on the path to solving its most significant problems. The Ane Osiobe International Foundation aims to say that if a country gets additional/excess USDs in its nation's reserve for solving the world's issues, policymakers should spend it in the best possible way, which is this report's primary contribution to the literature on global issues. The real problem goes back to determining the right priorities, and the right questions are brought forth to determine if the current list reflects the world's view and not just the opinions of the elitists.

#	Challenges	Priority Solutions
	Table 3[7]	

Table 3[7]
The Copenhagen Consensus Youth Form Ranking of the World's top Challenges.

#	Challenges	Priority Solutions
1	Malnutrition and Hunger	• The creation of health and nutrition programs to train locals. • The provision of micronutrient supplements for children such as vitamin A, iron, iodized salt, and zinc. • Community-based nutrition promotion. • The provision of malaria prevention supplies, treatment supplies, and the expansion of immunization programs.
2	Diseases	• TB case finding and treatment. • Total sanitation campaign. • Deworming at school age. • HIV prevention. • Biofortification. • Improving surgical capacity at the district hospital level. • Heart attack acute management. • Inspection and maintenance of diesel vehicles.
3	Water	• Facilitation of rural water supply projects and the creation programs to train locals on how to treat and maintain the system. • The construction of a larger multipurpose dam in Africa.
4	Education	• Provision of scholarship and voucher programs. • Implementing the DDA. • Over-the-horizon guarantees. • Increase and improve girls' schooling.
5	Women	• Provide support for women's reproductive role. • Affirmative action.
6	Air Pollution and Global Warming	• Improved stove intervention. • Package of adaptation, R&D followed by mitigation. • Bio-sand filters for household water treatment. • Low sulfur diesel for urban road vehicles. • R&D in low-carbon energy technologies. • Tobacco tax. • Diesel vehicle particulate control technology. • Increased proactive response.
7	Terror and Conflicts	• Packaged aid, spending limit, peacekeeping guarantee. • Post-conflict aid. • Improving trade and migration reform. • Inking aid to military spending limits. • Augmented defensive measures. • Targeted countries are to change their foreign policies.
8	Trade	• Conditional cash transfers. • Microfinance. • Greater international cooperation. • Rich nations drop trade barriers to emerging nations

Source: The 2008 CCYF |
https://www.copenhagenconsensus.com/sites/default/files/results_of_copenhagen_consensus_2008_youth_forum.pdf

This is what spurred the creation of the Copenhagen Consensus Youth Forum (CCYF), which is comprised of 80 young people worldwide. To join the CCYF, the members needed to meet two requirements: they were in a university and spoke English. Most of the group was from emerging countries, and the list of challenges and solutions they created in Table 3 was very similar to that of the dream team list in Table 2.

My World.org asked the same question presented to the Nobel economist at the Copenhagen Summit as an open survey to the world. Table 4 shows the distribution of the source of the votes.

Table 4 shows the statistical distribution of their data sources, while Figure 1 shows the prioritization of their needs.

Table 4		
Source	Headcount	As a % of home page votes
Website	619,878	6.37%
Ballot	8,047,796	82.66%
SMS	471,715	4.84%
Unknown vote source	597,095[8]	6.13%
Total votes from the website, ballot, and SMS	9,139,389	N/A
Votes on the Home Page	9,736,484	100.00%
Source: http://data.myworld2015.org/?source=Ballot (10/5/2019).		

From Figure 1, it's safe to say that the Ane Osiobe International Foundation is on the right path, as education ranks #1. Figure 2 shows countries by their vote.

Figure 1: What does the world want?
Source: http://data.myworld2015.org/ (10/4/2019)

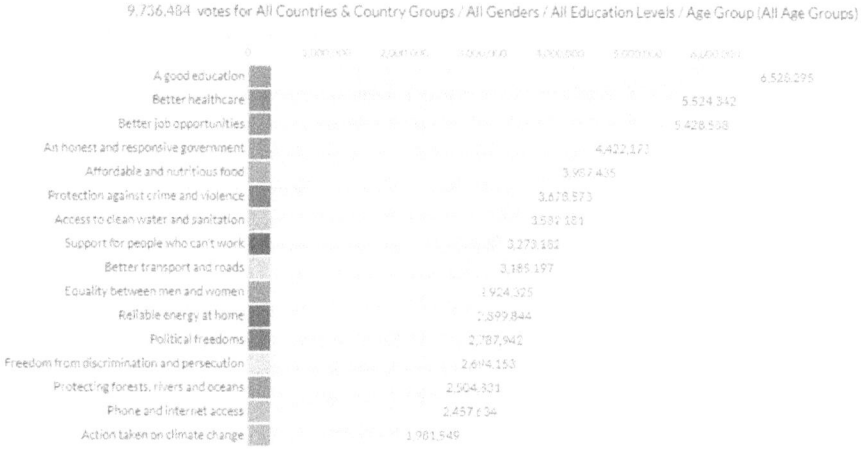

9,736,484 votes for All Countries & Country Groups / All Genders / All Education Levels / Age Group (All Age Groups)

Figure 2

Country	HDI	Votes	Votes%	Male	Female	≤15	16-30	31-45	46-60	≥61	Some Primary	Finished Primary	Finished Secondary	Beyond Secondary
Nigeria	Low	2735062	28.1%	53%	47%	41%	40%	13%	4%	2%	8%	46%	16%	30%
Mexico	High	1978589	20.3%	46%	50%	20%	55%	16%	6%	2%	7%	16%	25%	52%
India	Medium	902920	9.3%	49%	47%	40%	47%	6%	1%	0%	17%	30%	23%	24%
Pakistan	Low	701933	7.2%	46%	53%	3%	84%	13%	0%	0%	16%	21%	14%	48%
Sri Lanka	Medium	665533	6.8%	54%	46%	0%	100%	0%	0%	0%	0%	15%	30%	54%
Yemen	Low	413591	4.2%	72%	28%	1%	54%	38%	3%	1%	18%	22%	29%	30%
China	Medium	321853	3.3%	53%	47%	4%	53%	20%	15%	8%	16%	11%	17%	56%
Dominican Republic	Medium	228721	2.3%	45%	54%	23%	40%	20%	11%	6%	35%	27%	26%	11%
Philippines	Medium	107426	1.1%	45%	55%	35%	38%	17%	7%	2%	17%	31%	22%	29%
Republic of Korea	Very High	97531	1.0%	28%	72%	3%	36%	30%	25%	6%	1%	5%	5%	89%
United States of America	Very High	81543	0.8%	39%	61%	10%	43%	18%	18%	11%	5%	17%	15%	62%
Australia	Very High	73585	0.8%	42%	55%	15%	31%	16%	15%	15%	6%	27%	22%	40%

Source: http://data.myworld2015.org/ (10/4/2019)

128

With these findings, we can comfortably say there is a path ahead to start the conversation about our priorities, essential solutions, and where we could potentially begin. Let's not concentrate on solutions that require a high cost with little progress. Instead, let's focus on what we can do better, with little effort and low cost today, which will translate and multiply (to/for) the future.

AN IMPACT ANALYSIS ON THE NIGERIAN ECONOMY

INTRODUCTION

85% of the world's poor live in Asia and Africa, and 12% are from Nigeria. According to Katayama. R, an economist, and Wadhwa. D, a data scientist; in a 2015 study published by the World Bank (WB), 50% of the world's poorest people live in just five countries. Out of the five, two are from South Asia. Of the two from South Asia, 24% are from India and 3% from Bangladesh. The remaining three nations are from Sub-Saharan Africa. Of the Sub-Saharan nations', 12% are from Nigeria, 7% are from the Democratic Republic of the Congo (Congo, Dem Rep.), and 4% are from Ethiopia.

The two regions, "South Asia and Sub-Saharan Africa," together account for 85% (629 million) of the world's poor, according to the dataset of 2015. In 2018, the number was 700 million, or 10% of the world's population. Therefore, to make significant progress towards meeting goal 1, "ending poverty in all its forms everywhere" out of the 17 sustainable

Figure 1:
Global percentage of people living with less than $1.90 a day by region and country
Source: https://blogs.worldbank.org/opendata/half-world-s-poor-live-just-5-countries

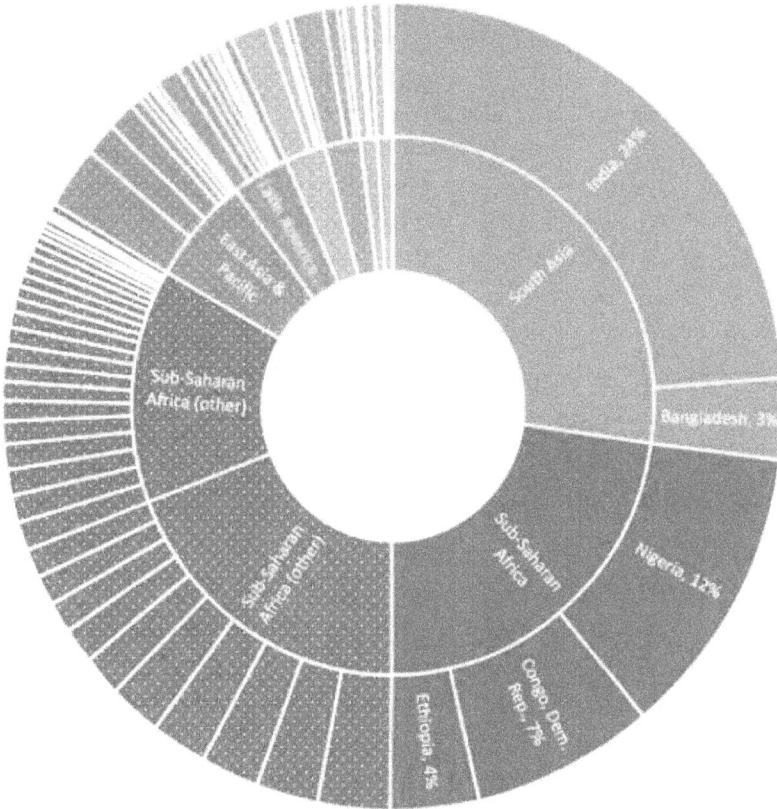

Povcal Net, World Development Indicators, World Economic Outlook,
Global Economic Prospects

development goals, the Ane Osiobe International Foundation aims to provide programs that spread the gift of hope in the nation of Nigeria by giving data-driven studies and helping kids who have potential, with opportunities that level the playing field. At the foundation, our primary goal is to help the Nigerian public gain an understanding of themselves while learning how they can develop their skills. Our goals would help foster the United Nations' target of reducing global poverty by 3% by 2030. The reductions in poverty in these five countries will be crucial as each nation has a high population to landmass density.

Figure 2:
Population trend of the five identified countries in the report (1960 – 2018)
Source: WDI

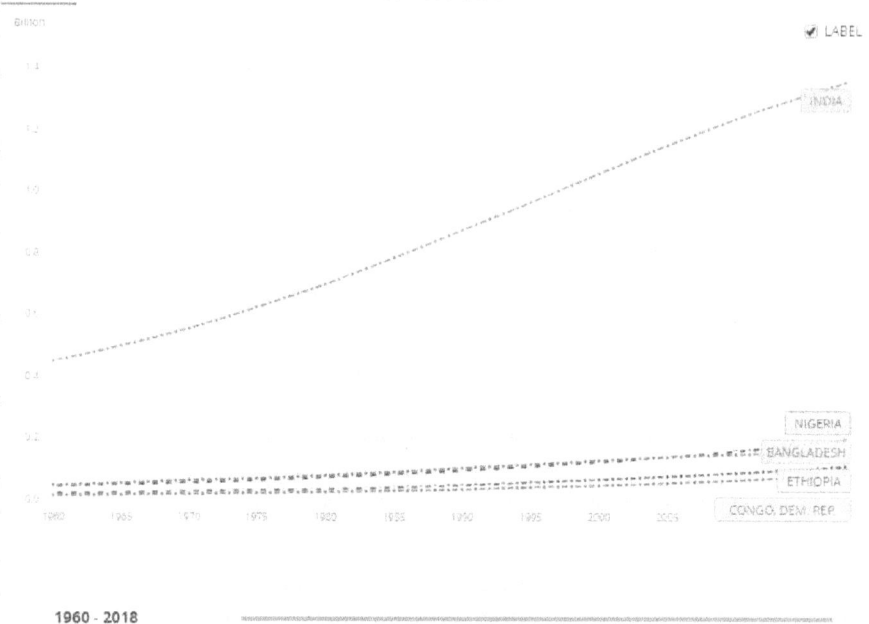

1960 - 2018

https://data.worldbank.org/

India

India's population is about 1.4 billion people, equivalent to 18.18% of the world population. The nation's landmass is about 2.4% of the world's land area. India's economy is the 6th largest in the world, with a Gross Domestic Product (GDP) of USD 2.30 trillion. Converted to GDP Purchasing Power Parity (PPP), it is the third-largest economy in the world with a GDP-PPP of

USD 8.52 trillion, and the country has a population density of 460 per Km2 (1,192 people per mi2).

Nigeria

The Federal Republic of Nigeria's population is about 201 million, equivalent to 2.6% of the world's population. The nation's landmass is about 356,667 mi²/910,770 Km². Nigeria's economy is the 31st largest in the world, with a GDP of USD 397,472 million. Nigeria's population density is 221 per Km2 (571 people per mi2), and the median age in the land is 18 years.

Figure 3:
Population trend of four identified countries in the report
((excluding India) (1960 – 2018))
Source: WDI

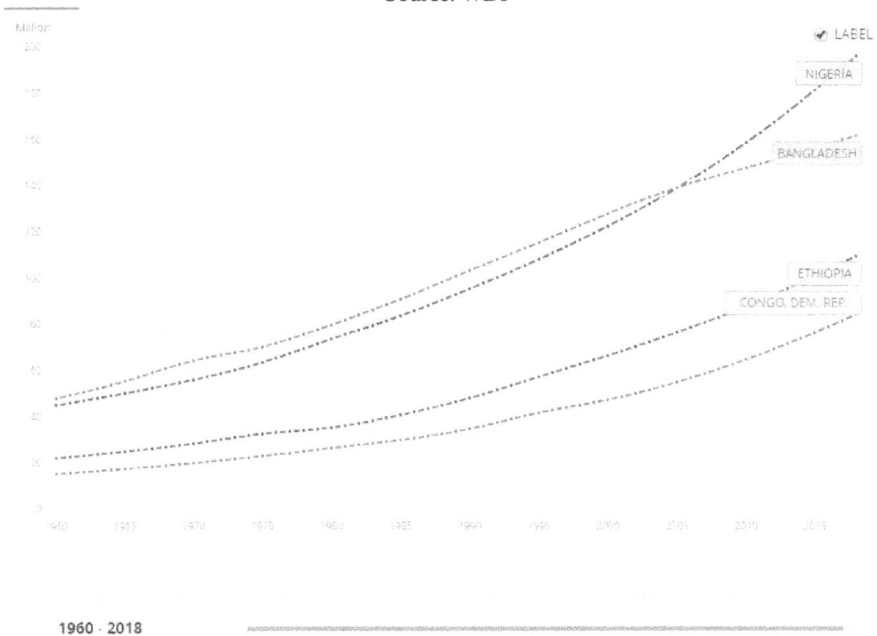

https://data.worldbank.org/

Bangladesh

Bangladesh's population is about 161 million people, equivalent to 20.09% of the world's population, and the median age in Bangladesh is 26 years. The total landmass of the nation is 130,170 Km2 (50,259 sq. miles) with a population density of 1291 per Km²2 (3,344 people per mi²). The economy of Bangladesh is market-based and is one of the fastest-growing economies in the world; the nation is ranked the 41st largest economy in the world in terms of nominal GDP and ranked the 30th largest economy by GDP-PPP.

Figure 4:
Projections of the most extreme poor nations' (2012 – 2030)
Source: https://blogs.worldbank.org/opendata/half-world-s-poor-live-just-5-countries

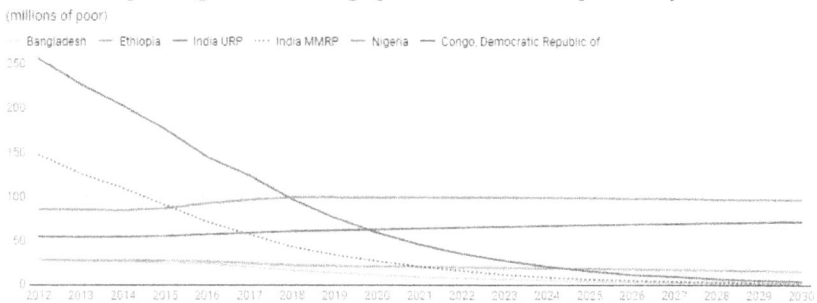

PovcalNet, World Development Indicators, World Economic Outlook,
Global Economic Prospects

Figure four shows the projections of the top five most impoverished nations from 2012 to 2030. From Figure four, one can infer that Bangladesh and India (Uniform Reference Period (URP) and Modified Mixed Reference Period (MMRP)) show a fast-declining rate, which implies that these nations' standard of living has been improving over time between 2012 – 2019 and projected 2020 – 2030. Ethiopia showed a slowly declining rate, which implies that the national standard of living is gradually improving. In Nigeria and the Congo, Dem and Rep showed a flat decline. This means these nations would remain relatively the same between 2020 – 2030 at their current economic (standard of living) status.

Ethiopia

The Federal Democratic Republic 's population is about 110.5 million people, equivalent to 1.43% of the world population, and the median age in Ethiopia is 19 years. The total landmass of the nation is 1,000,000 Km² (386,102 mi²), with a population density of 110 per Km² (285 people per mi²). Ethiopia's economy is market-based, ranked number 12 in the list of countries (and dependencies).

Figure 5:
Projections of the most extreme poor nations ((2012 – 2030) (Highlighting Nigeria))
Source: https://blogs.worldbank.org/opendata/half-world-s-poor-live-just-5-countries

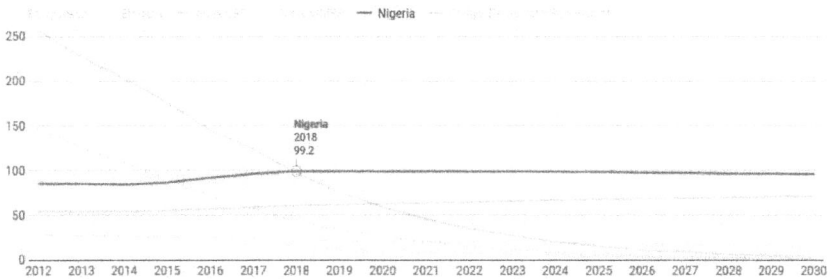

PovcalNet, World Development Indicators, World Economic Outlook,
Global Economic Prospects

Figure five shows the nation of Nigeria trend, which is relatively flat from 2012 – 2030. This implies that Nigeria needs to invest in its economy. Still, by the public and private sector, a joint sector agreement would foster economic growth and development much faster over time.

135

The Democratic Republic of the Congo

The current population of the Congo, Dem, is 87 million, equivalent to 1.12% of the world population. The nation has a median age of 17 years. The nation's landmass is about 2,267,050 Km²/875,313 mi². The economy of Congo, Dem, and Rep ranks 16th in the countries' dependency ratio by population.

Table 1:
Ranking of identified countries GDP per capita (PPP) with other 191 countries; from lowest to highest (where 1 = lowest; while 191 = highest

Rank	Country	USD GDP – Per Cap.
3	Congo, Dem, Rep	791
25	Ethiopia	2,517
50	Bangladesh	4,993
55	Nigeria	6,098
68	India	8,484

Source: IMF https://www.imf.org/external/pubs/ft/weo/2016/02/weodata/index.aspx

Table one shows the ranking of identified countries in this report's GDP per capita (PPP) with other 191 countries. Where 1 = lowest; while 191 = highest. The one shows Congo's Dem, Rep. as the lowest country in GDP – Per Cap, followed by Ethiopia, Bangladesh, Nigeria, and India. At this point, there will be no further explanation; there will be a reputation to build a stronger Nigeria, and we need every Nigerian's HELP.

According to figures 4 and 5, the projections of the declining poverty rate/ratio are based on a county's growth rate pattern that is correlated with its past growth rates related to the regional average over the last ten years. Extreme-poverty nations' such as India and Bangladesh, will approach zero by 2030, but extreme-poverty nations' like Nigeria, the Congo, Dem, Rep, and Ethiopia remain pretty elevated.

The uneven progress across these five countries indicates the broader uneven growth and development globally. An outcome where extreme poverty is nearly eliminated in some regions worldwide except in others (the Sub-Saharan African areas) certainly does not portray a picture of a world free of poverty. As emphasized in the Poverty and Shared Prosperity Report 2018, we should go beyond the focus on reducing the global poverty rate to below 3% and strive to ensure that all countries and all people can share in the benefits of economic development. Although this may be challenging, the Ane Osiobe International Foundation *"gives back to Nigeria, even when we're struggling ourselves because we know that there is always someone somewhere much worse off, and there but for the grace of GOD go I!!."*

Figure 6:
The selected five countries GDP – PPP (constant 2011 international $)

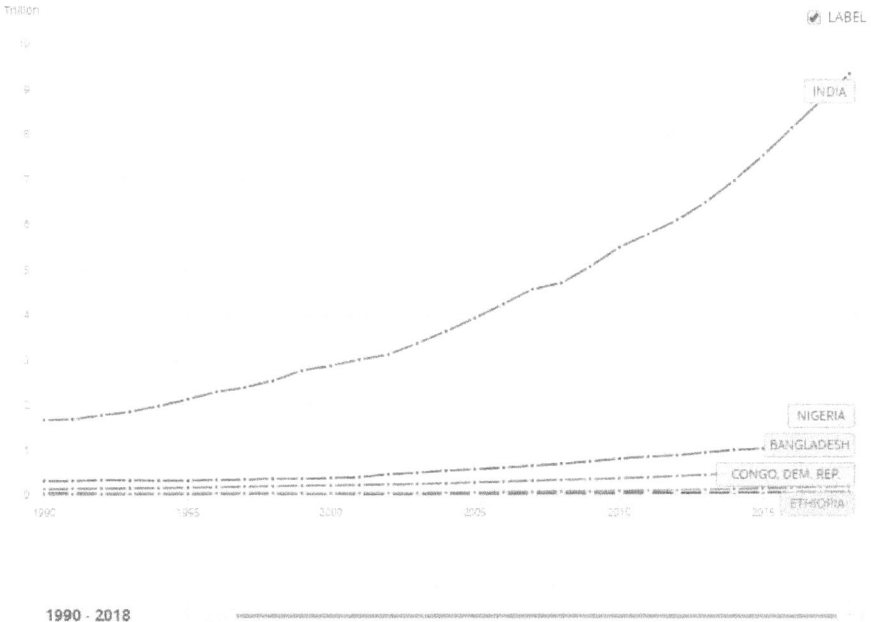

1990 - 2018

Source: WDI https://data.worldbank.org/indicator/NY.GDP.MKTP.PP.KD

Figure six shows the GDP – PPP (constant 2011 international $) of the selected five countries, with India ranked #1 among the chosen five countries, followed by Nigeria, Bangladesh, and Congo. Dem. Rep. and Ethiopia.

Figure 7:
The selected four countries (excluding India) GDP, PPP
(constant 2011 international $)
Source: WDI

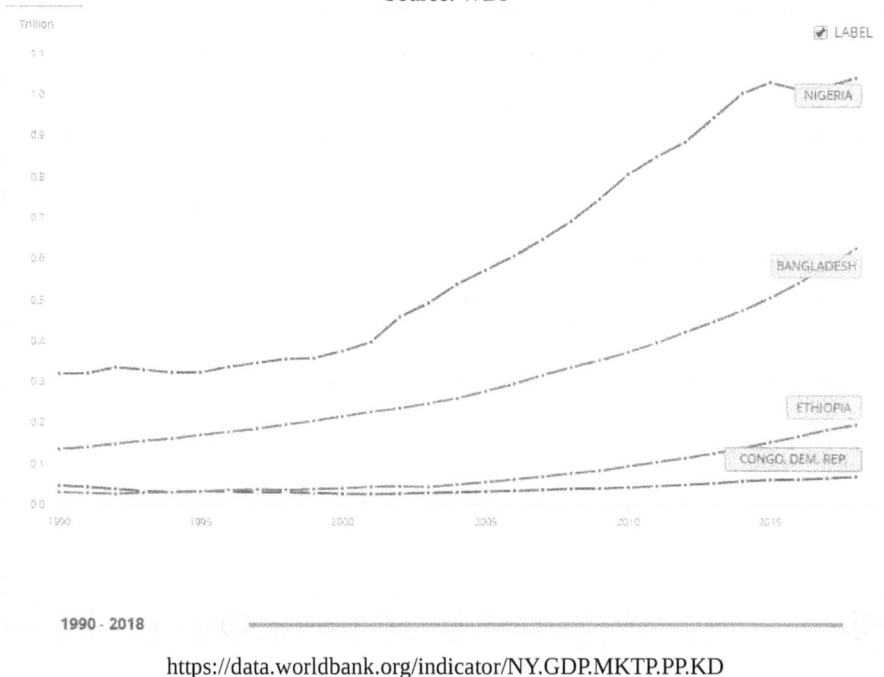

https://data.worldbank.org/indicator/NY.GDP.MKTP.PP.KD

Figure seven shows the selected four countries (excluding India) GDP and PPP (constant 2011 international $), with Nigeria ranked #1, followed by Bangladesh and Congo. Dem. Rep; and Ethiopia.

REFERENCE

[1] Beyond GDP - Report by the Commission on the Measurement of Economic Performance and Social Progress

[2] Central bank and monetary authority websites:
 https://www.bis.org/cbanks.htm

[3] Global Finance Magazine Beyond GDP - Report by the Commission on the Measurement of Economic Performance and Social Progress

[4] Global news and insight for corporate financial professionals

[5] International Monetary Fund (IMF) World Economic Outlook (WEO) database, October 2014

[6] New York Times: "The Rise and Fall of the G.D.P."-are there better ways to measure a country's wealth and happiness?

[7] The World Bank Country Profiles: https://data.worldbank.org/

[8] The World Bank: Blog: https://blogs.worldbank.org/opendata/half-world-s-poor-live-just-5-countries

[9] WEO Database October 2014-IMF

ERADICATING MALARIA

INTRODUCTION

There is a strong desire to eradicate malaria worldwide, and several attempts and strategies are being employed to make our world malaria-free. The death tolls due to the disease worldwide and the demography affected mainly by these malaria deaths have necessitated the need and urgency in devising and implementing efficient strategies. This report critically looks at malaria deaths worldwide and how the death tolls have fared over the years. It also looks at the countries, continents, and demography most affected. The report looks at the strategies implemented for controlling malaria. Also, it identifies the challenges of controlling malaria in Sub-Saharan Africa, the region with the highest malaria incidence. To understand the report's focus, we must define the following terminologies.:

- *Controlling Malaria*: The main aim is to reduce malaria transmission to a level that doesn't pose a public health issue.
- *Eliminating Malaria* is the complete wipeout of the disease in a region.
- *Eradicating Malaria*: is the elimination of malaria on a global scale.

140

The Impact of Malaria Worldwide

The most recent world malaria report released on November 2018 by the World Health Organization (WHO) recorded 219 million cases of malaria in the year 2017 (World Health Organization, 2018). The report showed a 0.92% rise from the 2016 report (World Health Organization, 2018). The deaths due to malaria worldwide dropped by 3.68.3% from 451,000 in 2016 to 435,000 in 2017 (World Health Organization, 2018). However, the data from the Institute of Health Metrics and Evaluation (IHME)[1] (www.healthdata.org) is significantly higher than that presented by WHO (Roser & Ritchie, 2017). IHME began publishing malaria mortality data in 1990, while WHO only began publishing the data in 2000. To present a holistic view and substantial data for comparison, we will present the data published by both reputable organizations.

Malaria Death Estimates from WHO

WHO began publishing the global estimates of the malaria death toll in 2000. From 2000 to 2015, the world's malaria death toll dropped by 50% (Roser & Ritchie, 2017). Africa had the highest death toll among the other continents, and in 2015, Africa accounted for 90% of the total death toll in the world. On the brighter side, Africa also recorded the most progress. Between 2000-2015, the African death toll dropped by 51.7 % from 764,000 to 395,000 (Roser & Ritchie, 2017).

Figure 1:
Global Malaria Deaths by WHO (2000 – 2015)

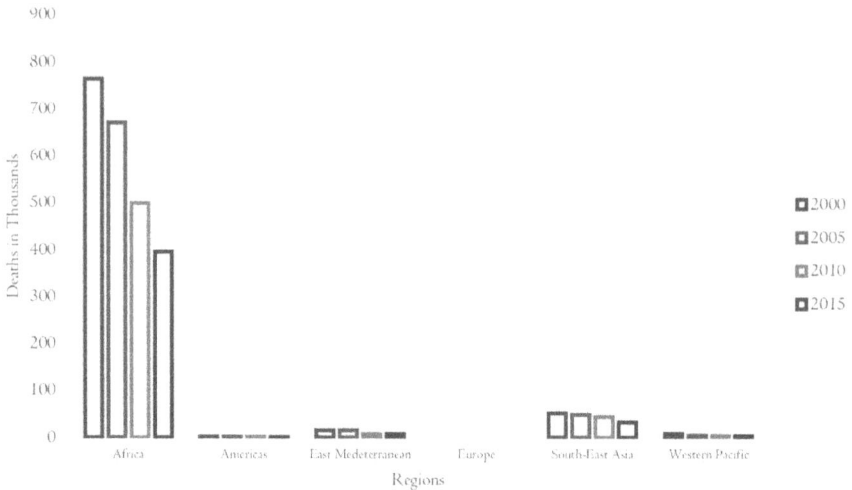

Source: https://ourworldindata.org

Figure one shows the global malaria deaths by WHO. It shows deaths caused by malaria in every region have been decreasing, with Africa showing a significant change, followed by East Mediterranean, South–East Asia, Western Pacific, America, and Europe.

Malaria Death Estimates from the Institute of Health Metrics and Evaluation

The IHME has been providing malaria death estimates since 1990. Although their number estimates are significantly higher than that of WHO and are divergent on the malaria death tolls of other regions, both datasets concur on the death toll in the African region, reflecting the 90% contribution to the worldwide deaths.

Figure 2:
Global Malaria Deaths by Region (1990 – 2015)

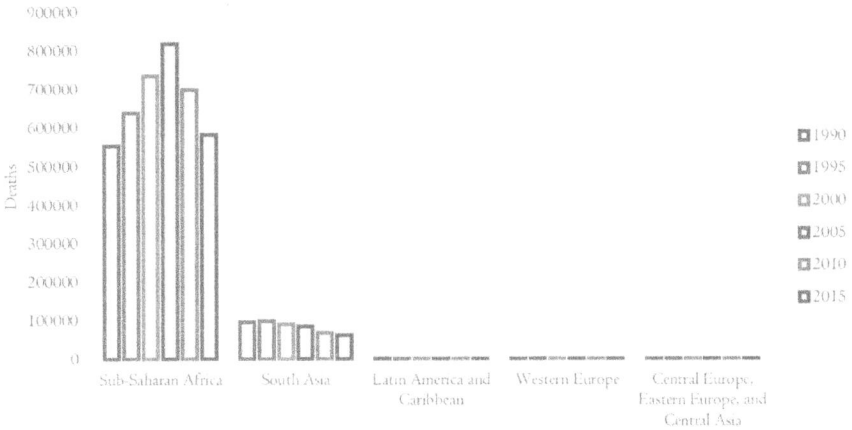

Source: Our World in Data
(IHME)

Figure two shows the global malaria deaths by region, with Sub–Saharan Africa having a standard distribution death toll curve, with 2005 as its peak, South Asia has a decreasing death toll, while Latin America and the Caribbean, Western Europe, Central Europe, Eastern Europe, and Central Asia were relatively flat.

The Malaria Death Toll by Age Group

The IHME has also published the demography of malaria death toll by age group since 1990. From 1990 up to date, children under age five have been the most affected over the years. The number of children under five years who die due to malaria is astounding. In 2016, an estimated 72% of the global malaria death toll was children under 5 (Roser & Ritchie, 2017).

These high numbers are because the immune system of children under five years of age is not yet fully developed, which means that they have very little resistance to malaria parasites and other potential health threats. Hence, they must be protected from exposure to these health threats. The same trend occurs when Nigeria data is analyzed.

Figure 3:
The World Malaria Death by Age Groups (2017)

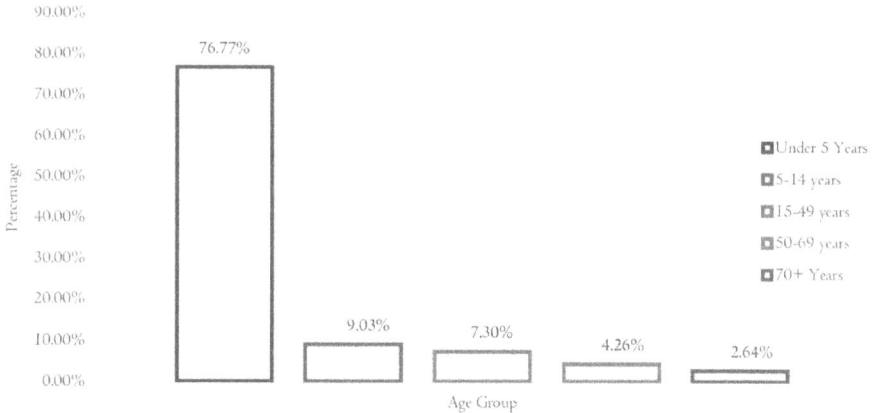

Source: Our World in Data
(IHME)

Figure three shows the world malaria death by age groups with 0 – 4 years at 76.77%, 5 – 14 years at 9.03%, 15 – 49 years at 7.30%, 50 – 69 years at 4.26%, and 70 + years at 2.64%. Based on the above descriptive statistic, one can hypothesize that the older one gets living in a malaria-infected area, the more resistant the person becomes to the Plasmodium.

Figure four shows malaria deaths by age group in Nigeria, with 0 – 4 years with an average of 144,326 deaths per year taking the most brutal hit, followed by 15 – 49 years with an average of 17,798 deaths per year, 50 – 69 years with an average of 12,456 deaths per year, 5 – 14 years with an average of 12,247 deaths per year, and 70+ years with an average of 7,010 deaths per year.

Figure 4:
Malaria Deaths by Age Group in Nigeria (1990 – 2015)

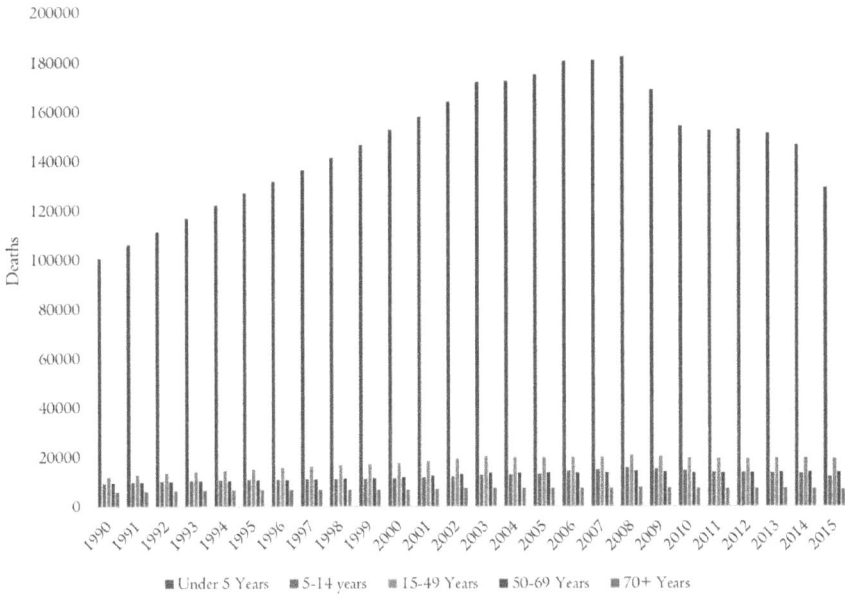

Source: Our World in Data
(IHME)

Malaria-Free Countries

Consistent efforts are being made worldwide to achieve the eradication of malaria. Although this global goal is yet to be achieved, world nations are making reasonable efforts to narrow the line between what is desired and what is obtainable. Worth noting is that there are countries where malaria never existed. In some nations with the sickness, the disease disappeared without any specific measure carried out by the nation or its people. Table one shows the data presented by the WHO on malaria-free certified nations. The certification is given to countries that report zero malaria cases for three consecutive years (World Health Organization, 2019).

145

Table 1:
Malaria-free countries

Country/Territory Countries certified malaria-free	Countries where malaria never existed or disappeared without specific measures

Africa

Algeria 2019
Lesotho 2012
Mauritius 1973
La Réunion (France) 1979
Seychelles 2012

Eastern Mediterranean

Bahrain 2012
Jordan 2012
Kuwait 1963
Lebanon 2012
Libya 2012
Morocco 2010
Qatar 2012
Tunisia 2012
United Arab Emirates 2007

Europe

Albania 2012
Andorra 2012
Armenia 2011
Austria 1963
Belarus 2012
Belgium 1963
Bosnia and Herzegovina 1973
Bulgaria 1965
Croatia 1973
Cyprus 1967
Czechia 1963
Denmark 1963
Estonia 2012
Finland 1963

France (Metropolitan) 2012
Germany 1964
Greece 2012
Hungary 1964
Iceland 1963
Ireland 1963
Israel 2012
Italy 1970
Kazakhstan 2012
Kyrgyzstan 2016
Latvia 2012
Lithuania 2012
Luxembourg 2012
Malta 1963
Monaco 1963
Montenegro 1973
Netherlands 1970
Norway 1963
Poland 1967
Portugal 1973
Republic of Moldova 2012
Romania 1967
Russian Federation 2012
San Marino 1963
Serbia 1973
Slovakia 1963
Slovenia 1973
Spain 1964
Sweden 1963
Switzerland 1963
The former Yugoslav
   Republic of Macedonia 1973
Turkmenistan 2010
Ukraine 2012
The United Kingdom
   and Northern Ireland 1963
Uzbekistan 2018

Americas

Antigua and Barbuda 2012
Argentina 2019
Bahamas 2012
Barbados 1968
Canada 1965
Chile 1968
Cuba 1973
Dominica 1966
Grenada 1962
Jamaica 1966
Paraguay 2018
Saint Kitts and Nevis 2012
Saint Lucia 1962
Saint Vincent and the 2012
  Grenadines
Trinidad and Tobago 1965
United States of America 1970
Uruguay 2012

South-East Asia

Maldives 2015
Sri Lanka 2016

Western Pacific

Australia 1981
Brunei Darussalam 1987
Cook Islands 1963
Fiji 1963
Japan 2012
Kiribati 2012
Marshall Islands 1963
Micronesia (the 1963
Federated States of)
Mongolia 1963
Nauru 1963
New Zealand 1963

Niue 1963
Palau 1963
Samoa 1963
Singapore 1962
Tonga 1963
Tuvalu 2012

Source: World Health Organization

Table 1 shows the countries certified malaria-free by WHO and the year they were certified. Column 1 of the table lists the countries/territories; column 2 lists the year the countries were confirmed to be malaria-free, and column 3 shows countries where malaria never existed or disappeared without any specific measure.

The above table inferred that Saint Lucia and Grenada were certified malaria-free in 1962; Kuwait, Austria, Belgium, Czechia, Finland, Iceland, Ireland, Malta, Monaco, Norway, San Marino, Slovakia, Sweden, Switzerland, The United Kingdom of Great Britain and Northern Ireland, Cooks Island, Fiji, Marshall Islands, Micronesia, Mongolia, Nauru, New Zealand, Niue, Palau, Samoa and Tonga were all certified malaria-free in 1963. Germany, Hungary, and Spain were all certified malaria-free in 1964. Bulgaria, Canada, Trinidad, and Tobago were all certified malaria-free in 1965. Dominica and Jamaica were certified malaria-free in 1966. Cyprus, Poland, and Romania were all certified malaria-free in 1967. Barbados and Chile were certified malaria-free in 1968. Italy, the Netherlands, and the United States of America were certified malaria-free in 1970. Mauritius, Bosnia and Herzegovina, Croatia, Montenegro, Portugal, Serbia, Slovenia, the former Yugoslav Republic of Macedonia and Cuba were certified malaria-free in 1973. Australia was certified malaria-free in 1981. Singapore was accredited malaria-free in 1982. Brunei Darussalam was approved as malaria-free in 1987. The United Arab Emirates was certified malaria-free in

149

2007. Morocco and Turkmenistan were both approved malaria-free in 2010. Armenia was accredited malaria-free in 2011. Lesotho, Seychelles, Bahrain, Jordan, Lebanon, Libya, Qatar, Tunisia, Albania, Andorra, Belarus, Denmark, France, Greece, Israel, Kazakhstan, Latvia, Lithuania, Luxembourg, Republic of Moldovia, Russian Federation, Ukraine, Antigua and Barbuda, Bahamas, Saint Kitts and Nevis, Saint Vincent and the Grenadines, Uruguay, Japan, Kiribati and Tuvalu were all certified malaria-free in 2012. Kyrgyzstan and Sri Lanka were certified malaria-free in 2016. Uzbekistan and Paraguay were both approved malaria-free in 2018. Algeria and Argentina were confirmed malaria-free in 2019 also; looking at Table 1, you will quickly observe that only four nations (Algeria, Mauritius, Lesotho, and Seychelles), out of the fifty-four countries in the African continent, have attained the malaria-free status by the WHO. Thus, the a large concentration of malaria deaths from this region.

Malaria Treatment and Prevention – Interventions

Controlling malaria is made possible by a couple of prevention methods, and the choice of the intervention employed depends on the level of malaria transmission in the area of interest. These malaria treatment prevention interventions are:

- Case management (diagnosis and treatment) of malaria: This is the prompt diagnosis and treatment of malaria patients with recommended antimalarial drugs to prevent the disease from progressing and curtail the infection's spread within and outside the community (Centers for Disease Control and Prevention, 2018).
- Prevention: This can be done using the following methods, which are

not limited to the list below.

1. The insecticide-treated nets (ITN): ITNs are a form of personal protection from malaria. These Insecticide Treated Nets work by forming a protective barrier. They are treated with insecticides that kill mosquitoes as well as other insects. Treated bed nets are more effective than untreated nets (Centers for Disease Control and Prevention, 2019).

2. The intermittent preventive treatment of malaria in pregnant women (IPTp): This is the administration of curative doses of antimalaria drugs (usually Sulfadoxine- Pyrimethamine popularly known as SP) to all pregnant women during their pregnancy period without testing if they are infected with the malaria parasite or not. IPTp is a preventive measure because women lose some of their immunity to malaria infection during pregnancy. Malaria infection during pregnancy can affect both mother and fetus adversely. Malaria during pregnancy can lead to maternal anemia and fetal loss delivery of low birth-weight infants (Centers for Disease Control and Prevention, 2018).

3. The infant's periodic preventive treatments (IPTi): Administering a therapeutic dose of antimalaria drugs (Sulfadoxine-Pyrimethamine) to infants at risk of malaria regardless of their malaria infection status. This dosage is administered through the Extended Program on Immunization (EPI) following the same intervals, corresponding to other routine vaccination schedules recommended for infants. IPTi is usually administered to infants at ten weeks, 14 weeks, and nine months of age (Centers for Disease Control and Prevention, 2015).

4. Indoor residual spraying (IRS): This is the spraying of insecticides

on a house's walls and other surfaces. IRS does not prevent people from being bitten by mosquitoes but kills the mosquito after they have probably fed on a victim and come to on the sprayed surface. Thus, the IRS aims to prevent malaria transmission to other people (Centers for Disease Control and Prevention, 2019).

The four malaria prevention interventions are employed in countries laden with high malaria transmission. Also, in areas of low malaria transmission, IPT is usually discouraged (Centers for Disease Control and Prevention, 2018). Occasionally, two other interventions are used. These are:

- Larva control and vector control intervention focuses on the Larva stage of the malaria vector. Mosquito breeding sites are located, treated, and sometimes removed to prevent breeding. Larva control is implemented through environmental modification, such as draining and filling or through larvicides (chemicals used to kill mosquito larvae). Larva control can also be achieved biologically by introducing fish and other aquatic animals to feed on the larvae (Centers for Disease Control and Prevention, 2018).
- Mass drug administration and mass fever treatment: This is the administration of antimalarial drugs to residents of a defined geographical area simultaneously and often at repeated intervals (Centers for Disease Control and Prevention, 2019).

Malaria control in Africa

By now, you already know that malaria exacts its most substantial burden in Africa. Efforts have been made to control the disease in Africa; this has proved extremely difficult for specific reasons:

- High malaria intervention cost that is difficult to bear in the region: As of 2015, the funding for the global fight against malaria totaled $2.9bn (World Health Organization, 2016). The funding for malaria control worldwide was majorly provided by the United States of America (35%), followed by the United Kingdom of Great Britain and Ireland (16%), while governments of endemic malaria countries provided about 31% of the funding. The $2.9bn is still 55% shy of the $6.4bn funding target for 2020 (World Health Organization, 2016). Despite the funding support from the U.S.A. and UK, more funding is still needed, including much more funding from the malaria-endemic governments affected the most by this infection.

- Weak infrastructures to combat the disease: Poor healthcare facilities, access to healthcare by a relative minority, and poor road network to the rural areas more prone to malaria than urban centers among other infrastructural challenges, make the fight against the disease in Africa very challenging.

- High prevalence of the deadliest parasite species in the area: The two most deadly human malaria parasites - P.vivax and P-falciparum, are most commonly found in the African continent (World Health Organization, 2016).

- Highly efficient species of mosquitoes that transmit the disease: The most effective malaria vector, Anopheles gambiae, is the most prevalent in Africa and the most difficult to control (World Health Organization, 2016).

- Favorable climate for the vector to thrive: Without sufficient rainfall, mosquitoes will not survive, and the parasites will not survive without adequate warmth (Centers for Disease Control and

Prevention, 2018). Most of Africa is in the tropics, characterized by insufficient rainfall and green vegetation. Africa is also the hottest continent in the world (World Atlas, 2018). These two climatic conditions make Africa a good breeding location for mosquitoes and malaria parasites.

Further Study

The Ane Osiobe International Foundation is working on a more theoretical and empirical driven analysis based on our pre–proposed hypothesized preposition:

H_O – *The older one gets living in a malaria–infected area, the more resistant the person becomes to the Plasmodium.*
H_a = *H_O will not hold to be true.*

CONCLUSION

Although the disease burden in Africa is very high, through the implementation of malaria prevention interventions, the support of global health organizations, and the commitment of African nations to drastically reduce the figures of malaria cases and death toll from malaria in the region, we continue to record commendable decline in the malaria cases and death toll from the disease in the area. For example, from WHO's global malaria death estimate publication (2000-2015), the death toll in Africa has dropped by 50% (Roser & Ritchie, 2017).

REFERENCES

Centers for Disease Control and Prevention. (2015, June 10). *Intermittent Preventive Treatment During Infancy (IPTi)*;
https://www.cdc.gov/malaria/malaria_worldwide/reduction/ipti.html

Centers for Disease Control and Prevention. (2018, July 23).
https://www.cdc.gov/malaria/malaria_worldwide/reduction/dx_tx.html

Centers for Disease Control and Prevention. (2018, July 23).
https://www.cdc.gov/malaria/malaria_worldwide/reduction/iptp.html

Centers for Disease Control and Prevention. (2018, July 23). *Larval Control and Other Vector Control Interventions*.
https://www.cdc.gov/malaria/malaria_worldwide/reduction/vector_control.html

Centers for Disease Control and Prevention. (2018, November 14). *Malaria*.
https://www.cdc.gov/malaria/about/biology/index.html

Centers for Disease Control and Prevention. (2019, January 4). I*ndoor Residual Spraying*. https://www.cdc.gov/malaria/malaria_worldwide/reduction/irs.html

Centers for Disease Control and Prevention. (2019, January 4). *Insecticide-Treated Bed Nets*. https://www.cdc.gov/malaria/malaria_worldwide/reduction/itn.html

Centers for Disease Control and Prevention. (2019, January 4). *Use of Antimalarials to Reduce Malaria Transmission*.
 https://www.cdc.gov/malaria/malaria_worldwide/reduction/mda_mft.html

Centers for Disease Control and Prvention. (2018, July 23).
https://www.cdc.gov/malaria/malaria_worldwide/reduction/index.html

Roser, M., & Ritchie, H. (2017, December 11). *Malaria*.

World Atlas. (2018, January 5). *Africa Weather*. Retrieved from World Atlas:
https://www.worldatlas.com/webimage/countrys/afweather.htm

World Health Organization. (2016, April 16). *Do all mosquitoes transmit malaria?* Retrieved from World Health Organization: https://www.who.int/features/qa/10/en/

World Health Organization. (2016, December 13). *Malaria control improves for vulnerable in Africa, but global progress off-track.* Retrieved from World Health Organization: https://www.who.int/news-room/detail/13-12-2016-malaria-control-improves-for-vulnerable-in-africa-but-global-progress-off-track

World Health Organization. (2018). World Malaria Report, 2018. *World Health Organization*(ISBN: 978 92 4 156565 3), xii-xix. Retrieved July 17, 2019, from https://apps.who.int/iris/bitstream/handle/10665/275867/9789241565653-eng.pdf?ua=1

World Health Organization. (2019, May 22). *Countries and territories certified malaria-free by WHO.* Retrieved from World Health Organization: https://www.who.int/malaria/areas/elimination/malaria-free-countries/en/

World Health Organization. (2019, March 27). *Malaria.* Retrieved from World Health Organization: https://www.who.int/news-room/fact-sheets/detail/malaria

NIGERIA'S JOBLESS RECOVERY

INTRODUCTION

This chapter examines jobless recovery and its effect on Nigeria's economy. The underlying objective of this chapter is to evaluate the trend between the increasing gross domestic product and the unemployment rate in Nigeria. To empirically analyze the impact of the jobless recovery in the nation, we estimated a two-stage least square regression from 1986 to 2018, and our results support the view that the nation's increasing real gross domestic product is associated with the country's jobless recovery status.

Every economy experiences bearish and bullish times according to the Business Cycle Theory (BCT) building on (Lucas, 1980) work; this chapter will define BCT as the economic expansion, peak, recession, trough, and recovery. The recovery, expansion, and peak periods are characterized by economic growth, increased productivity, and a low unemployment rate, while the recession and trough periods are the opposite. An economy is declared to be in a recession when the economy's Real Gross Domestic

Product (RGDP) reduces consecutively for two quarters. However, when an economy experiences a positive relationship with RGDP and the unemployment rate, that country is said to be in a jobless recovery state. The relationship between growth, poverty, and inequality has been the focus of economic growth theory and the interest of many scholars such as ((Romer, 1989 & 1990), (Osiobe, 2019) (Mankiw et al., 1992), (Lucas 1988), and (Fosu & Gafa, 2020)).

Fosu & Gafa (2020) found that the poverty level in Africa has declined over the past few decades due to the rise in Real Gross Domestic Product per capita $RGDP_{per\ capita}$, which is consistent with the global economy. Inequality, which this chapter will use the GINI index as a proxy, is defined as the extent to which income and consumer expenditure distribution among individuals and households within an economic region diverges from an equilibrium distribution state (World Development Index (WDI), 2020). This index is appropriate because it is the primary driver of changes in poverty within a community and has played a significant and complementary role in economic growth and income (re)distribution in some countries like Kenya, Nigeria, Ghana, and South Africa, with a GINI of 40.8, 43.0, 43.5, and 63.0, respectively (WDI, 2020).

Our study builds on (Mbaku, 2020) by aiming to blend the general and specific in probing the complex issue of Nigeria's jobless recovery. While also contributing to the literature on Nigeria's economic growth theory and empirically analyzing the socio-economic impact of the nation's jobless recovery, critically examining the widespread optimism about Africa (Frankema & Waijenburg, 2018) and probing the rising problem of inequality and precarious work environment in Africa. Nigeria's economy is a prime case study because the country had some compelling economic indicators in the last fiscal cycle. These indicators include but are not limited to the nation's RGDP growth of 2.3% in 2019, an inflation rate of 11.3%, fiscal revenue of 7% below the country's Gross Domestic Product (GDP), increased public spending financed mainly by borrowing, a public debt of 83.9 Billion (bn) United States Dollars (USD) (68% domestic and 32% foreign), which is 14.6% higher than 2018, and a poverty rate higher than the national average of 69% in rural communities (Africa Development Bank Group (ADBG), 2020).

According to ADBG (2020), the status quo of the Nigerian economy can be attributed to the low skill limit opportunities for employment in the mainstream economy. In Nigeria, inconsistent with the Western world economic recovery, the unemployment rate has been increasing. A prolonged jobless recovery seems unrealistic because, in most recovery periods, the unemployment rate reduces, consumer confidence rises, M1 & M2 money supply increases (((M1) monies that are the most liquid example (e.g.), cash and debit cards) ((M2) less liquid monies, e.g., stocks)), and aggregate demand increases; promoting economic growth. Weller (2014) corroborates this, stating that the labor market and industries pivot toward economic recovery after a recession. The chapter aims to evaluate the effect of the jobless recovery phenomenon in the Nigerian economy using a Two-Stage Least Square ($2SLS$). Our result shows that increasing $lnRGDPt$ and lnPop_t will hurt the nation URt. The $2SLS$ results imply that the quality and type of work are central to the growth rate of inequalities in Nigeria. The International Labor Organisation's (ILO) decent work agenda established a utile measuring scale for labor at the international level (ILO, 2020). According to Obeng-Odoom (2014), Africa, on the rise, is the new persona replacing the continent's negative image. The re-imaging of Africa has generated considerable interest among scholars that the region has been the center of the world's socio-economic crisis jokes. Mackett (2020) found that higher-paid professionals tend (not always) to have a decent occupation compared to low-skilled workers in elementary occupations. On the other hand, the higher a person is on the occupational ladder, the lower the individual scores in other economic indicators, such as decent working time and balancing work—family—and—personal life and vice-versa.

The Concept of Jobless Recoveries

The United Nations Development Program (UNDP, 1993) defines jobless growth as a phenomenon in which an increase in employment lags far behind an increase in output. Thus, jobless growth refers to a situation whereby the growth in real GDP moves at a faster rate than the employment growth. In other words, the unemployment rate is also rising as GDP grows. In 1996, the UNDP gave a broader view on jobless growth as growth in output that generates little or no employment, suppresses wages, makes working conditions dreary, and brings about precarious livelihoods.

Study Area

Nigeria is a nation located in West Africa with 36 states and the Federal Capital Territory (FCT) and a population size of 195 Million (mn) people as of 2018 (WDI, 2020). The FCT lies between latitude 8° 25' and 9° 25' North of the equator and longitude 6° 45' and 7° 45' East of the Greenwich meridian. It is located in the middle belt of Nigeria (Osiobe, 2018).

Figure 1:
Map of Nigeria showing the FCT, Abuja municipal area, and Gwagwalada area

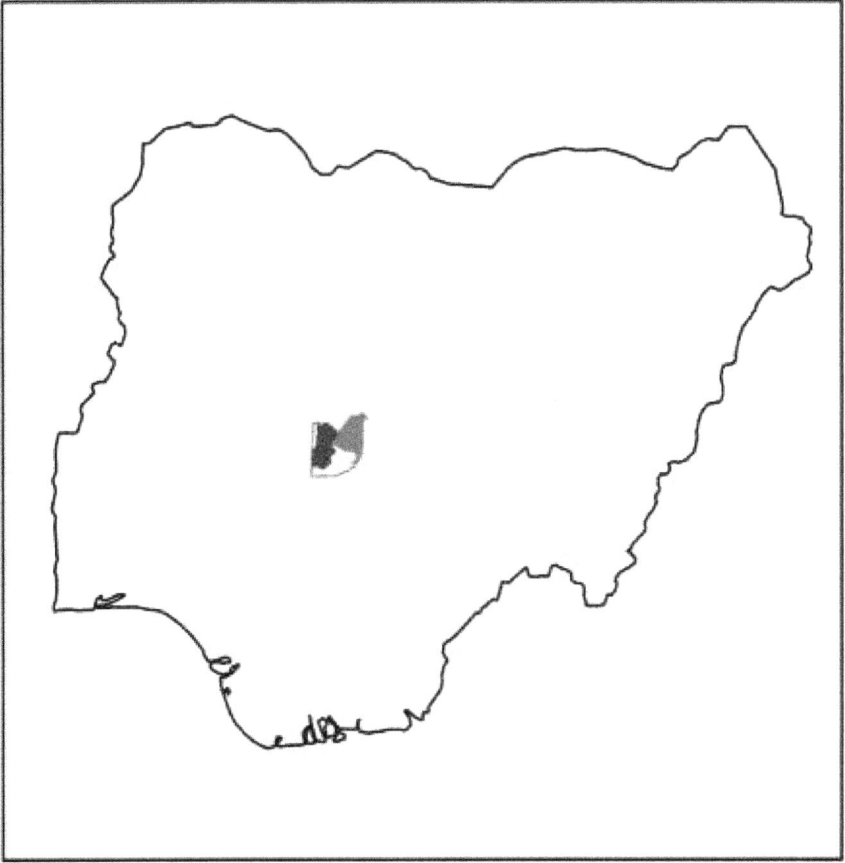

Coordinate System: GCS WGS 1984

Study Area

- Nigeria Border
- FCT Boundary
- Lugbe, Abuja
- Gwagwalada Gwagwalada

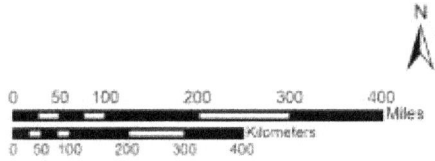

The country is multicultural, with over 250 ethnic groups, with Hausa, Igbo, and Yoruba being the largest ethnic groups with over 500 unique native languages. According to the (WDI, 2020), it is an emerging nation and the regional power of Africa.

LITERATURE

Graetz and Michaels (2017) state that since the early 1990s, recovery from recessions in the United States (US) has. According to them, a possible explanation for these jobless recoveries is founded on technological change. The chapter adopted data on recoveries from 71 recessions in 28 industries and 17 countries from 1970-2011. The aim was to compare the US jobless recoveries with those of other developed countries with a good technology base. The results suggest that though GDP recovered more slowly after recent recessions, the employment rate did not. The authors' findings indicate that technology does not cause jobless recoveries in developed countries outside the US.

Sanusi (2012) examines the dynamic relationships between output growth and unemployment in Nigeria. The chapter employed a generalized method of moments and linear estimation of data for the period 1970-2010. The results from the linear estimates point out that the short-run relationship between output and unemployment is negative, but in the long-run, it is positive. Therefore, this result supported the hypothesis of non-linearity in the dynamic relationship between output and unemployment and confirmed that the dynamic relationship is non-linear and hump-shaped.

Samavati and Stumph (2004) examine the effect of the 2003-2004 jobless recovery on income and poverty in the US. The chapter shows a disproportionate number of single mothers and children make up the poor class; the chapter goes on to study the effect of declining income and rise in the overall poverty rate on the most vulnerable groups in society (minorities, women, and children). The findings suggest that jobless growth worsened the rate of poverty.

Workforce Flow Chart

Figure 2 shows the workforce flow chart of any economy. For our study, we will assume that the Total Population (T_{Pop}) is 190 Mn people, which is the starting point of the flow. Within the population sample, an economy will have the Dependent Population (D_P), which are people within the age groups of (0 – 15 years (yrs)) and older people, which are persons' within the ages of (65+ yrs). Within the total population sample, an economy also has the Institutionalized Group (I_G), which comprises people who are in correctional academies, prisons, and hospitals. To get the adult population or labor force, we utilize equation (1):

$T_{Pop} - (D_P + I_G) =$ *Adult population/labor force* (1)

The labor force comprises the population group within the age group of (16 – 64 years). The labor force is employed (worked at least one hour in the previous week) and unemployed (people actively looking for a job within the past four weeks). The final is the retired population, students, family members like the house who help with house chores, and the discouraged group. From 1970-1998, Africa's poverty rose by 55% from 11% to 66% despite a period when foreign aid inflows were at their highest level. But Foreign aid may be beneficial as a soothing when targeted at specific, narrow objectives, such as the prevention and eradication of diseases like malaria, tuberculosis, HIV/AIDS, smallpox, and diarrhea. Other economic woes that have plagued African nations include but are not limited to lack of decent work-(places), attractive investment opportunities, capital flight, and minimum-risk high-interest investment in Western countries. The United

Nations (UN) coined the term decent work, and the decent work agenda was not only to establish a definition of good practice, which can be used as a yardstick for workers, but also to create unity among workers, governments, and employers (Mackett, 2020).

The decent work agenda is based on the understanding that work is not only a source of income but, more importantly, a source of personal dignity, family stability, peace in [the] community, and economic growth that expands opportunity for productive jobs and employment" (Cohen & Moodley, 2012). The term's growing popularity also suggests the importance of moving labor market debates beyond the employment/ unemployment discussion. This is especially important, given that labor market wages are the primary source of income in many countries. This indicates that inequality in the quality of jobs and the subsequent wages and opportunities will also translate to broader societal disparities.

Figure 2:
Workforce Flow Chart

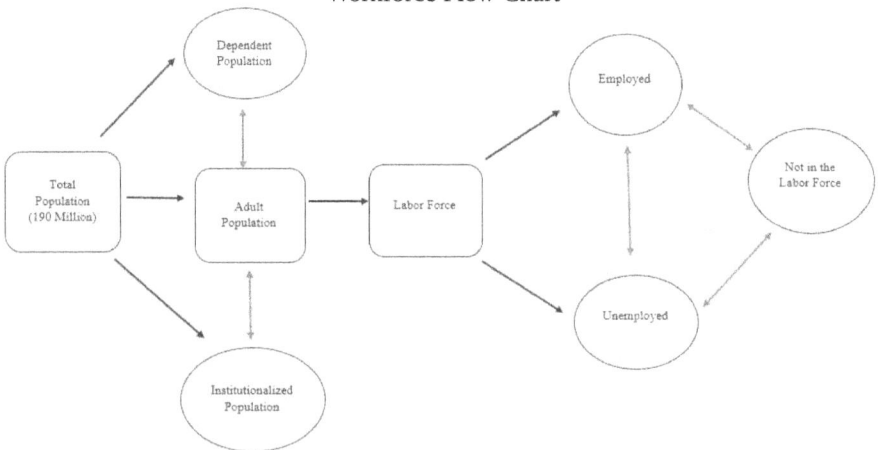

METHODOLOGY

Analysis of the Two-Stage Least Square (2SLS) and the Ordinary Least Squares (OLS) Methods

The OLS linear regression assumes equation (2) to be a zero systematic error:

$$y_n = \sum_{i=0}^{k} \beta_i x_{ni} + \varepsilon_n \qquad (2)$$

The matrix notation of n . 1 and a vector notation of n . k (the matrix); k . 1 (vector); and the result is n . 1

n . 1 (3)

where $\varepsilon[e] = 0$

The 2*SLS* implemented when some of the independent variables correlate with ε_n and face an endogeneity problem.

$$\theta_{2SLS} = \left(z_p' Z\right)^{-1} Z_p' y \qquad (4)$$

where $Z_p' Z = Z_P' Z_p$ which is the *OLS* of y on Z_p.

Variables

This chapter sourced its data from the ((Central Bank of Nigeria (CBN), 2019), (Index Mundi (IM), 2019), and (CEIC, 2019)). The variables adopted for the empirical analysis include the Unemployment rate (URt), the explained variable in the base equation (8). UR_t is defined as the number of people within the labor force who do not have jobs but are actively looking for one (source (IM, 2019)). Real Gross Domestic Product ($RGDP_t$) is an explanatory variable; it is the total value of economic output produced within any sovereign economy each year and adjusted for inflation (source (CBN, 2019)). Foreign Direct Investment (FDI_t) is an explanatory variable that refers to the total value of investment made in a country by a foreign government, agencies, or even multi-national corporations (source (IM, 2019). Population (Pop_t) refers to the total number of people living within a geographical location (source (CEIC, 2019)). The inflation rate (Inf_t) is a dropped explanatory variable after a robustness test and model sensitivity test. Inf_t is the rise in the general price level of goods and services in an economy, and ""t"" is the time from 1986 – 2018.

Model Specification

The OLS equation before the robustness and sensitivity test is:

$$UR_t = \beta_0 + \beta_1 \, lnRGDP_t \, \beta_2 \, FDI_t + \beta_3 \, lnPop_t + \beta_4 \, lnf_t + \omega_t \text{ (5)}$$

And then operationalized to our base model as:

$$UR_t = \partial_0 + \partial_1 \, lnRGDP_t + \partial_2 \, FDI_t + \partial_3 \, lnPop_t + \mu_t$$

Endogeneity exists between UR_t $RGDP_t$, and FDI_t. Hence, we predict using FDI_t and $lnPop_t$. $ln\widehat{RGDP}_t$

$$lnR\widehat{GDP}_t \equiv lnRGDP_t = \gamma_0 + \gamma_1 FDI_t + \gamma_2 lnPop_t + \varepsilon_t \qquad (7)$$

The Endogeneity Relationship

According to Iloabuchi (2019), after analyzing the effects of the unemployment rate in Nigeria and economic growth, the author found that there is a unidirectional Granger causal relationship between unemployment and economic growth, supporting the assertion of endogeneity between UR_t and $lnRGDP_t$ in our study. Gross & Ryan's (2008) paper that investigated the effects of employment projection laws and contract jobs on Japanese firm-level FDI in Western Europe in the '80s' and '90s' found that these protections matter in the location choice of Japanese investors and hurt FDI-related employment size. (Fung et al., 1999) found that increasing FDI in a nation can affect the economic dynamics of a country positively and negatively, supporting the supposition of endogeneity between UR_t and FDI_t in our model.

Osiobe (2019) analyzed the effects of Australia's declining fertility rate and found an inverse relationship between fertility rate and income per capita from the model used in the chapter; there is a - 0.11%-point relationship between (Table 1 of the chapter), population and real gross domestic product per capita and population. This chapter can be used to defend the endogeneity relationship between UR_t and $lnPop_t$. To operationalize the base equation (6), we substitute $lnRGDP_t$ with as the new base model equation (8): $lnR\widehat{GDP}_t$

$$UR_t = \delta_0 + \delta_1 ln\widehat{RGDP}_t + \delta_2 FDI_t + \delta_3 lnPop_t + \varphi_t \qquad (8)$$

Data Analysis and Results

Table 1: Summary Statistics of the Variables (log)
Source: Authors' calculation

	UR_t	$RGDP_t$	Pop_t	FDI_t	Inf_t
Mean	9.37	366.2	133151.3	3120	
		(10.37)	(11.76)		19.92
Median	9	289.5	128667	1880	
		(10.27)	(11.76)		12.22
Maximum	22	698.1	195875	8840	
		(11.15)	(12.19)		72.84
Minimum	1.9	15237.99	85819	193	5.38
		(9.63)	(11.36)		
Std. Dev.	5.61	194.1	33008.99	2590	18.29
		(0.52)	(0.24)		

n = 33

The Balance of Payment Account (BOP A/C)

The *BOP a/c* is a record of all payments or monetary transactions between a country and the rest of the world during a specific period. The equation for the *BOP a/c* is:

BOP A/C = Current Account (*C a/c*) +

Capital Account (*K a/c*) + Financial (*F a/c*) (9)

With the assumption/hope that:

C a/c = *K a/c* + *F a/c*

Result Interpretation

Table 2: 2*SLS* Results
1%***; 5%**; 10%*

	Coefficient	T-value	P-value
$ln\widehat{RGDP}_t$	13.47	3.53	0.00***
FDI_t	-1.98	-1.09	0.28
$lnPop_t$	-7.46	-2.65	0.01***
Adj-R^2	20%		

Authors' calculation

Table 2 shows our empirical findings. It can be inferred from the chapter that a 1% increase in $ln\widehat{RGDP}_t$ will lead to a 0.13%-point rise in UR_t. According to Anyaehie & Areji (2015), Nigeria is a mono-commodity (petroleum) based economy and is plagued by the Dutch disease (Otaha, 2012). Due to the country's oil sector's heavy dependence on foreign experts, the energy sector significantly influences the nation's economy by acting as a prime mover. Hence, the country is in a vicious circle because it has zero competitive, comparative, or price advantage over its main exports (crude oil) and imports (refined produce) (Ayadi et al., 2002). Our result implies that most skilled workers' jobs in Nigeria, especially in the oil industry, are handled by qualified experts (white-collar employees). These experts (in most cases in the oil industry) (Ogunwa, 2012) have little ties to the country, hence reducing their net Marginal Propensity to Consume (MPC) in Nigeria. This reduction in the foreign experts' MPC within the country will negatively impact the nation's economy (directly, indirectly, and induced). As a result of this shift in capital flight and remittances, the net multiplier of money within the country will decrease, resulting in a reduction in the nation's Marginal Propensity to Save (MPS).

Subsequently, as capital flight and remittance for foreign experts continue to increase, the net demand for the naira in the money market will reduce, causing the currency to lose its value while increasing the value of other hard currencies like the USD. Hence, it fosters economic growth and development outside Nigeria. Studies like ((Ballard, 2003) (Siddique et al., 2012) (Fayissa & Nsiah, 2010) (Pradhan et al., 2008) (Adams, 2006) (Adams & Page, 2005) (Adam, 2011)) showed a positive impact on growth and reduced poverty in the developing world. At the margin, they spend less on consumer goods and more on investment goods like education and housing. Concerning this chapter, we associate the positive statistical relationship between UR_t and capital flight and the outflow of remittances through the K a/c and F a/c (see equations 9 & 10) via transfer payment and FDI to their friends, families, and lucrative businesses abroad. This analysis with the BOP a/c is justified because it allows economists and policymakers to identify any long-run trends (jobless recovery) that could harm the economy. $(ln\widehat{RGDP}_t)$

Figure 3 shows the remittance flowing from the developed world to the developing world. The red and black parallel lines linked to the BOP a/c show the remittance movement from Nigeria to the rest of the world, and the redline indicates more FDI flows out of the country. According to the WDI (2019), global remittances from high-income countries reached 689 billion (Bn) USD in 2018, up from 633 billion USD in 2017. However, Nigeria has a high share of remittances as a share of GDP, which is 21% of its GDP (The World Bank Group, 2019). Ang (2007) analyzed the 3rd largest recipient of remittances in the world after the nations India and Mexico, the Philippines, which received about 11 billion USD in 2005 and accounted for 10% of the nation's GDP. Aug (2007) confirmed ((Taylor, 2006) & (Ballard 2003)) presupposition that although remittance may contribute to economic growth, there is a need to create economic policies that promote active development in the region. These remittances do not solve the problems of necessary infrastructure, access to credit, and other development problems.

Figure 3:
Flow Chart of Remittances
Source: Authors' creation

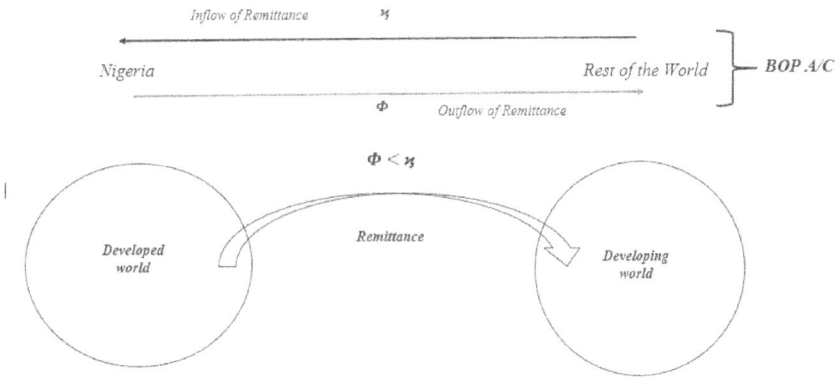

Our findings support those of (Leon-Ledesma & Piracha, 2004), whose results showed the impact of remittances on unemployment depends on their effect on productivity growth and investment. The authors analyzed 11 transition countries from 1990 – 1999 and found a positive impact on productivity and employment directly and indirectly through its effect on investment. Javid et al. (2012) support the finding that remittances have a substantial and statistically significant impact on poverty reduction, thus suggesting significant potential benefits associated with international migration for poor people in developing countries like Pakistan.

Our results show that an increasing will increase UR_t, which can be associated with an increasing capital flight and outflow of remittances from

Nigeria, an emerging economy, to the rest of the world. Ceteris Paribus, this implies that the foreign experts who work in the mono-economy, primary industry (the oil sector) with zero ties to the country; hence, they will send a large share of their net income to their home country. Thus reducing their overall net MPC and MPS and increasing capital flight and outflow of remittances. Our results also show that a 1% increase in $lnPopt$ will lead to a 0.75%-point decrease in UR_t. This implies that as the fertility rate in the country increases, UR_t decreases. The result can be explained using the steady-state, where all endogenous variables are constant. $(ln\widehat{RGDP}_t)$

$$\dot{c} = \dot{x} = \dot{\mu} = \dot{k} = \dot{l} = 0 \tag{11}$$

Translating into our base-equation (7):

$$\dot{c} = \dot{x} = \dot{\mu} = \dot{k} = \dot{l} = 0 \tag{12}$$

Operationalizing the golden rule as capital accumulates and population growth increases, Figure 4 is assumed, and it shows the effect of $lnPop_t$ on URt at the steady-state. Where R_1 represents white-collar jobs. R represents blue-collar jobs, τ_1 represents white-collar-pay, τ represents blue-collar-pay, Q is associated with τ, R, and $\dot{r} = 0$ that shows the time reallocation towards white-collar employment and away from the blue-collar jobs in the Nigerian economy justifying the saying that *"monopolist never set the price in the inelastic range of the demand curve."*

The deadweight loss due to this movement will result in higher pay for white-collar jobs, moving from point τ to τ_1, increasing the outflow of remittances and capital flight from Nigeria to the rest of the world. This affects the Nigerian job market, while the country's productivity level keeps rising, and the unemployment rate keeps increasing. On the other hand, blue-collar jobs will increase their supply, resulting in lower wages, strongly

Figure 4:

Steady-state and the Dynamic Transition System associated with UR_t and $lnPop_t$

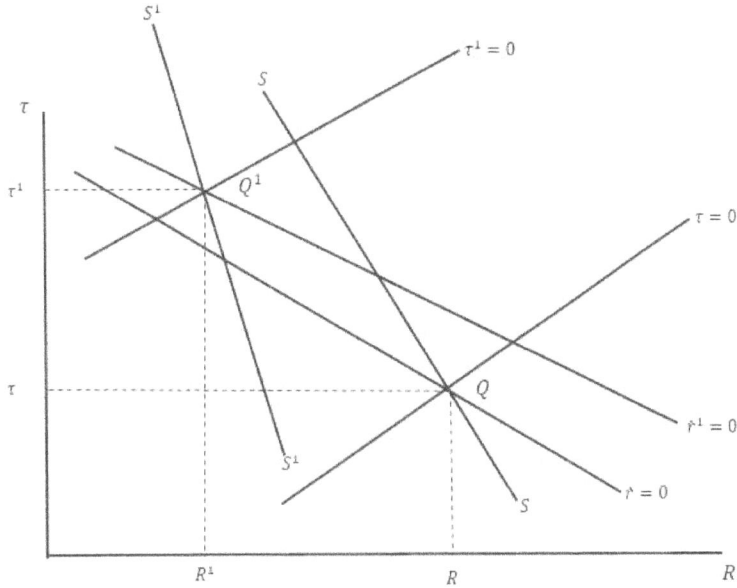

Source: Authors' creation

associated with increasing MPC on consumer goods and decreasing MPS, creating an intertemporal substitution effect that will reduce capital accumulation in the economy, reducing investment and productivity. Figure 4 assumes S_1 to be elastic and S is inelastic.

According to Wang et al. (1994), the sign of the correlation depends crucially on which shock initiates the motion on the relative reactive reactions of labor and capital stock input. The empirical evidence on the movement between the growth rate of Real Gross Domestic Product per capita and population growth has been inconclusive (Kormendi & Meguire,

1985). Barro & Becker (1989) examined how families and macroeconomy interreact, while (Becker et al., 1990) led the understanding of long-term growth and recognized much economic investment is directed towards human beings and physical capital.

DISCUSSION, FINAL THOUGHTS, POLICY IMPLICATION, AND CONCLUSION

Discussion and Implication

In the context of the base model (equation 8), the potential foreign expert may observe growing employment at home. Still, higher wages work in the Nigerian oil industry as an expert (Figure 4 S_1 curve) if allowed to move within a defined period, usually between (3-9 yrs). A traditional migration model will expect that outmigration would increase at a low unemployment rate in one's country of origin. Immigration will decrease, but it is reasonable to assume that the potential immigrant (oil foreign expert) may feel more confident about the benefits of moving if they expect to return to their home country within a specified period. Hence, immigration increases, but so does capital flight and outflow of remittances (see Figure 4). According to Obeng-Odoom (2018), the major criticism of modern-day mainstream development economics is that the industry does not provide a practical approach to studying inequality and is too Western-centric in its concepts, methodology, and vision of an ideal society. Some of the available analytical problems have contributed to worsening African social conditions because they have shaped African development policies.

The relationship between RGDP and unemployment in emerging countries has been well debated. There are two views; the negative view holds that an increasing RGDP will increase unemployment, capital flight, and residents' dependency on remittances from friends and family working abroad. This scenario distorts the economic growth and development process since the animal spirit of the economy (optimism and pessimism) leans more pessimistic. The other view is that an increasing RGDP will reduce the unemployment rate, which is one of the critical factors in poverty alleviation, which is growing the middle-class population. According to Leon-Ledesma & Piracha (2004), each region's job structures and economic circumstances differ. Migrants from relatively emerging to developed countries may perceive migration as enhancing long-term job prospects in any labor market by acquiring skills and experience or accumulating savings, which will be used to finance future self-employment by creating small businesses.

Policy Recommendation and Conclusion

Based on theoretical reviews, empirical reviews, and analysis, we recommend the implementation of the economic diaspora to stimulate economic growth and development in the country. For this chapter, the economic diaspora will be defined as people who have roots in a particular nation either through ancestor or birth but live in different parts of the world and have economic skills or finance that the country needs or outsource to foreign experts. The opening of the People's Republic of China to the capitalist world led by President Jimmy Carter and Deng Xiaoping after 1979 was done in a spatial sequence designed to mobilize the resources of China, with the special economic zones located in crucial areas of migrant origins. Most of the significant FDI inflow into China has come from the Chinese diaspora (Smart & Hsu, 2007).

Uduku (2007) analyzes how the Igbo community, primarily the hometown union/associations activities in the diaspora of the World Igbo Congress (WIC), have maintained links with the hometown communities via fostering small and large-scale economic ventures, including but not limited to capital construction project, local investments, and occasionally local recruitment project for the international market from home towns (often small villages) in Eastern Nigeria. If other regions can imitate, not ignoring the remarkable efforts already made by local NGOs, these efforts will help flatten the $S^{\wedge}1$ curve in (Figure 4), making it more inelastic. Vietnam's economic growth has implemented the returning diaspora more recently. Pham (2011) examined the recent government policy towards the Vietnamese diaspora, and the official contributions reveal that the economic diaspora used informal networks as their main route to make investments in the nation. The economic diaspora would be sufficient to support our recommendation that will flatten the $S^{\wedge}1$ curve (see Figure 4). Other countries that have practiced economic diaspora in recent times include but are not limited to, India. The nation's economic policies have undergone a paradigm shift (Kapur, 2004), which analyzed the impact of transborder flows of ideas transmitted through international migration and return by Indian intellectuals and entrepreneurs on the policy preferences of governing elites.

Kapur (2004) argued that while these ideas transmitted are significant to growth and development, they are also the least evident. It is important to note that economic diaspora is not a fix-all pill to the jobless recovery state of the Nigerian economy but a step in the right direction. Other economic policies will need to support the initiative if implemented, like but not limited to enforcing the rule of law, property rights, and converting the democratic system from a nepotism system to a meritocracy system. With the economic growth in sub-Saharan African countries, Sub-Saharan Africa has experienced 20 years of virtually uninterrupted growth since the mid-1990s and, combined with more excellent political and macro-economic stability in the region. Economists and policymakers expect this growth to lift the region's millions of people out of poverty by 2030. This assertion is analyzed using three geo-social-economic success and region-specific-development trajectories: 1) Britain's capital-intensive path, 2) Japan's labor-intensive way, and 3) Ghana's land-extensive growth path. The analysis in this chapter has relevance even outside the context of the studies' base model (equation 8) and underlining presupposition. For instance, our analysis of impacts on remittances, capital flight, migration, and consumption will contribute to testing the validity of the chapter.

Overall, the empirical evidence from previous studies ((Graetz & Michael, 2017) (Sanusi, 2012) (Samauati & Stumph, 2004)) on jobless recoveries supports the hypothesis that a non-linear dynamic relationship exists between output and unemployment. Our results show that an increase will increase UR_t, and increasing $lnPopt$ will decrease UR_t at the 1% significant level. Our findings bridge the gap between Western-centric approaches to locating these problems within the realm of ideas and look to the nexus between ideas, materialism, and history (Obeng-Odoom, 2018) while backing our findings with empirical analysis. Africa's poverty levels have steadily declined since the '90s, and this progress has been driven by $GDP_{per\ capita}$ – growth, which is consistent with the global evidence. $(ln\widehat{RGD}P_t)$

Inequality plays a complementary role in the rise of jobless recovery rates and poverty rates, and it is the primary driver of socioeconomic changes in most developing and developed countries. Reducing inequality has increasingly become the main focus of economic growth, development, and economic stability, but poverty reduction is at the forefront of the development discourse in Africa. Although relative poverty has been on the decline in most countries, absolute poverty levels remain on the rise in Africa as population growth has been increasing exponentially, for example, Nigeria, which has been offsetting the fall in poverty rates within the region.

Economists and policymakers agree that a higher pace of poverty alleviation programs will require a more intensive process of structural economic transformation that includes but is not limited to 1) increasing per capita productivity in agriculture, industry, and services sectors; 2) the transformation of per capita low productivity sectors into high productivity sectors (e.g., subsistence agriculture, informal economy); 3) a relatively egalitarian process between the poorest and affluence demographics of Africa. Existing literature suggests that countries' fundamental characteristics, growth, and redistributive policies are the underlying factors behind poverty reduction. Fosu (2015) has observed that the progress on poverty since the early-mid 1990s may be primarily attributable to income growth, presumably linked to the resurgence of GDP growth. However, improvements in income distribution have been complimentary.

Today, compared to other sub-regions, the progress in sub-Saharan Africa (SSA) on poverty has been slow, and poverty levels remain relatively high (Thorbecke, 2013). The evolution of rural-urban exchange is not a linear growth trend. According to (Frankema & Waijenburg, 2018), three generalizations are valid. 1) the current process of urbanization in Africa is stimulating economic growth via enhanced consumer-side demand; 2) the agglomeration effects are raising labor per capita productivity by increasing the division of labor and specialization, resource sharing, access to public goods, e.g., healthcare and education, and positive economic growth spill-overs; 3) the domestic market integration strengthens the forward and backward linkages between the agricultural, manufacturing, and service industries. Nigeria ranks among the bottom quintiles on the poverty gap. It squared the poverty gap concerning the direct effect. Redistribution of resources from the rich to the poor segment of society is likely to reduce poverty, even with negligible growth (Bourguignon, 2003). But, according to (Fosu, 2015), inequality may or may not promote poverty reduction, depending on a country's income level. While reducing inequality would generally decrease poverty, redistribution may exacerbate poverty in developing countries.

Nevertheless, Nigeria has also grown tremendously in terms of *GDP per capita* (WDI, 2020) and failed to generate a significant increase in income growth, presumably due to the dominance of capital-intensive sectors (oil industry) in the country. They support the slope differentiation in (Figure 4) that at higher standards of poverty, more significant efforts on growth and inequality reduction are required to alleviate poverty. While in many African countries, people with low incomes seem to have benefited from economic growth, this trickle-down effect has been limited in other countries such as Nigeria. One of Africa's growth and development problems is that the very norm of economic growth and development is not conceived of at the African level but at the international level by institutions such as the World Bank and the International Monetary Fund. The strategies for the continent's growth and development path are not empirically studied from primary data investigations from grassroots researchers. Development is about the welfare and development of human capital, which can be defined as education and training (formal, informal, and cultural); knowledge; labor; skills (general, firm, job, and task-specific); experience (Osiobe, 2020) but, not just about RGDP growth. Development must not be limited to the stated definition but must be centered around human capital while integrating his beliefs and relationship with his fellow man. That is, development should be the organic outcome of a people's value system, perceptions, concerns, and endeavors with a path for improving and understanding other cultures.

Studies Limitation and Future Studies

Although the data limitations constrained our empirical results and gave little space for further analysis, our results are theoretically consistent and statistically robust. Our findings display a negative relationship between $(ln\widehat{RGDP_t})$ UR_t and; a positive correlation between $lnPop_t$ and UR_t within the Nigerian economy. Further research is necessary to analyze the jobless recovery phenomenon using different methodologies and variables.

Takeaways

The overwhelming reliance on revenues from natural resource extraction (oil and gas industry) has stimulated the 'jobless recovery' epidemic in the nation, conspicuous consumption, and slight employment expansion in other industries with smaller profit margins. Scholars of different disciplines are divided about the extent to which recent growth is also driven by improved governance (Work, 2002), increased levels of education and investment (Osiobe, 2019 & 2020), growing urban middle classes (Daramola & Ibem, 2010), deepening financial markets (Onwumere et al., 2012), Information and Communication Technology revolutions/evolution (Ogunsola & Aboyade, 2017), and rapid demographic growth as a result of significant improvements in human health (Iwejingi, 2011). The wage gaps between African economies and late industrializing countries in Asia, e.g., Vietnam, Bangladesh, and China, are not nearly as large as the gap between Britain and Japan around 1900. Hence, labor-intensive exported industrialization seems harder to realize for Africa in a world where Asian manufacturing is still building on its momentum.

This chapter addressed the jobless recovery phenomenon in Nigeria for which ongoing debates of why RGDP can lead to an increasing unemployment rate and how the federal government of Nigeria can implement the economic diaspora policy to foster economic growth development and reduce the unemployment rate in the region. This chapter has presented the 2SLS approach to address the jobless recovery phenomena in the country. Our study can be used to provide valuable information to guide future researchers interested in this topic and policymakers when creating and implementing new and amending existing growth and development policies.

Final Thoughts

This chapter investigated the effect of $(ln\widehat{RGDP_t})$ and UR_t in the Nigerian economy. The authors' argument is based on theoretical and empirical backing. The results are inversely different (developed to emerging country) migration. This is consistent with findings from previous works on the impact of RGDP and unemployment in the traditional economic growth theory, in which economic growth and development are associated with a low unemployment rate. However, the jobless recovery phenomenon exists in Nigeria, and the chapter's empirical findings provide evidence.

REFERENCES

Adams, R.H., Jr., & Page, J. (2005). Do international migration and remittances reduce poverty in developing countries? *World Development*, pp. 1645-1669. https://doi.org/10.1016/j.worlddev.2005.05.004

Adams, R.H. (2006). International Remittances and Household: Analysis and Review of Global Evidence. *Journal of African Economics*, pp. 393-425. https://doi.org/10.1093/jafeco/ejl028

African Development Bank Group. (2020, May 10). *Nigeria Economic Outlook*. Retrieved from https://www.afdb.org/en/countries-west-africa-nigeria/nigeria-economic-outlook

Ang, A.P. (2007). Workers' Remittances and Economic Growth in the Philippines. *Dynamics Economics Growth, and International Trade Conference Papers*.

Anyaehie, M.C., & Areji, A.C. (2015). Economic Diversification for Sustainable Development in Nigeria. *Open Journal of Political Science*. https://doi.org/10.4236/ojps.2015.52010

Ayadi, F.O., Chatterjee, A., & Obi, P.O. (2000). A vector autoregressive analysis of an oil-dependent emerging economy - Nigeria. OPEC Review, pp. 329-349. https://doi.org/10.1111/1468-0076.00087

Ballard, R. (2003). Remittances and Economic Development. *International Development Committee: Evidence*, pp. 157-168.

Banerjee, A.V., & Duflo, E. (2011). *Poor Economics: A Radical Rethinking of the Way to Fight Global Poverty*. New York: Public Affairs.

Barro, R.J., & Becker, G.S. (1989). Fertility choice in a model of economic growth. *Econometrica*, pp. 481-501. https://doi.org/10.2307/1912563

Becker, G.S., Murphy, K.M., & Tamura, R. (1990). Human Capital, Fertility, and Economic Growth. *Journal of Political Economy*. https://doi.org/10.1086/261723

Bolt, P.J. (1996). Looking to the Diaspora: The Overseas Chinese and China's Economic Development, 1978-1994. *Diaspora: A Journal of Transnational Studies,* pp. 467-496. https://doi.org/10.1353/dsp.1996.0019

Bourguignon, F. (2003). The Growth Elasticity of Poverty Reduction: Explaining Heterogeneity across Countries and Time Periods. In T.S. Ericher & S.J. Turnovsky, *Inequality and Growth: Theory and Policy Implication.* London: The MIT Press.

Brown, J.M. (2006). *Global South Asians: Introducing the Modern Diaspora.* Cambridge: Cambridge University Press. https://doi.org/10.1017/CBO9780511807657

CEIC. (2019, April 12). Retrieved from https://www.ceicdata.com/en

Central Bank of Nigeria. (2019, April 12). *CBN-Data & Statistics.* Retrieved from https://www.cbn.gov.ng/documents/data.asp

Cheung, G.C. (2004). Chinese Diaspora as a Virtual Nation: Interactive Roles between Economic and Social Capital. *Political Studies,* pp. 664-684. https://doi.org/10.1111/j.1467-9248.2004.00502.x

Cohen, T., & Moodley, L. (2012). Achieving decent work in South Africa? *African Journal Online,* pp. 320-344. https://doi.org/10.4314/pelj.v15i2.12

Daramola, A., & Ibem, E.O. (2010). Urban environmental problems in Nigeria: Implications for sustainable development. *Journal of Sustainable Development in Africa,* pp. 124-145.

Enyinnaya, J., & Osiobe, E. (2017). *Cost-Benefit Analysis: The Ane Osiobe Altruism Farm of the Edison 3.0 Project 2017 Price Value.* Abuja: The Ane Osiobe International Foundation.

Fayissa, B., & Nsiah, C. (2010). The impact of remittances on Economic Growth and Development in Africa. *The American Economist,* pp. 92-103. https://doi.org/10.1177/056943451005500210

Fosu, A.K. (2015). Growth, Inequality, and Poverty in Sub-Saharan Africa: Recent Progress in a Global Context. *Oxford Development Studies*, pp. 44-59. https://doi.org/10.1080/13600818.2014.964195

Fosu, A.K., & Gafa, D.W. (2020). Progress on poverty in Africa: How have growth and inequality mattered? *African Review of Economics and Finance*, pp. 61-101.

Frankema, E., & Waijenburg, V. M. (2018). Africa Rising? A Historical Perspective. *African Affairs*, pp. 543-568. https://doi.org/10.1093/afraf/ady022

Fung, M.K-y., Zeng, J., & Zhu, L. (1999). Foreign Capital, Urban Unemployment, and Economic Growth. *Review of International Economics*, pp. 651-664. https://doi.org/10.1111/1467-9396.00190

Graetz, G., & Michaels, G. (2017). Is Modern Technology Responsible for Jobless Recoveries? *American Economic Review*, pp. 168-173. https://doi.org/10.1257/aer.p20171100

Gross, D.M., & Ryan, M. (2008). FDI location and size: Does employment protection legislation matter? *Regional Science and Urban Economics*, pp. 590-605. https://doi.org/10.1016/j.regsciurbeco.2008.05.012

Iloabuchi, C.C. (2019). Analysis of the Effect of Unemployment on the Economic Growth of Nigeria. *IOSR Journal of Economics and Finance (IOSR-JEF)*, pp. 82-89.

Indexmundi. (2019, April 12). Retrieved from https://www.indexmundi.com/nigeria/

International Labor Organisation. (2020, May 10). *Decent Work*. Retrieved from https://www.ilo.org/global/topics/decent-work/lang--en/index.htm

International Labor Organization. (2020, May 10). *Decent work and the 2030 Agenda for sustainable development*. Retrieved from https://www.ilo.org/global/topics/sdg-2030/lang--en/index.htm

Iwejingi, S.F. (2011). Population Growth, Environmental Degradation, and Human Health in Nigeria. *Pakistan Journal of Social Sciences*, pp. 187-191.

Javid, M., Arif, U., & Qayyum, A. (2012). Impact of Remittances on Economic Growth and Poverty. *Academic Research International*, pp. 433-447.

Kapur, D. (2010). Ideas and Economic Reforms in India: The Role of International Migration and the Indian Diaspora. *India Review*, pp. 364-384. https://doi.org/10.1080/14736480490895723

Kormendi, R.C., & Meguire, P.G. (1985). Macroeconomic determinants of growth: Cross-country evidence. *Journal of Monetary Economics*, pp. 141-163. https://doi.org/10.1016/0304-3932(85)90027-3

Leon-Ledesma, M., & Piracha, M. (2004). International Migration and the Role of Remittances in Eastern Europe. *International Migration*, pp. 65-83. https://doi.org/10.1111/j.0020-7985.2004.00295.x

Lever-Tracy, C., Ip, D., & Tracy, N. (1996). *The Chinese Diaspora and Mainland China*. New York: St. Martin's Press, Inc. https://doi.org/10.1057/9780230372627

Levi, S.C. (2002). *The Indian Diaspora in Central Asia and its Trade*, 1550-1900. Brill.

Lucas, J.R. (1988). On the Mechanics of Economic Development. *Journal of Monetary Economics*, 22, 3-42. https://doi.org/10.1016/0304-3932(88)90168-7

Lucas, R.E. (1980). Methods and Problems in Business Cycle Theory. *Journal of Money, Credit, and Banking*, pp. 696-715. https://doi.org/10.2307/1992030

Mackett, O. (2020). The measurement of decent work in South Africa: A new attempt at studying quality of work. *African Review of Economics and Finance*, pp. 203-247.

Mackett, O. (2020). The measurement of decent work in South Africa: A new attempt at studying the quality of work. *African Review of Economics and Finance*, pp. 203-247.

Mankiw, N.G., Romer, D., & Weil, N.D. (1992). A Contribution to the Empirics of Economic Growth. *The Quarterly Journal of Economics*, 107(2), 407- 437. https://doi.org/10.2307/2118477

Mbaku, J.M. (2020). Comment on 'Poverty in Africa: How have growth and inequality mattered?'. *African Review of Economics and Finance*.

Nwoke, C. (2020). Rethinking the idea of independent development and self-reliance in Africa. *African Review of Economics and Finance*, pp. 152-170.

Obeng-Odoom, F. (2015). Africa: On the Rise, But to Where? *Forum for Social Economics*, pp. 234-250. https://doi.org/10.1080/07360932.2014.955040

Obeng-Odoom, F. (2018). Critique of development economics. *The Japanese Political Economy*, pp. 59-81. https://doi.org/10.1080/2329194X.2019.1617637

Ogunsola, L.A., & Aboyade, W.A. (2017). Information and Communication Technology in Nigeria: Revolution or Evolution. *Journal of Social Sciences*, pp. 7-14. https://doi.org/10.1080/09718923.2005.11892487

Ogunwa, S.A. (2012). Globalization and Developing Countries: A Blessing or a Curse in Nigeria. *Insight on Africa*, pp. 1-18. https://doi.org/10.1177/0975087814411143

Onwumere, J.U., Ibe, I.G., Ozoh, F.O., & Mounanu, O. (2012). The Impact of Financial Deepening on Economic Growth: Evidence from Nigeria. *Research Journal of Finance and Accounting*, pp. 64-71.

Osiobe, E. (2019). Forecasting how Crude Oil Export is Changing the Dynamics of Nigeria's Economy 1970 -2030. *Lead City Journal of The Social Sciences*.

Osiobe, E.U. (2018). *The National Economic Impact from Agriculture*. Abuja: The Ane Osiobe International Foundation.

Osiobe, E.U. (2019). A Literature Review of Human Capital and Economic Growth. *Business and Economic Research*, 9(4), 179-196. https://doi.org/10.5296/ber.v9i4.15624

Osiobe, E.U. (2019). The Effect of Australia's Declining Fertility Rate 1978 -2016. *International Journal of Human Resource Studies*, pp. 95-100. https://doi.org/10.5296/ijhrs.v9i4.15717

Osiobe, E.U. (2020). Human capital, capital stock formation, and economic growth: A panel granger causality analysis. *Journal of Economics and Business*, pp. 569-582. https://doi.org/10.31014/aior.1992.03.02.221

Otaha, J.I. (2012). Dutch Disease and Nigeria Oil Economy. *African Research Review*, pp. 82-90. https://doi.org/10.4314/afrrev.v6i1.7

Pham, A.T. (2011). *The Returning Diaspora: Analyzing overseas Vietnamese (Viet Kieu) Contribution toward Vietnam's Economic Growth*. Political Sciences.

Pradhan, G., Upadhyay, M., & Upadhyaya, K. (2008). Remittances and economic growth in developing countries. *The European Journal of Development Research*, pp. 497-506. https://doi.org/10.1080/09578810802246285

Romer, P. (1989). *Human Capital and Growth: Theory and Evidence*. NBER Working Paper No. 3173. https://doi.org/10.3386/w3173

Romer, P. (1990). Endogenous Technological Change. *Journal of Political Economy*, 98(5), 71-102. https://doi.org/10.1086/261725

Safarai, S., Stern, M., Flusser, D., & van Unnik, W. C. (1988). Chapter Thirteen: The Social and Economic Status of the Jews in the Diaspora. In S. Safari, S. Flusser, D. Flusser, sser, & W.C. van Unnik, *The Jewish People in the First Century* (pp. 701-727). Brill. https://doi.org/10.1163/9789004275096_004

Samavati, H., & Stumph, C. (2004). Do the Poor Get Poorer? Women, Children, and America's Jobless Recovery. *Proceedings of the Midwest Business Economics Association*, pp. 72-81.

Sanusi, A.R. (2012). *Macroeconomic Policy, Output, and Unemployment Dynamics in Nigeria: Is there evidence of jobless growth?* SSRN. https://doi.org/10.2139/ssrn.2135752

Sharma, K. (2010). The Impact of Remittances on Economic Insecurity. *Journal of Human Development and Capabilities*, pp. 555-577. https://doi.org/10.1080/19452829.2010.520923

Siddique, A., Selvanathan, E.A., & Selvanathan, S. (2012). Remittances and Economic Growth: Empirical Evidence from Bangladesh, India, and Sri Lanka. *The Journal of Development Studies*, pp. 1045-1062. https://doi.org/10.1080/00220388.2012.663904

Smart, A., & Hsu, J-Y. (2007). The Chinese Diaspora, Foreign Investment, and Economic Development in China. *The Review of International Affairs*, pp. 544-566. https://doi.org/10.1080/1475355042000241511

Taylor, E.J. (2006). *International Migration and Economic Development*. Turin: International Symposium on International Migration and Development.

The World Bank Group. (2019). *Migration and Remittances: Recent Development and Outlook*.

The World Bank Group. (2019, April 8). *Record High Remittances Sent Globally in 2018*. Retrieved from https://www.worldbank.org/en/news/press-release/2019/04/08/record-high-remittances-sent-globally-in-2018

The World Bank Group. (2020, March 14). *The World Development Index*. Retrieved from http://data.worldbank.org/country/nigeria

Thorbecke, E. (2015). Multidimensional Poverty: Conceptual and Measurement Issues. *The Many Dimensions of Poverty*, pp. 3-19. https://doi.org/10.1057/9780230592407_1

Uduku, O. (2002). The Socio-economic basis of a diaspora community: Igbo bu ike. *Review of African Political Economy*, pp. 301-311. https://doi.org/10.1080/03056240208704615

UNDP. (1993). *Human Development Report: People's Participation*. Oxford: United Nations Development Program.

Wang, P., Yip, C.K., & Scotese, C.A. (1994). Fertility Choice and Economic Growth: Theory and Evidence. *The Review of Economics and Statistics*, pp. 255-266. https://doi.org/10.2307/2109880

Weller, M. (2014). *The Battle for Open: How openness won and why it doesn't feel like a victory.* London: Ubiquity Press. https://doi.org/10.5334/bam

Work, R. (2002). Overview of decentralization worldwide: A stepping stone to improved governance and human development. *Philippine Journal of Public Administration*, pp. 1-24.

World Development Index. (2019). *GINI index (World Bank estimate) South Africa, Nigeria, Kenya, Ghana.* Retrieved from https://data.worldbank.org/indicator/SI.POV.GINI?locations=ZA-MA-TN-DZ-EG-NG-KE-LR-SO-GH

World Development Index. (2020, April 9). *Gini Index (World Bank Estimate).* Retrieved from https://datacatalog.worldbank.org/gini-index-world-bank-estimate-1

PERFORMANCE MANAGEMENT: AN UNDERSTANDING

INTRODUCTION

The underlying presupposition and the supposition of performance management as a study field have been controversial or have a non-defined concept ever since the field was introduced to the mainstream economy. The chapter covers performance management as a business analyst, scrum master, archeologist, and leader. The research delves into the founding history of performance management and analyzes critical performance management tools. Our findings show that performance management should be seen, managed, and played as an infinite game while creating incentives for the players who will, in turn, drive productivity in any industry.

Sports analogies are overused in the Performance Management (PMT) industry, which is a wrong analogy because a sports game is a finite game with an agreed set of rules and a set time for it to be over. It's played with the purpose to win. Instead, an infinite game analogy is best suited for the industry. Performance Managers' (PM) primary goal is to keep the game going (ensure that their product stays relevant over time) and bring as many people as possible to increase their market share. There are no set rules or time for the game to be over (free entry and exit), and the aim is not to win; the objective is to continue playing.

PMT is a branch of applied behavior analysis, which is a branch of behavior analysis. The chapter's underlining presupposition and supposition on how a PM should act and how the PMT industry should function are built on (Nash, 1950a;1950b;1951) strategic interaction and rational decision-making and Landes's (1998) philosophy of how an economy (which is a perfect example of an infinite game) should best function which is based on trust and the welfare of the entry group. This chapter contributes to the PMT's literature and serves as a precise and accurate navigating tool for PMs in the industry. The primary aim of a PM is to govern an enterprise using behavioral and persuasive analysis to create a workplace environment that brings out the best in people, ensuring the business runs efficiently, effectively, and profitably while generating the highest values (wealth, economics of scale and scope) for the organization.

Baer et al. (1968) explained that analytic behavioral application is a self-examining, self-evaluating, discovery-oriented research procedure for studying behavior; hence, all experimental behavioral research is "according to the usual strictures of modern training." The authors stated that the difference between applied and basic research is not "discovery" and "application" but the chapter sample. Non-applied research looks at behaviors and variables that may conceivably relate to the topic, while applied research is constrained to variables that can improve the behavior. Similarly, applied research is constrained to examining actions that are

192

socially important rather than convenient for study. It also frequently implies the chapter of those behaviors in their usual social settings rather than in a "laboratory" setting. Therefore, analytic behavioral applications, by definition, achieve experimental control of the processes they contain. Still, since they strive for this control against formidable difficulties, they achieve it less often per study than a laboratory-based attempt. According to Daniels and Bailey (2014), PMT is a branch of applied behavior analysis focusing on workplace success.

REVIEW

A company's goal, mission, and vision bring its different departments, from sales, information technology (IT), business analysis (BA), and, not limited to, the PM, to what constitutes a functioning enterprise. The PM is the glue that combines different parts of a company to function as a single entity. According to Ammons and Roenigk (2020), successful PMT requires devolved decision authority. That is, meaningful decision-making must be placed in the hands of managers at the program level (department and sub-unit levels), where those best equipped with insights can make needed changes. The authors' analysis sampled 62 selected cities and counties. Their empirical findings showed a positive relationship between devolved decision authority and reported PMT success. Especially when managers both have and perceive that they have meaningful discretion. The conceptual underpinnings of PMT are outlined in what has been called PMT doctrine (Moynihan, 2008). Included are principles and practices thought to be integral to a successful PMT.

Moynihan (2008) focuses on the principle of devolved decision authority and its importance as an element of PMT success. Devolved decision authority, the author suggests, becomes most effective when both the grant of authority is real and managers are willing to acknowledge that they have it. The presence of both conditions substantially increases the likelihood of PMT success. PMT is the purposeful use of performance information to make decisions, including improving operations and services (Moynihan, 2008; Moynihan et al., 2012; Poister et al., 2015; Van Dooren et al., 2010). It suggests, however, that granting greater discretion to operating managers matters, especially when managers recognize and acknowledge that they have the authority they need to make necessary decisions to get the job done.

Instances where managers failed to acknowledge the decision authority granted to them revealed the importance of manager attitude. It is not enough for governments to grant devolved decision authority to pursue performance management success if managers continue to believe they have insufficient decision authority to improve operations and achieve desired results. An attitude of powerlessness can essentially negate the benefits of devolved decision authority. Schaerer and Swaab (2019) analyzed the Illusion of Transparency (I-T). The I-T concept contemporizes a situation in which people focus on their feelings, biases, and intentions that they over-or-underestimate how their worlds and words come across to others—resulting in vagueness, which may, in most cases, lead to misinterpretation of their real intent. I-T is one of the most common causes of misunderstandings when communicating with others.

Schaerer and Swaab (2019) hypothesized that managers suffer from I-T when delivering feedback. In their study, the authors surveyed 173 managers and 566 employees at a multinational nonprofit organization.

The questionnaire asked employees and managers to rate:

- **Employees:** How well did they think they had performed in a recent performance appraisal?
- **Managers:** what they thought the employees would say.

Employees perceived their feedback as being more optimistic than their managers thought they would. The effect was more substantial as the feedback leaned more to the negative side of the spectrum. Schaerer and Swaab (2019) tried to understand how to reduce this gap between managers' and employees' perceptions.

The authors' presupposition was aligned with the assumption that managers fall prey to I-T because they aren't sufficiently motivated to consider how their employees will perceive their comments. This is due to the managers' busy schedule and is most often shared during the end-of-year period. To analyze the effect of an intervention that will alert managers on their IT and lead to a more accurate interpretation of employees'-to-managers' non-verbal cues (Schaerer and Swaab, 2019), sampled 117 Master of Business Administration (MBA) students who stood as a proxy for "managers" and paired them up with random individuals who stood as a proxy for "employees" and then created an online panel.

Procedure:

- Participants were told to imagine that they were going through an appraisal process.
- Proxy managers' were given data about how well employees scored on various capabilities.
- Proxy managers' were asked to deliver reviews to the employees.

Schaerer and Swaab (2019) conclude and point to several ways to combat IT.

- Firms can/should increase feedback frequency: managers should adjust annual appraisals to quarterly or monthly feedback and reminders.

- Firms should schedule ongoing training within the company and departments and structure weekly or monthly "*pulse checks*" to enhance communication. Hence, the authors concluded that the data shows that giving feedback more frequently makes it more accurate.
- Firms should provide candid feedback moving back and forth between employees before appraisals.

In performance management, assessment is often designed to identify the environmental variables contributing to individual employee performance problems. Despite their differences, most Organizational Behavior Management (OBM) assessment techniques are designed to guide intervention, not prevention. Safety assessments may assist managers or consultants in increasing safety concerning a specific task within an organization. Behavioral Systems Analysis (BSA) enables managers and consultants to improve how essential processes are conducted and managed across units and people within the organization.

Performance management assessments enable a manager or consultant to intervene on the specific antecedent or consequence events contributing to performance problems. Assessment procedures in OBM can also be described based on their topography. Historical assessments involve examining information that has been previously gathered (Bumstead and Boyce, 2005). An indirect, or informant, assessment consists of asking an employee or manager about the environmental events contributing to a performance problem and is often conducted using a questionnaire (e.g., the Performance Diagnostic Checklist [PDC]) or a specific process (e.g., the PIC/NIC analysis; (Daniels and Bailey, 2014).

A descriptive analysis (sometimes called a direct assessment) includes direct observation and recording of the antecedents and consequences surrounding a target performance (Fante et al., 2010). The experimental analysis involves manipulating relevant antecedent or antecedent and consequence events to the target performance (Therrien et al., 2013). Using a systems analysis tool often includes creating and examining a visual representation of a process or system (e.g., process map; (Brache and Rummler, 1995). One method for identifying the function of problem behavior is conducting a functional analysis (FA) (Iwata et al., 1994), an analog assessment that systematically manipulates and evaluates the effects of environmental variables on the occurrence of problem behavior. Since the introduction of the FA in 1982, numerous procedural variations have been evaluated. One such variation was the brief functional analysis, which adapted aspects of the original FA, such as session length, to address the needs of patients who presented to a one-time 90-minute outpatient. Relative to problem behavior maintained by negative reinforcement, several studies have demonstrated that access to positive reinforcers can decrease escape-claimed problem behavior when delivered contingent on compliance with a task.

Companies fail due to a lack of social, cultural, and environmental adaptability (SCEA). In times of uncertainty, discontinuities, and global competition, SCEA is essential for any organization's success and continuity. When building an objective and subjective business model, SCEA is crucial to add to the equation.

- Objectively + SCEA business model: they are structured and interdependent operational relationships between a firm and its customers, suppliers, complements, partners, and other stakeholders, and among its internal units and departments (functions, staff, operating departments, etc.).

- The subjective + SCEA business model represents these mechanisms, delineating how it believes the firm relates to its environment.

Hence, for this chapter, business models will be defined as cognitive structures providing a theory of how to set boundaries for the firm, create value, and organize its internal structure and governance.

Performance Management System and its Value to a Company

The Performance Management System (PMS) is a one-word practicality. The PMS is not a generalized abstract theory; it sets specific actions for increasing desired performance and decreasing undesired ones. The PMS procedures have been validated against measurable results in a wide variety of applications. Most firms that have successfully used the PMS have reported higher Returns on Investments (ROI) ranging from 4:1, 32:1, and 60: 1 in their first year (Daniels and Bailey, 2014)

$$ROI = \frac{Net\ Return\ on\ Investment}{Cost\ of\ Investment} \cdot 100\%$$

or

$$ROI = \frac{Final\ Value\ of\ Investment - Initial\ Value\ of\ Investment}{Cost\ of\ Investment} \cdot 100\%.$$

The PMS can be used both for short-term results. According to (Fein, 1981;1983), the PMS has benefited the engineering, research, and development industries, safety, distribution, transportation, and customer service industries.

- *It is easy to understand*: the PMS is easy to understand and requires no formal psychological training.

- *It maximizes all kinds of performance in most industries*: PMS is based on knowledge acquired through the scientific study of behavior and feedback, and the principles apply to behavior wherever it occurs.

- *The PMS creates a flexible working environment*: the PMS gives both the PM and their crew work-life-balance and can also enhance relationships at work, at home, and in the community.

Performance Management System as a (Social)-Science

Social science studies human beings, societies, and the relationships between them, while science is the intellectual and practical systematic approach in disproving an idea. While PMS is a (Social)-Science, it has its roots in Operant Conditioning (OC), a branch of psychology. OC is sometimes referred to as instrumental conditioning, a method of training that employs a rewards and punishments system for behavior.

Through OC, an association is made between a behavior and a consequence (whether negative or positive) for that behavior. Skinner, who is the father of OC, but his work was based on Thorndike's law of effect, introduced a new term into the law of effect and reinforcement. The reinforcement tends to be repeated and strengthened, while behavior that is not reinforced tends to diminish and weaken. Skinner (1936) defined OC as changing behavior metanoia using reinforcement given after the desired response. He identified three primary responses or operant that can follow behavior.

Neutral operant, which neither increases nor decreases probability repetition, can either encourage positive behavior and discourage negative behavior in economics. This is called the 'Token Economy,' and the punishers reduce the likelihood of repeated behavior. The Business Model Canvas BMC is a good tool in structuring a token economy. The BMC shows how PM decides when you have encountered an obstacle so big that you should quit and do something else because it is counterproductive? And how not to get into counterproductive persistence.

Table 1: Sample of a Business Model Canvas (BMC)

Key Partners	Key activities	Value propositions	Customer relationship	Customer segment
	Key resources		Channels	
Fixed and Variable Cost Structure			Revenue streams	
Author's Creation				

The BMC (see Table 1) outlines critical steps in visualizing the PM decision-making channels. Skinner (1953) established the fundamental principles that we still employ today: conditioning, extinction, stimulus discrimination, motivation/drive, schedules of reinforcement, and outlined the possibility of the science of human behavior, saying that "science is first a set of attitudes. It is a disposition to deal with facts rather than what someone said about them."

Skinner (1953) work provides the foundation for PMT's practice today, and the most valuable principle is reinforcement, which in this chapter is defined as the consequence that follows a behavior that increases the probability it will occur again next time. Hence, if a PM wants its company to be successful1, wants something done more or less often, or in some cases, to do it differently because, in the long run, it will be more effective, Skinner's OC theory has been proven effective.

PM as an Archeologist

A good PM always tries to understand the causes of positives and, most importantly, negative results to ensure it doesn't happen again. A good PM must investigate any situation like an Archeologist to understand the causes of any results. The PM must recreate the scenario, dig through historical records, and [try to] recreate the situation. To be a proactive PM, one must define the results that one needs and then determine the behaviors that will produce and manage that behavior as they occur.

When a PM manages behavior daily, the PM is creating the future results that the organization values; because " [a] business is behavior." Within the last few years, businesses have become more aware of the need to change behaviors and staff members. Before the doctoring of the OC methodology, companies tried to achieve their goals by downsizing, moving staff around, and re-engineering these change methods used because people get confused with the difference between changing culture, behavior, and people. According to Peters and Waterman (1982), managers who understand behavior are more likely to know when to manage closely and when to relax their supervision in a way that still elicits the best performance from their direct reports.

Our knowledge of the principles of behavior does not change how they affect our behavior. Still, it guides us in developing effective, efficient, and satisfactory interactions with others at work and home. Deming (1986) stated that employees should not be held accountable for results when the system was out of control in the first place.

What is Performance?

A performance consists of a situation, one or more behaviors, tasks, and results combined to produce a specific accomplishment. In this chapter, ' behavior will be defined as little actions repeated every day, usually in autopilot mode; therefore, 'lazy,' which in this chapter will be defined as not showing enthusiasm in an endeavor, is not a behavior. Pinpointing the business case (result) is a challenging task, but a PM will need an essential skill to fix the performance problem.

Hence, it is safe to say that if a PM or any managerial staff member wants to improve performance, the key to [his/her] success begins with precisely defining or pinpointing the outcomes. The term 'pinpointing' in this chapter will be defined as being precise about behavior. Hence, next to delivering constructive and positive reinforcement, pinpointing is the next most crucial skill for a PM to have. Therefore, performance can be described as [*'result of an outcome' or 'products of behavior'*]. In general, a pinpoint(s) must be measurable, observable, and reliable 2

What is the Difference between Results and Behavior?

A result is what's left after the behavior, while the behavior can be observed directly. People's behavior is what they say to each other; listening and active listening are essential categories of behavior (Skinner, 1957). According to Thompson (1978), from a profit of view, what people say to each other and how they say it [to each other] probably influences any different type of interaction in the private industry.

Thompson (1978) concludes verbal interaction can make or break a company. Hence, You can't incentivize performance; you can only incentivize behavior. Other behavioral tools that a PM can use include but are not limited to:

- The Antecedent, Behavior, and Consequence Model (ABCM), the three-term contingency model, analyzes and understands workplace behavior. The model builds on the fact that every behavior has an antecedent that precedes (prompts) and affects its future probability.
- The Positive Immediate and Certain (PIC) and Negative Immediate and Certain (NIC) analyses are used in performance management to analyze why people act the way they act. The PIC and NIC analysis assess different influences on behavior and identify how strong or weak the contingencies maintain them. It allows us to examine the antecedents and consequences that affect a given behavior in detail.

However, by using the PIC and NIC analysis, we can examine the external environment for causes we can do something about. The PIC and NIC aim to understand behavior from the performer's standpoint. To be successful at the PIN and NIC, you must relate to the other person's experiences: walking a mile in their shoes as the expression goes.

Table 2: PIC and NIC Analysis

Key:

Antecedents	Behavior	Consequences	P/N	I/F	C/U

P = Positive – will strengthen behavior
N = Negative – will weaken behavior
I = Immediate – while the behavior is occurring
F = Future – delays beyond the immediate
C = Certain – always follow the behavior; high probability
U = Uncertain – may or may not follow the behavior; low probability
Author's Creation

Table 2 shows a sample of the PIC and NIC tables. Positive or negative consequences are determined by the performer's reinforcement history, not by whether you like the result.

Antecedent

An antecedent is a deliberate attempt to change or maintain behavior by presenting some stimulus before the action occurs or anything a person senses (see, hear, [and/or] touch) that contains information about behavioral consequences and increases the likelihood that they will respond. Generally, antecedents don't cause behavior. If they did, everyone would pick up their phones when they heard it ring.

The visualization techniques that have become popular, particularly in sports, are often an antecedent approach to changing performance. The founding scholars' positive thinking approach (Carnegie, 1936; Mandino, 1986) has attempted to change behavior through antecedents in the form of advice. Advertising uses antecedents to influence behavior. Packaging, commercials, and direct mail campaigns all indirectly manipulate antecedents to encourage purchasing.

Common ways to use antecedents effectively include but are not limited to when they immediately precede a behavior, when they signal a consequence desired by the catalyst, and when the correlation between the antecedent and the desired result is high. For an antecedent to be adequate, it must have the following characteristics: it must come before the desired behavior, it must pass precise information, and the consequences are sometimes the antecedents.

After Action Reviews

An After-Action Review (AAR) is a well-structured debriefing process used by PM to analyze a situation or a past event on:

- What happened?
- Why did it happen?
- How can it be done better next time?

Many PMs conduct an AAR to extract lessons from past projects and apply the learned lesson (s) to new projects. One major shortcoming with the AAR is that with little practice and teams implementing the lessons learned from their past projects, team(s') can "[re]-discover" the same mistakes all over again.

Transforming your AAR from Diagnoses of Past Failure into Aids for Future Success

Understanding the difference between lessons and learning is critical. A PM needs to understand lessons, which isn't the same as learning the lessons. This is a misconception between the identification gap stage 3, the implementation gap stage, and the results gap in the PMT industry. PMs need to see the AAR as an ongoing learning process—rather than a one-time meeting, report, or postmortem. These distinctions made the AAR rigorous at the identification stage before the implementation stage, leading to the result stage without overlooking the intended results, anticipated challenges, and lessons from previous similar situations.

Today, most PMs conduct a per-AAR after each project milestone—, holding everyone accountable for quickly applying critical lessons in the next project phase. Companies that [can] master this process gain and sustain a competitive advantage over those that don't. They [can] avoid repeating past errors and build value for their stakeholders. Generally, a reinforcer is any event, action, or object that has increased the frequency of a behavior. At the same time, reinforcement is any procedure by which those events or objects increase the behavior.

A PM cannot tell if an antecedent, review, or feedback is a positive or negative reinforcer based on one application. The PM must repeat the behavior before you know that the addition causes behavior. The difference between a reinforcer and reinforcement is the former is any event, action, or object that has increased the frequency of a behavior. At the same time, the latter is described as any procedure by which those events or objects increase the behavior.

The Product Manager's Prioritization Technique

Figure 1 shows the PM's prioritization technique, also known as a scale of economic preference and sometimes confused with opportunity cost6. It shows the three pillars necessary for a PM to build, organize, and reorganize an enterprise. The first pillar is to have good financial analytical skills and understand the implications of the enterprise's cost and benefits results. The second is ensuring the business is focused on its business Mission, Vision, and Goals (MVG). The third is creating and understanding the implication of business Strengths, Weaknesses, Opportunities, and Threats (SWOT).

The business SWOT analysis tracks how an organization gets information from inside and outside sources. In other words, how much does it depend on information that is not directly or indirectly correlated to the business MVG and financial results?

Figure 1: The PM's Foundational Prioritization Technique
Mission & Motivation, Vision, and Goal (MVG)

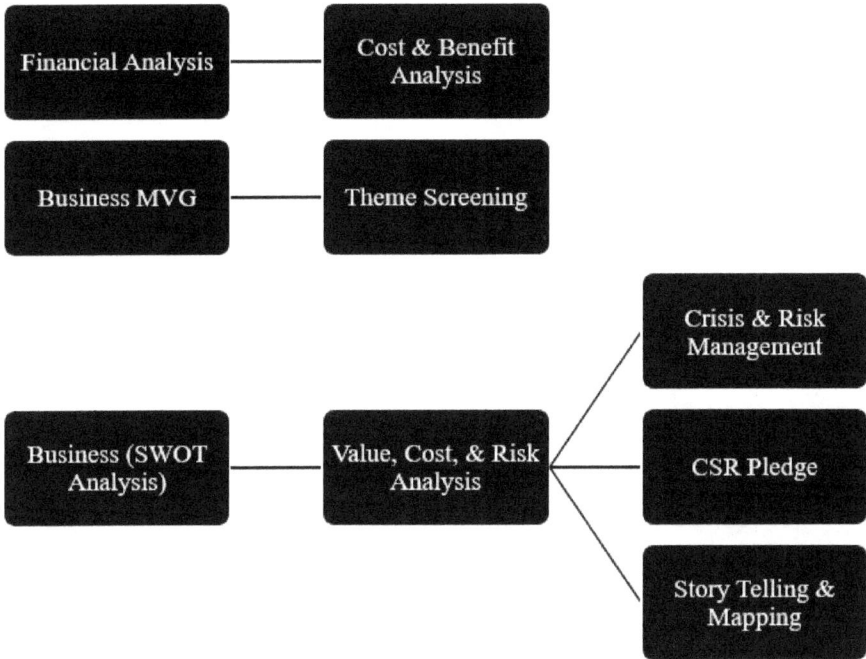

Civil Social Responsibility Pledge (CSR Pledge)
Author's creation

The Kano Prioritization Model of Product Development and Satisfaction

Noriaki Kano developed, the Kano Prioritization Model, a Japanese researcher from the Tokyo University of Science and Quality Management, in 1984 (Kano et al., 1984).

The model helps a PM determine customers' (projected and current) satisfaction levels with an enterprise product. The Kano Model is built on the following premises: customer satisfaction, measured on the vertical line in Figure 2. The positive vertical axis represents customer satisfaction, while the negative axis represents customer dissatisfaction. Conversely, the horizontal axis represents the customer's realization scale after using the product. The positive horizontal axis indicates that the firm met the customer's expectations, while the negative axis means the customers' expectations were not met.

Figure 2: The Kano Prioritization Model

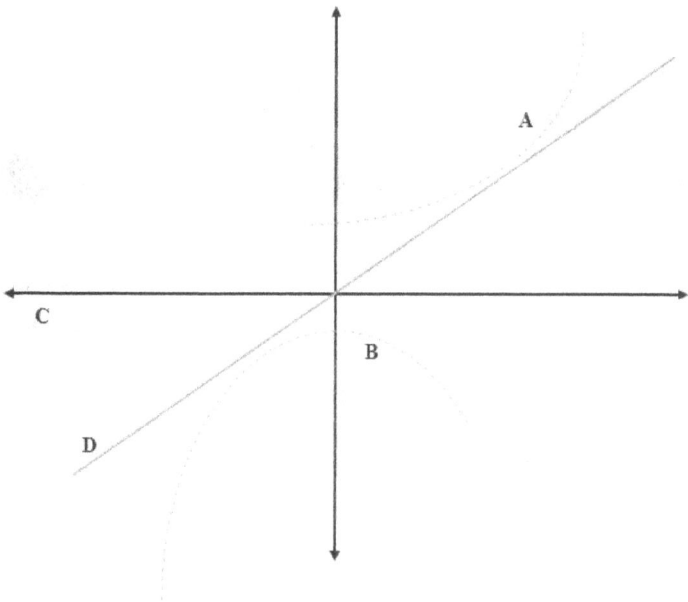

Where the:
Vertical line = Customer Satisfaction ((+) = satisfaction; (-) = dissatisfaction)
Horizontal line = Realization scale ((+) = fully fulfilled; (-) not fulfilled)
A = Delighters (didn't expect but like the result)
B = Basic (expected result and can decrease satisfaction)
D = desired qualities and movements
Author's creation

Figure 3: The Kano Prioritization Metrics Table

		Satisfaction						
		Exceeded expectation	Above expectation	Met expectation	Neutral	Fell-short of expectation	Below expectation	Dissatisfied
	Exceeded expectation							
	Above expectation							
	Met expectation							
Realization	Neutral							
	Fell-short of expectation							
	Below expectation							
	Dissatisfied							

Author's creation

According to Rotar and Kozar (2017), Kano proposes two dimensions to represent how customers feel about our products. Kano *et al*. (1984) 4 first dimension is the satisfaction scale (also called Delight and Expectation) to total dissatisfaction (didn't meet expectation). The other is the realization/investment/sophistication or implementation dimension, representing how much the product meets the customers' realization expectations.

Quality Function Deployment/House of Quality

Quality Function Deployment (QFD) or House of Quality (HQ) is another method that Yoji Akao, a planning specialist, originated in Japan in 1966. The QFD/HQ application is beneficial in the PMT industry due to its valuable tool that allows PMs to focus on products and product design processes from different dimensions that address the (why, what, and how) question(s) (Akao, 1988).

Figure 4: Quality Function Deployment or House of Quality

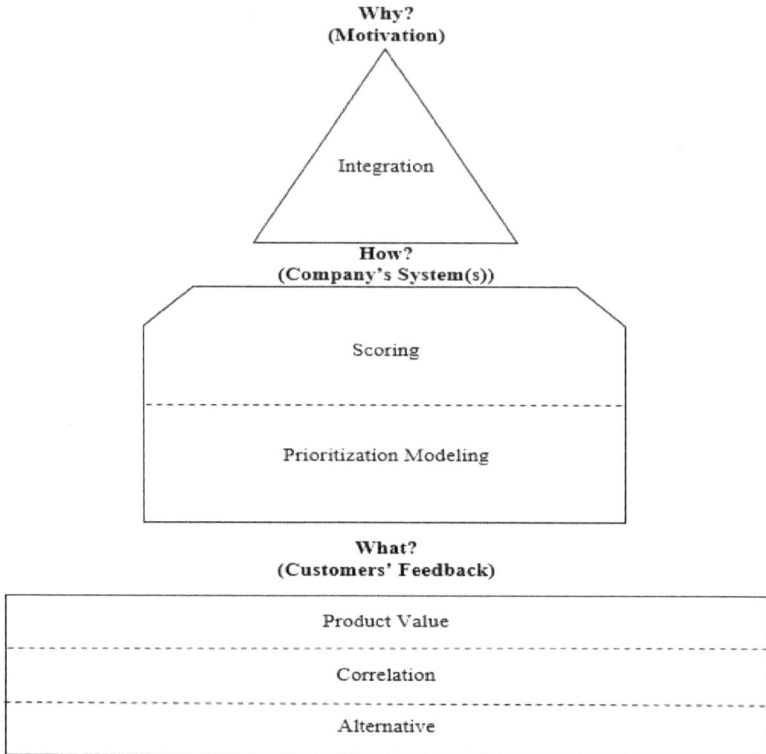

The "what" section of the QFD/HQ identifies:

- Consumers' needs: this involves identifying potential products that customers may need.
- Consumers' wants involve resolving or producing products that address customers' current issues.
- Creating alternatives: with the help of a SWOT analysis, PMs can identify the next best step. The "how" section of the QED?HQ identifies:

- Creates the prioritization and scoring models using a matrix table (see Figure 3). The "why" section integrates the QED/HQ.

Outcome-Driven Innovation

They developed the Outcome-Driven Innovation (ODI) technique that builds on the presupposition that people buy goods and services that satisfy their needs or get the required job done. Hence, producers value their feedback in understanding the satisfaction level(s) of their product(s). This feedback (See Figure 5) creates opportunities for innovation in underserved areas and outlines managerial strategies in overserved areas (analyzing the opportunity cost of inputs in that economy sector).

Figure 5: Outcome-Driven Innovation

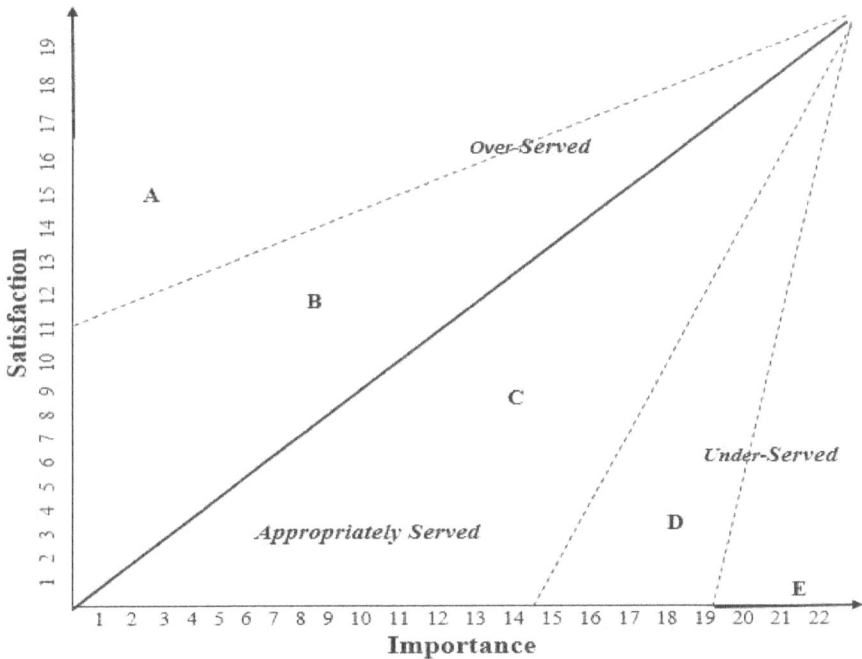

211

Author's Creation
Software/Process (S & P) Architecture

S & P architecture manages complexity to produce simplicity by breaking the complex into smaller manageable modules. Software architecture comprises patterns, principles, and guidelines that follow documentation-structure, process-structure, and system-structure.

Figure 6: S & P Architecture

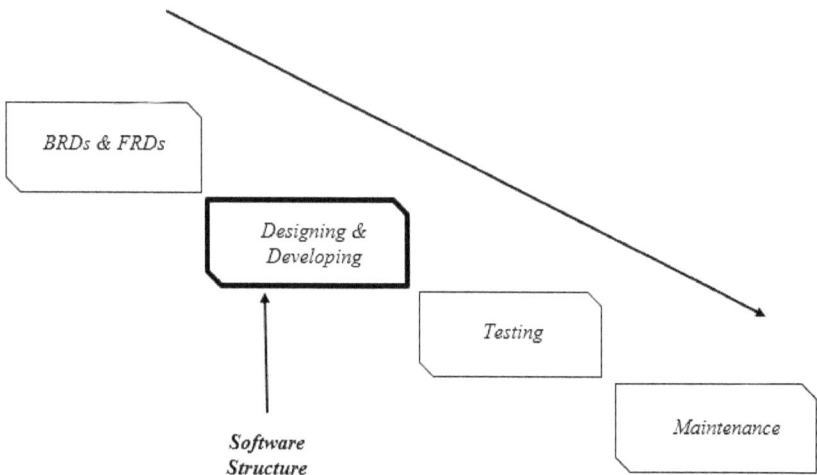

Author's Creation

Figure 6 shows a simple S & P architecture system from the Business Requirement Documentation (BRDs) to the Functional Requirement Documentation (FRDs) to the design and development stage, testing maintenance. Layouts, models, and communication systems categorize S & P architecture. They are designed by domain-driven, objective-oriented, layered, message-driven, client-driven, and N-Tier architecture. Figure 7 shows a more complex S & P architecture with a dynamic communication system between peers and clients from a single database system.

Figure 7: S & P Architecture Communication Stream

Where

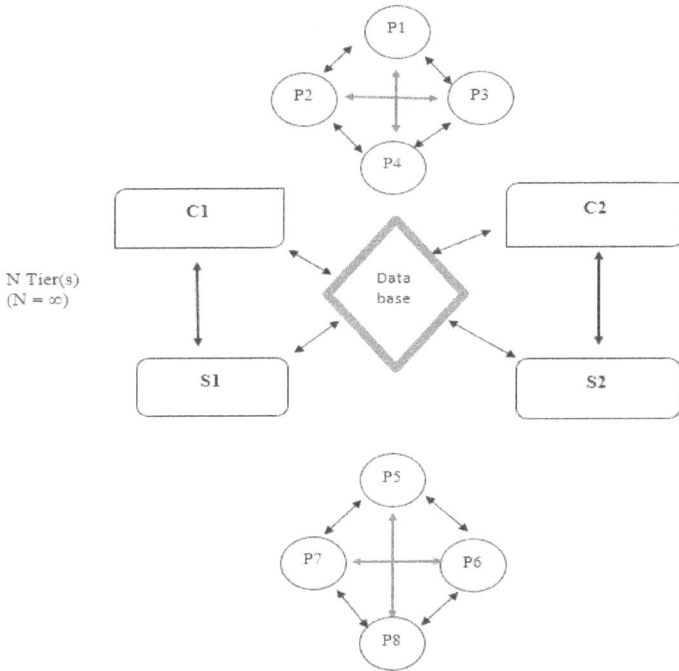

N Tier(s)
(N = ∞)

C = clients
P = peer
Author's Creation

Story Mapping

Patton (2015) created the story mapping model. Story Maps states that single-list product backlogs are inefficient, and a better prioritization model is needed. A Story Mapping can be organized in the following way (See Figure 8):

213

Figure 8: User Story Mapping

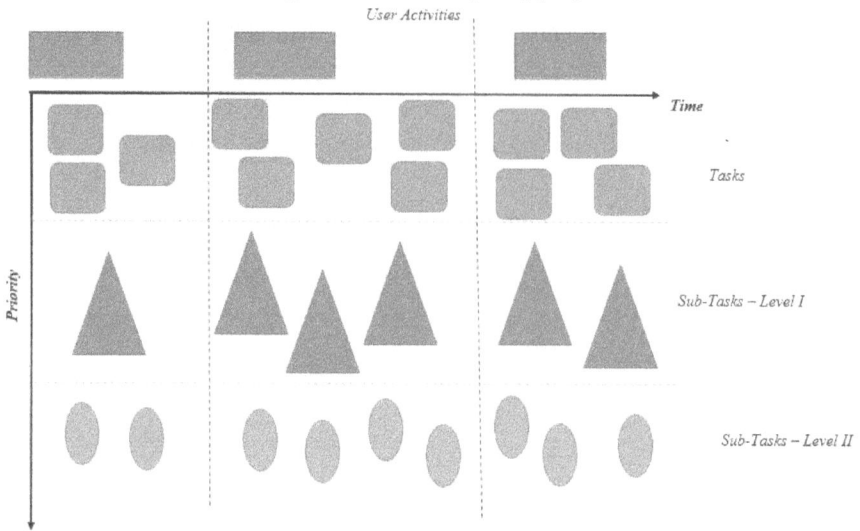

Author's Creation

The horizontal axis represents usage and time sequence; user tasks are placed along this axis in the row where they are performed. In contrast, the vertical line represents the user activities' levels of priority in the story map; user tasks are arranged vertically as to how important they are (task, sub-task—level I, and sub-task—level II). Equally important tasks are sometimes kept at the same level, but it is always better to differentiate to create efficient plans.

The Must-Should-Could-Won't-Have (MoSCoW) method is used to reach an agreement on what is more important to producers, shareholders, stakeholders, and customers.

Marketing Requirement Document (MRD) translates the customer's needs and wants for goods and services.

Business Requirement Document (BRD): is a transcript from the client to the scrum master of the project requirements, objectives, and prototype of the project's functionality.

214

Product Requirement Document (PRD): transcribes the product's capabilities and is helpful for type one and two error testing.

Functional Requirement Document (FRD): This is a formal statement from the scrum master to the IT department of the application's requirement.

The IDEA MODEL: The IDEAS model seen in Figure 9 is a tool like the business model canvas or a business plan that consists of practical tools for designing, creating, and implementing change. It supports a design process that includes but is not limited to value-proposition, innovation, in-depth customer requirements, prototypes, and a build-test-learn cycle (Browne and Keeley, 2007; Cohen, 2009; Facione and Gittens, 2016).

Figure 9:

IDEA--MODEL

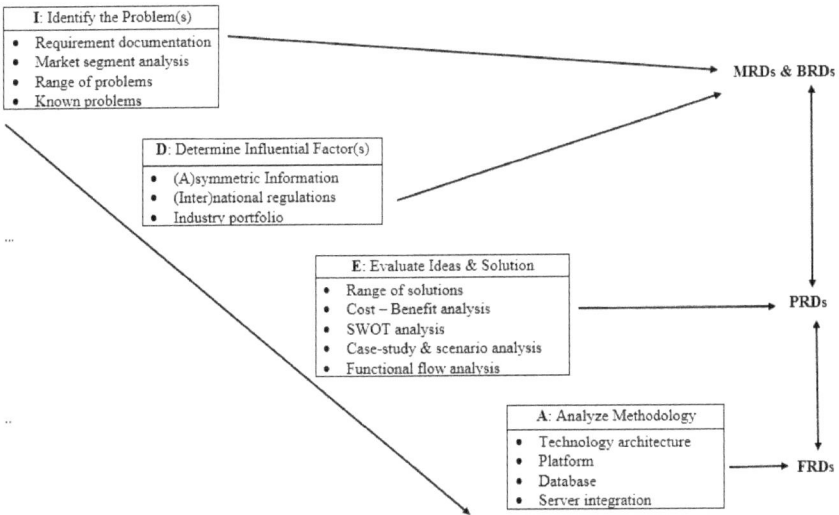

Author's Creation

CONCLUSION

The chapter analyzed the performance management industry from a behavioral perspective, building on Skinner (1936) Skinner (1953) Skinner (1957) and Nash (1950a) Nash (1950b) Nash (1951) studies. The chapter covers performance management as a business analyst, scrum master, archeologist, and leader. The research delves into the founding history of performance management and analyzes critical performance management tools. And concludes that performance management should be seen, managed, and played as an infinite game while creating incentives for the players who will, in turn, drive productivity in any industry. The chapter contributes to the existing literature on performance management by reviewing and delving into the main concepts of the performance management system. The chapter examines performance management in managerial science literature and will serve as a precision and accurate navigating tool in the performance management industry.

The chapter contributes to the existing literature on performance management by reviewing the field in a single article and delving into the main concepts of the performance management system. The chapter is one of the few papers that have examined performance management in managerial science literature, and it aims to serve as a precision and accurate navigating tool for performance managers in the industry.

REFERENCES

Akao, Y. (1988). *Quality function deployment: Integrating customer requirements into product design*. Productivity Press.

Ammons, D. N. and Roenigk, D. J. (2020). Exploring devolved decision authority in performance management regimes: The relevance of perceived and actual decision authority as elements of performance management success. *Public Performance and Management Review*: 28-52. Available: https://doi.org/10.1080/15309576.2019.1657918

Baer, D. M., Wolf, M. M. and Rislley, T. R. (1968). Some current dimensions of applied behavior analysis. *Journal of Applied Behavior Analysis:* 91-97. Available: https://doi.org/10.1901/jaba.1968.1-91

Brache, A. P. and Rummler, G. A. (1995). Invited reaction - performance improvement: A methodology for practitioners. *Human Resource Development Quarterly*: Available: https://doi.org/10.1002/hrdq.3920060104

Browne, M. N. and Keeley, S. M. (2007). *Asking the right questions: A guide to critical thinking*. Pearson Education, Inc.

Bumstead, A. and Boyce, T. E. (2005). Exploring the effects of cultural variables in the implementation of behavior-based safety in two organisations. *Journal of Organizational Behavior Management*: 43-63. Available: https://doi.org/10.1300/J075v24n04_03

Carnegie, D. (1936). *How to win friends and influence people*. Simon and Schuster: New York.

Cohen, E. D. (2009). *Critical thinking unleashed*. Rowman and Littlefield Publishers, Inc.

Daniels, A. C. and Bailey, J. S. (2014). *Performance management: Changing behavior that drive organizational effectiveness*. Aubrey Daniels International, Inc: Atlanta.

Deming, W. E. (1986). *Out of the crisis*. MIT Press: Cambridge.

Facione, P. and Gittens, C. A. (2016). *Think critically*. Pearson.

Fante, R., Gravina, N., Betz, A. and Austin, J. (2010). Structural and treatment analyses of safe and at-risk behaviors and postures performed by pharmacy employees. *Journal of Organizational Behavior Management*: 325-38. Available: https://doi.org/10.1080/01608061.2010.520143

Fein, M. (1981). *Improshare: An alternative to traditional managing*. Institute of Industrial Engineers.

Fein, M. (1983). *Improshare: An alternative to traditional managing.-USA*. California.

Iwata, B. A., Dorsey, M. F., Slifer, K. J., Bauman, K. E. and Richman, G. S. (1994). Toward a functional analysis of self-injury. *Journal of Applied Behavior Analysis*: 197-209. Available: https://doi.org/10.1901/jaba.1994.27-197

Kano, N., Seracu, N., Takahashi, F. and Tsuji, S. (1984). Attractive quality and must-be quality. *The Journal of Japanese Society for Quality Control*: 39-48.

Landes, D. S. (1998). *The wealth and poverty of nations*. W. W. Norton and Company: New York.

Mandino, O. (1986). 'The greatest salesman in the world', (New York: Bantam Books).

Moynihan, D. P. (2008). *The dynamics of performance management*: Constructing informal information. Georgetown University Press: Washington, DC.

Moynihan, D. P., Pandey, S. K. and Wright, B. E. (2012). Setting the table: How transformational leadership fosters performance information use. *Journal of Public*

Administration Research and Theory: 143-64. Available: https://doi.org/10.1093/jopart/mur024

Nash, J. F. (1950a). Equilibrium points in n-person games. *National Academy of Sciences*: 48-49. Available: https://doi.org/10.1073/pnas.36.1.48

Nash, J. F. (1950b). The bargaining problem. *Econometrica*: 155-62. Available: https://doi.org/10.2307/1907266

Nash, J. F. (1951). Non-cooperative game. *Annals of Mathematics*: 286-95. Available: https://doi.org/10.2307/1969529

Patton, J. (2015). *Using story mapping.* O'Reilly Verlag GmbH and Co: KG.

Peters, T. J. and Waterman, R. H. (1982). *In search of excellence.* Harper and Row: New York.

Poister, T. H., Aristigueta, M. P. and Hall, J. L. (2015). *Managing and measuring performance in public and nonprofit organizations: An integrated approach.* 2nd edn: Jossey-Bass: San Francisco CA.

Rotar, L. J. and Kozar, M., 2017. "The use of the Kano Model to enhance customer satisfaction." In *Organization*.

Schaerer, M. and Swaab, R. (2019). *Are you sugarcoating your feedback without realizing it?* Havard Business Review.

Skinner, B. F. (1936). Conditioning and extinction and their relation to drive. *Journal of General Psychology*: 296-317. Available: https://doi.org/10.1080/00221309.1936.9713156

Skinner, B. F. (1953). Some contributions of an experimental analysis of behavior to psychology as a whole. *American Psychologist*: 69-78. Available: https://doi.org/10.1037/h0054118

Skinner, B. F. (1957). Verbal behavior. Available: https://doi.org/10.1037/11256-000

Therrien, K., Wilder, D. A., Rodriguez, M. and Wine, B. (2013). Preintervention analysis and improvement of customer greeting in a restaurant. *Journal of Applied Behavior Analysis*: 411-15. Available: https://doi.org/10.1901/jaba.2005.89-04

Thompson, D. W. (1978). *Managing people: influencing behavior*. The C. V. Mosby Company: St. Louis.

Van Dooren, W., Bouckaert, G. and Halligan, J. (2010), 'Performance management in the public sector'.

REFORMING AND CREATING A

BUSINESS-FRIENDLY ENVIRONMENT

IN NIGERIA

INTRODUCTION

As a religious country, the people's faith has influenced business behavior and actions. Some residents view their religion as a culture, way of life, trust currency, and/or a segregation index. Previous studies have analyzed and attributed corruption in Nigeria as the primary cause of the dwindling economy, attributing a direct and sometimes indirect correlation to the nation's focus on religion as the catalyst of the country's problem. This article is an internal whitepaper of the Ane Osiobe International Foundation's activities, utilizing its operation costs and estimated budget for future projects to analyze the economic impact of corruption on the Nigerian economy's business-friendly environment, attraction, and retention. The impact results show the direct, indirect, and induced effects of a hostile business environment as non-profit organizations try to help residents of the Nigerian economy. The government places a heavy tax burden on their donations under section 12-A of the Nigerian tax code and the indirect bureaucratic corrupted processes on every activity that can promote economic growth and development within the region, which is simply an indirect, self-induced economic war against the Nigerian people that in turn creates a vicious domino-and-multiplier effect against the nation in the international market. The recommendation from the chapter builds on the premise that the most valuable asset to combat this hostile virtuous cycle is trust and transparency not only at the national level but where it is most needed, which is the individual level.

Nigeria is a very religious [Christianity, Islam, and Paganism (polytheism or ethnic-tradition)] country. The nation is known for its rich culture, afro-music, natural resources, and multilingual ethnicity. Still, this chapter will focus on its business environment from a non-profit perspective and how hostile it is to stakeholders. The Nigerian business environment can be summarized in one word, both from the banking, natural resource, education, and non-profit sectors: "corrupt." According to the Transparency International Index, corruption abuses entrusted power and privileges for private gain. Nigeria ranks 154 out of 180 countries with a score of 24/100 based on 2021 (Corruption Perception Index (CPI), 2022). Eighty-five percent of the participants believe corruption in the country keeps increasing based on the chapter trends (Transparency International (TI), 2015). According to the Global Corruption Barometer (GCB), 43 percent thought corruption increased in the previous 12 months, and 44 percent of public service users paid a bribe during the last 12 months (GCB, 2019).

Figure 1: Corruption Perceptions Index
Source: (CPI, 2022)

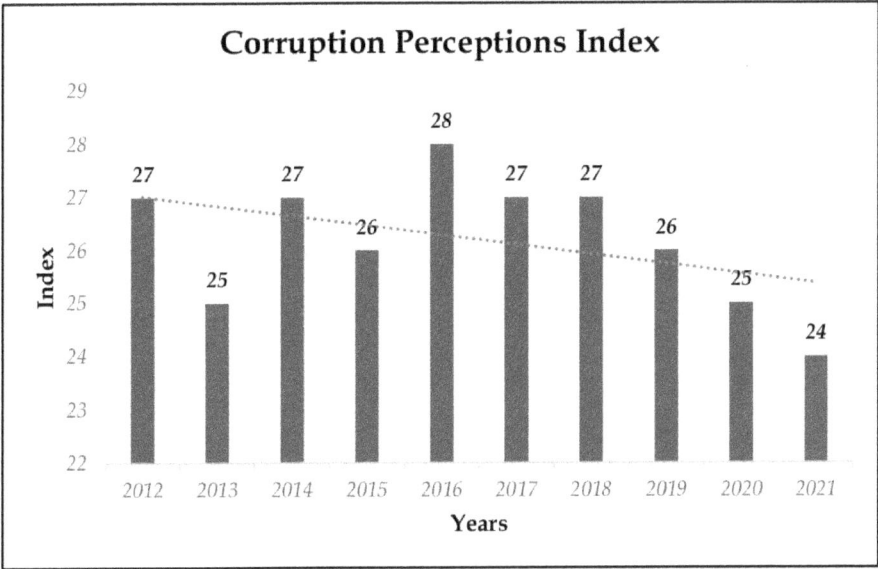

Figure 1 shows Nigeria's CPI; a low score out of 100 indicates the country is highly corrupt, while a high score indicates that the government is transparent in its dealings. Researchers such as but are not limited to (Ajie and Wokekoro, 2012 Egger and Winner, 2005 Anokhin and Schulze, 2009) have indicated that corruption can be linked to the economy (natural resources, trade, and international agreements) and non-economic (religion, trust, and culture) factors which have had a net negative impact on the growth and development of the country. Hence, associating most emerging economies located in South America, Africa, and Asia with low CPIs, between 39 (*Colombia, Ethiopia, Guyana, Kosovo, Morocco, North Macedonia, Suriname, Tanzania, and Vietnam*) – and 11 (*South Sudan*) with (*Denmark, Finland, and New Zealand*) ranking top of the list with 88/100 (CPI, 2022) in both the private and public sectors.

Figure 2: CPI 2022
Source: (CPI, 2022)

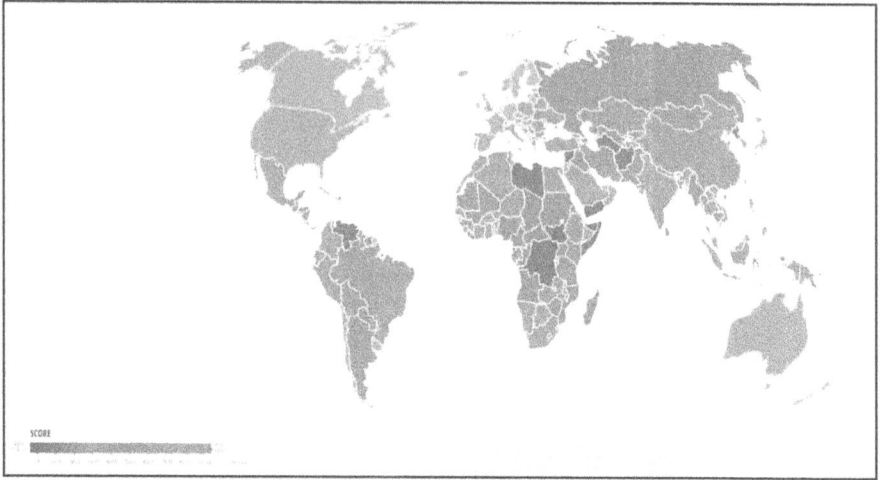

Figure 2 shows the CPI of the 180 countries on the continental map of the world, with 100/light yellow, meaning less corrupt or very clean, and 0/dark red, meaning highly corrupt, for the year 2021. According to Transparency International, the global average of CPI remained the same for the last decade, at 43/100 points. Despite multiple commitments by sovereign governments, 131 nations have made zero significant progress against corruption in the previous ten years (2011 – 2021). Two-thirds of countries on the world map and 100% of the countries in Africa score below 50, indicating severe corruption problems, while 27 countries are at their lowest score ever. Based on the Transparency International analysis (CPI, 2022), human rights are crucial in the fight against corruption: countries with well-protected civil liberties generally score higher on the CPI, while countries that violate civil liberties tend to score lower.

Figure 3 shows that Nigeria scores below the world's CPI average with a 24/100, tying with (The Central African Republic and Lebanon) which indicates that the country is highly corrupted with a declining trend see Figure 1.

Figure 3: CPI 2022
Source: (CPI, 2022)

Table 1 shows that the Nigerian Naira is Africa's 12th weakest and most valuable currency, weaker than the Zimbabwean dollar. The monetary policy power of the Central Bank of Nigeria is so weak that the black market rate at the exchange market overpowers the CBN official rate. Today, the naira has little value among its African pairs and is even weaker against other countries worldwide. According to the World Development Index (WDI), Nigeria is the biggest economy on the continent, ranked as the 26th-largest economy in the world in terms of nominal GDP, with 432.3 billion USD as Gross Domestic Product (GDP) as of 2020 (WDI), 2022), most of its citizens live in poverty which has a high correlation to the level of the nation's corruption. Nevertheless, its leaders still borrow money from foreign countries like China and international organizations like the World Bank and the International Monetary Fund (IMF), putting pressure on its local currency regarding the interest rate. This effect is not due to borrowing but to using the funds. The evidence will show that the money is not used for capital investments but for consumption only, which is plagued with a high

225

corruption CPI. Due to the weakening economy and public fund mismanagement, the nation is faced with a high rate of brain drainage.

Table 1: Top 25 Worst Currencies in Africa

Source: (Baha, 2022)

Ranking	Country (*Name of Currency*)	1 USD to
1	Sao Tome & Principe (Dobra)	20,901
2	Sierra Leonean (Leone)	10,105
3	Guinea-Bissau (West-African CFA Franc)	9,953
4	Guinea (Guinean Franc)	9,930
5	Equatorial Guinea (Central African CFA franc)	9,905
6	Malagasy (Ariary)	3,735
7	Uganda (Shilling)	3,671
8	Tanzania (Shilling)	2,319
9	Burundi (Franc)	1,944
10	Rwanda (Franc)	987
11	Malawi (Kwacha)	765
12	Nigeria (Naira)	625
13	Somali (Shilling)	585
14	Burkina Faso (West African CFA Franc)	541
14	Cote d'Ivoire (West African CFA Franc)	541
14	Togo (West African CFA Franc)	541
14	Benin Republic (West African CFA Franc)	541
14	Mali (West African CFA Franc)	541
14	Niger (West African CFA Franc)	541
14	Senegal (West African CFA Franc)	541
21	Gabon (Central African CFA Franc)	540
21	Cape Verde (Central African CFA Franc)	540
23	Cameroon's (West African CFA Francs)	539
24	Comoros (Comorian Franc)	407
25	Zimbabwe (Zimbabwean Dollar)	362

The contribution of this chapter to the literature on business attraction, retention, and a business-friendly environment is that the research investigates how the corruption level in Nigeria has affected the country's business environment and the negative economic impact (direct, indirect, and induced) effects of deadweights on the economy. Our analysis utilizes the Ane Osiobe International Foundation's ((AOIF) Financial Records (AOIFFR)) as a case study for empirical analysis. The limitation of the chapter is that some of the analyses are based on projected expenditure numbers and not actual expenditure figures.

LITERATURE

Corruption is a social phenomenon that is hard to define empirically or theoretically because what is corrupt or unethical in one community can be seen as a way of life and ethical in another. Hence, to define corruption, factors like but not limited to history, politics, social and cultural norms, beliefs, the rule of law, and the economic status quo need to be factored into the definition. A theatrical-based study asserts that democracy [which universally is more favored as an economic system compared to dictatorship] has primarily led to the reduction of corruption and promoted economic growth and development (Treisman, 2000), which can be supported by the current standard of living in most democratic western countries. Westernized countries like the United States, Canada, Switzerland, and Israel that practice Western democracy are known for their higher level of residents' participation. As a result, their higher level of public involvement in the nation's governance leads to economic growth and development (Scully & Slottje, 1991; Vorhies & Glahe, 1988). According to (Alesina et al., 2003), ethical conflict is one of the essential determinants of political economy. Many believe that the lack of an ethical system that favors all residents in a nation will lead to fractured institutions, political instability, and a decline in economic growth and development. Alesina et al. (2003) support (Easterly &

Levine's, 1997) analysis that per capita GDP has an inverse relationship with ethnolinguistic fractionalization in African countries, arguing that much of their economic growth and development failure is due to ethical conflict.

METHODOLOGY

The author used the IMPLAN software to estimate a hostile business environment's direct, indirect, and induced economic impact(s). The result depicts the economic deadweight due to the Nigerian government's hostile dealings with businesses. The appropriateness of this model for this chapter is justified as IMPLAN is the only Input-Output data company with the aggregate labor force information in Nigeria (Osiobe, 2018).

Data

The chapter used publicly available data from the foundations' audited financial reports from 2015 to 2021 (AOIFFR, 2022).

Table 2: Data 1
Source: (AOIFFR, 2022)

Year	Expenditure Report ₦	Donations Reports ₦	Total Expenditure ₦	Change in Total Expenditure ₦
2015	791,350.00	-	791,350.00	-
2016	2,029,300.00	250,000.00	2,279,300.00	188.03%
2017	2,430,603.00	650,000.00	3,080,603.00	35.16%
2018	4,410,327.00	91,400.00	4,501,727.00	46.13%
2019	2,923,132.00	1,200,000.00	4,123,132.00	-8.41%
2020	1,150,027.00	9,000,000.00	10,150,027.00	146.17%
2021	15,000,000.00	-	15,000,000.00	47.78%
Total	**28,734,739.00**	**11,191,400.00**	**39,926,139.00**	-

Table 3: Data 2

Project Name	Estimated cost ₦
Project – Nayomee	101,000,000.00
Project – Evergreen	50,000,000.00
Project – Woodbury	50,000,000.00
Transactional Cost	49,000,000.00
Total	**250,000,000.00**

Source: (AOIF Unpublished Statements, 2022)

Methodology

The chapter methodology builds on (Osiobe, 2018 & 2019) while expanding on the model.

$$Y_i = \beta_i X_1 + \cdots + \beta_{i\,25} + X_{25} + + \varepsilon_i$$

The Input-Output model shows the relationships/multiplier effect of the monetary transaction from one industrial sector within an economy that may translate [become an input] to another industrial sector within the same economy—showing how dependent each industry is on the other, both as a demander of outputs and as a supplier of inputs.

$$A = \begin{pmatrix} \beta_{1,1} & \cdots & \beta_{1,25} \\ \vdots & \ddots & \vdots \\ \beta_{25,1} & \cdots & \beta_{25,25} \end{pmatrix}, B = \begin{matrix} b_1 \\ \vdots \\ b_{25} \end{matrix}, C = \begin{matrix} x_1 \\ \vdots \\ x_{25} \end{matrix}$$

Where:

A = input-output matrix

B = externa; demand vector

C = production level vector

$$Y = AC + B$$

Where:

$$A \text{ and } B \neq \begin{bmatrix} 0 \\ \vdots \\ 0 \end{bmatrix}$$

The chapter also builds on the Leontief Model [Leontief Inverse Matrix or Total Requirement Matrix] (Leontief, 1966):

$$I_n Y - AC = B$$

$$(I_n - A)Y = B$$

$$Y = (I_n - A)^{-1} B$$

Model Information

Table 4: Model Information

Source: (Implan 11 software and Database for Nigeria, 2022) & author's modification to current data (WDI,2022)

Software Year	2011
Model Status	Multiplier
Multiplier Specification	SAM
Gross Regional Production	₦ 35,106,462,154,698
Total Personal Income	₦ 21,315,290,000,000
Number of Industries in the model	25
Land Area (Square Miles)	356,667
Population	206,100,000
Average Household Income	₦636,084

FINDINGS

Figure 4: Expenditure Report
Source: (AOIFFR, 2022)

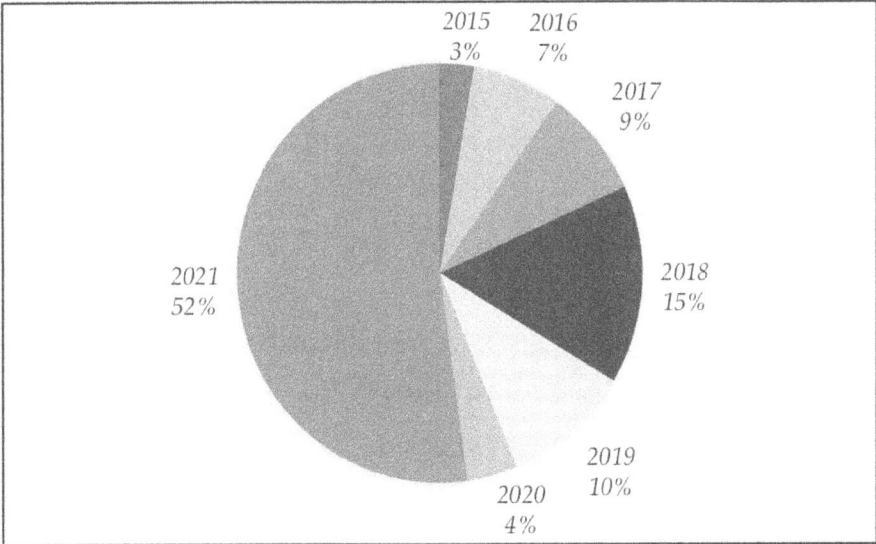

Figure four shows the expenditure report of AOIF from 2015 to 2021 as a percentage of the foundation's yearly spending. The pie chat shows 2021 at 52%, 2018 at 15%, 2019 at 10%, 2017 at 9%, 2016 at 7%, 2020 at 4%, and 2015 at 3%.

2015 Expenditure and Donation Economic Impact Results

Based on (AOIFFR 2022), the economic impact of the AOIF activities in the year 2015 based on our empirical analysis (see Table 10, in the Appendix Section (AS)), shows that the total labor income was ₦ 87,491; the mean labor income was ₦ 29,163.33k; the median labor income was ₦ 3,940; the range of the labor income was ₦ 77,634 (with a min of ₦ 2,958 and max of

₦ 80,592). The total employment effect was 0.2, with a 0.1 direct impact on employment and zero indirect and induced effect on employment. The total value added was ₦ 855,391; the mean value-added was ₦ 285,130.7k; the median value added was ₦ 76,565; the range of the value-added was ₦ 636,891 (with a min of ₦ 70,968 and a max of ₦ 707,859). The total output was ₦ 965,264; the mean output was ₦ 32,175.7k; the median output was ₦ 88,136; the range of the production was ₦ 705,572 (with a min of ₦ 85,778 and max of ₦ 791,350).

Based on the AOIF activities, the top ten industry gainers are (see Table 11 in the AS). On the aggregate level of the top ten industries, the total labor income was ₦ 86,312; the mean labor income of the top ten industries was ₦ 8631.2k; the median labor income of the top ten industries was ₦ 334; the range of the labor income of the top ten industries was ₦ 81,626 (with a min of ₦ 26 and a max of ₦ 81,652). The total value added of the top ten industries was ₦ 840,464; the mean value-added of the top ten industries was ₦ 84,046.4k; the median value-added of the top ten industries was ₦ 5,746.5k; the range value-added of the top ten industries was ₦ 715,265 (with a min of ₦ 1,899 and a max of ₦ 717,164). The total output of the top ten industries was ₦ 942,803; the mean output of the top ten industries was ₦ 94280.3k; the median output of the top ten industries was ₦ 7810.5k; the range output of the top ten industries was ₦ 798,298 (with a min of ₦ 3,455 and a max of ₦ 801,753).

2016 Expenditure and Donation Economic Impact Results

Based on (AOIFFR, 2022), the economic impact of the AOIF activities in the year 2016 based on our empirical analysis (see Table 12, in the AS) shows that the total labor income was ₦ 224,357; the mean labor income was ₦ 74,785.67k; the median labor income was ₦ 10,104; the range of the labor income was ₦ 199,081 (with a min of ₦ 7,586 and max of ₦ 206,667). The total employment effect was 0.4, with a 0.2 direct effect on employment, 0.1 indirect effect on employment, and 0.1 induced effect on employment. The total value added was ₦ 2,193,524; the mean value-added was ₦ 731,174.7k; the median value added was ₦ 196,339; the range of the value-added was ₦ 1,633,213 (with a min of ₦ 219,966 and a max of ₦ 1,815,199). The total output was ₦ 2,475,277; the mean output was ₦ 825,092.3k; the median output was ₦ 226,011; the range of the output was ₦ 1,809,334 (with a min of ₦ 219,966 and max of ₦ 2,029,300). The economic impact of the AOIF donations shows that the total labor income of donations was ₦ 27,640; the mean labor income of donations was ₦ 9,213.33k; the median labor income of donations was ₦ 1,245; the range of the labor income of donations was ₦ 24,525 (with a min of ₦ 935 and a max of ₦ 25,460). The total employment effect of donations was 0.1, and there was zero direct, indirect, or induced employment effect on the economy. The total value added of donations was ₦ 270,232; the mean value-added of donations was ₦ 90,077.33k; the median value-added of donations was ₦ 24,188; the range of the value-added of donations was ₦ 201,204 (with a min of ₦ 22,420 and a max of ₦ 223,624). The total output of donations was ₦ 304,942; the mean output of donations was ₦ 101,647.3k; the median output of donations was ₦ 27,843; the range of the output was ₦ 222,901 (with a min of ₦ 27,099 and a max of ₦ 250,000).

Based on the AOIF activities, the top ten industry gainers are (see Table 13 in the AS). On the aggregate level of the top ten industries, the total labor income was ₦ 221,334; the mean labor income of the top ten industries was ₦ 22,133.4k; the median labor income of the top ten industries was ₦ 856; the range of the labor income of the top ten industries was ₦ 209,317 (with a min of ₦ 67 and a max of ₦ 209,384). The total value added of the top ten industries was ₦ 2,155,246; the mean value-added of the top ten industries was ₦ 215524.6k; the median value-added of the top ten industries was ₦ 14,735.5k; the range value-added of the top ten industries was ₦ 1,834,190 (with a min of ₦ 4,871 and a max of ₦ 1,839,061). The total output of the top ten industries was ₦ 2,417,680; the mean output of the top ten industries was ₦ 241,768k; the median output of the top ten industries was ₦ 20,029; the range output of the top ten industries was ₦ 2,047,117 (with a min of ₦ 8,860 and a max of ₦ 2,055,977). On the aggregate donations level of the top ten industries, the total donations labor income was ₦ 27,267; the mean donations labor income of the top ten industries was ₦ 2,726.7k; the median donations labor income of the top ten industries was ₦ 105; the range of the donations labor income of the top ten industries was ₦ 25,787 (with a min of ₦ 8 and max of ₦ 25,795). The total donations' value-added of the top ten industries was ₦ 265,517; the mean donations' value-added of the top ten industries was ₦ 26,551.7k; the median donations' value-added of the top ten industries was ₦ 1,815.5k; the range donations' value-added of the top ten industries was ₦ 225,964 (with a min of ₦ 600 and a max of ₦ 226,564). The total donations output of the top ten industries was ₦ 297,845; the mean donations output of the top ten industries was ₦ 29,784.5k; the median donations output of the top ten industries was ₦ 2,467.5k; the range of donations' output of the top ten industries was ₦ 252,195 (with a min of ₦ 1,091 and a max of ₦ 253,286).

Figure five shows an upward trend of Foreign Direct Investment (FDI) in the form of donations flowing into the Nigerian economy.

Figure 5: Total Expenditure
Source: (AOIFFR, 2022)

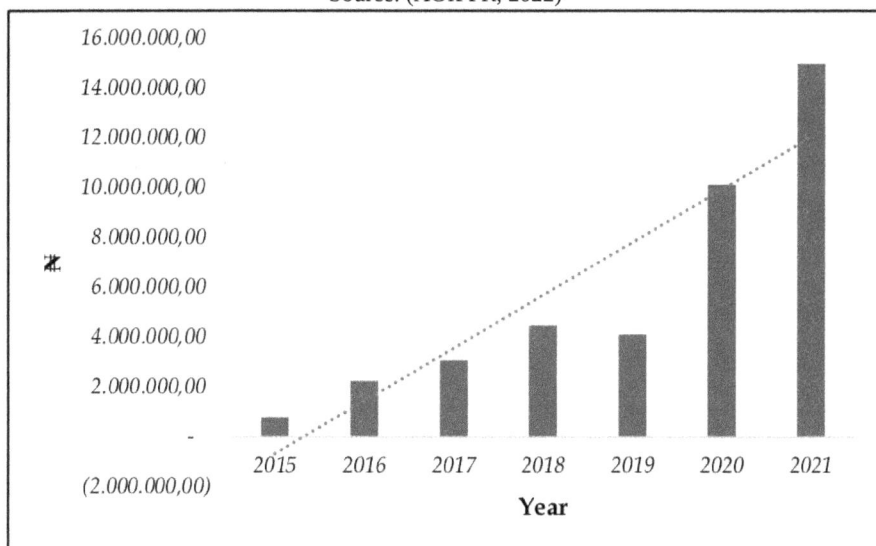

2017 Expenditure and Donation Economic Impact Results

Based on (AOIFFR, 2022), the economic impact of the AOIF activities in the year 2017 based on our empirical analysis (see Table 14, in the AS) shows that the total labor income was ₦ 268,725; the mean labor income was ₦ 89,574.67k; the median labor income was ₦ 12,102; the range of the labor income was ₦ 238,450 (with a min of ₦ 9,086 and max of ₦ 247,536). The total employment effect was 0.5, with a 0.3 direct effect on employment, 0.1 indirect effect on employment, and 0.1 induced effect on employment. The total value added was ₦ 2,174,162; the mean value-added was ₦ 875,767.7k; the median value added was ₦ 235,166; the range of the value-added was ₦ 1,956,187 (with a min of ₦ 217,975 and max of ₦ 2,174,162). The total output was ₦ 2,964,774; the mean output was ₦ 988,257.7k; the median output was ₦ 270,705; the range of the output was ₦ 2,167,138 (with a min of ₦ 263,465 and max of ₦ 2,430,603). The economic impact of the AOIF donations shows that the total labor income of donations was ₦ 71,863; the mean labor income of donations was ₦ 23,954.33k; the median labor income of donations was ₦ 3,236; the range of the labor income of donations was ₦ 63,767 (with a min of ₦ 2,430 and a max of ₦ 66,197). The total employment effect of donations was 0.1, 0.1 direct effect, and a zero indirect and induced employment effect on the economy. The total value added of donations was ₦ 702,602; the mean value-added of donations was ₦ 234,201; the median value-added of donations was ₦ 62,889; the range of the value-added of donations was ₦ 523,130 (with a min of ₦ 58,292 and a max of ₦ 581,422). The total output of donations was ₦ 792,850; the mean output of donations was ₦ 264,283.3k; the median output of donations was ₦ 72,393; the range of the output was ₦ 57,953 (with a min of ₦ 70,457 and a max of ₦ 650,000).

Based on the AOIF activities, the top ten industry gainers are (see Table 15 in the AS). On the aggregate level of the top ten industries, the total labor income was ₦ 265,104; the mean labor income of the top ten industries was ₦ 26,510.4k; the median labor income of the top ten industries was ₦ 1,025.5k; the range of the labor income of the top ten industries was ₦ 250,710 (with a min of ₦ 80 and max of ₦ 250,790). The total value added of the top ten industries was ₦ 2,581,456; the mean value-added of the top ten industries was ₦ 258,145.6k; the median value-added of the top ten industries was ₦ 17,649; the range value-added of the top ten industries was ₦ 2,196,910 (with a min of ₦ 5,834 and a max of ₦ 2,462,556). The total output of the top ten industries was ₦ 2,895,787; the mean output of the top ten industries was ₦ 289,578.7k; the median output of the top ten industries was ₦ 23,989.5k; the range output of the top ten industries was ₦ 2,451,944 (with a min of ₦ 10,612 and a max of ₦ 2,462,556). On the aggregate donations level of the top ten industries, the total donations labor income was ₦ 70,894; the mean donations labor income of the top ten industries was ₦ 7,089.4k; the median donations labor income of the top ten industries was ₦ 274; the range of the donations labor income of the top ten industries was ₦ 67,046 (with a min of ₦ 21 and max of ₦ 67,067). The total donations' value-added of the top ten industries was ₦ 690,341; the mean donations' value-added of the top ten industries was ₦ 69,034.1k; the median donations' value-added of the top ten industries was ₦ 4,720; the range donations' value-added of the top ten industries was ₦ 587,505 (with a min of ₦ 1,560 and max of ₦ 589,065). The total donations output of the top ten industries was ₦ 774,403; the mean donations output of the top ten industries was ₦ 77,440.3k; the median donations output of the top ten industries was ₦ 6,415.5k; the range of donations' output of the top ten industries was ₦ 655,707 (with a min of ₦ 2,838 and a max of ₦ 658,545).

2018 Expenditure and Donation Economic Impact Results

Based on (AOIFFR, 2022), the economic impact of the AOIF activities in the year 2018 based on our empirical analysis (see Table 16, in the AS) shows that the total labor income was ₦ 487,601; the mean labor income was ₦ 162,533.3k; the median labor income was ₦ 21,959; the range of the labor income was ₦ 432,667 (with a min of ₦ 16,487 and max of ₦ 449,154). The total employment effect was 1, with a 0.5 direct effect on employment, 0.2 indirect effect on employment, and 0.2 induced effect on employment. The total value added was ₦ 4,767,239; the mean value-added was ₦ 1,589,080;

the median value added was ₦ 426,708; the range of the value-added was ₦ 3,549,501 (with a min of ₦ 395,515 and max of ₦ 3,945,016). The total output was ₦ 5,379,579; the mean output was ₦ 1,793,193; the median output was ₦ 491,194; the range of the output was ₦ 3,932,269 (with a min of ₦ 478,058 and max of ₦ 4,410,327). The economic impact of the AOIF donations shows that the total labor income of donations was ₦ 101,051; the mean labor income of donations was ₦ 33,683.67k; the median labor income of donations was ₦ 4,551; the range of the labor income of donations was ₦ 89,666 (with a min of ₦ 3,417 and a max of ₦ 93,083). The total employment effect of donations was 0.2, 0.1 direct employment impact, zero indirect, and induced employment effect on the economy. The total value added of donations was ₦ 987,967; the mean value-added of donations was ₦ 329,322; the median value-added of donations was ₦ 88,431; the range of the value-added of donations was ₦ 735,601 (with a min of ₦ 81,967 and a max of ₦ 817,568). The total output of donations was ₦ 1,114,869; the mean output of donations was ₦ 371,623; the median output of donations was ₦ 101,796; the range of the output was ₦ 814,927 (with a min of ₦ 99,073 and a max of ₦ 914,000).

Based on the AOIF activities, the top ten industry gainers are (see Table 17 in the AS). On the aggregate level of the top ten industries, the total labor income was ₦ 481,029; the mean labor income of the top ten industries was ₦ 48,102.9k; the median labor income of the top ten industries was ₦ 1,860; the range of the labor income of the top ten industries was ₦ 454,914 (with a min of ₦ 145 and a max of ₦ 455,059). The total value added of the top ten industries was ₦ 4,684,048; the mean value-added of the top ten industries was ₦ 468,404.8k; the median value-added of the top ten industries was ₦ 32,024.5k; the range value-added of the top ten industries was ₦ 3,986,291 (with a min of ₦ 10,586 and a max of ₦ 3,996,877). The total output of the top ten industries was ₦ 5,254,403; the mean output of the top ten industries was ₦ 525,440.3k; the median output of the top ten industries was ₦ 43529.5k; the range output of the top ten industries was ₦ 4,449,050 (with a min of ₦ 19,255 and a max of ₦ 4,468,305). On the aggregate donations level of the top ten industries, the total donations labor income was ₦ 99,689; the mean donations labor income of the top ten industries was ₦ 9,968.9k; the median donations labor income of the top ten industries was ₦ 385.5k; the range of the donations labor income of the top

Figure 6: Change in Total Expenditure
Source: (AOIFFR, 2022)

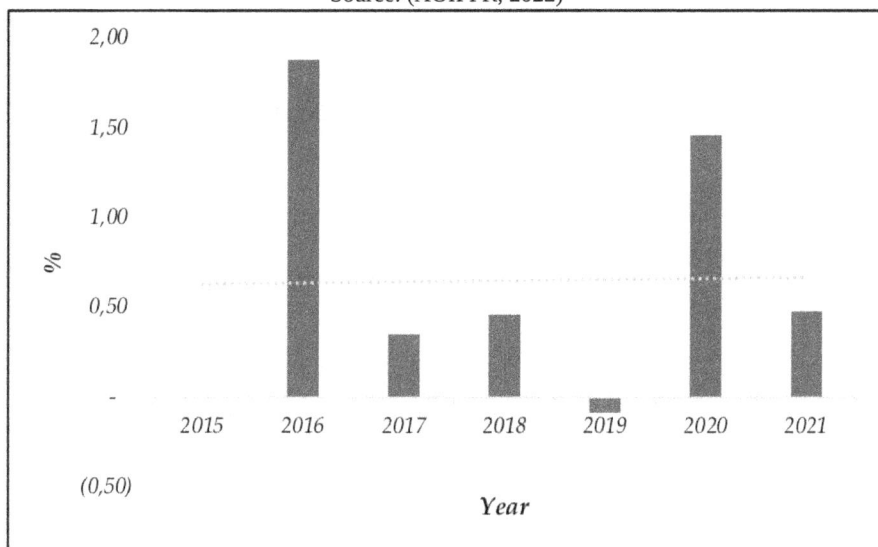

ten industries was ₦ 94,277 (with a min of ₦ 30 and max of ₦ 94,307). The total donations' value-added of the top ten industries was ₦ 970,725; the mean donations' value-added of the top ten industries was ₦ 97,072.5k; the median donations' value-added of the top ten industries was ₦ 6,636.5k; the range donations' value-added of the top ten industries was ₦ 826,122 (with a min of ₦ 2,194 and max of ₦ 828,316). The total donations output of the top ten industries was ₦ 1,088,925; the mean donations output of the top ten industries was ₦ 108,892.5k; the median donations output of the top ten industries was ₦ 9,021; the range of donations' output of the top ten industries was ₦ 922,025 (with a min of ₦ 3,990 and max of ₦ 926,015).

Figure six shows the percentage change in the FDI flows into the nation due to the AOIF activities in the country.

2019 Expenditure and Donation Economic Impact Results

Based on (AOIFFR, 2022), the economic impact of the AOIF activities in the year 2019 based on our empirical analysis (see Table 18, in the AS) shows that the total labor income was ₦ 323,179; the mean labor income was ₦ 107,726.3k; the median labor income was ₦ 14,555; the range of the labor income was ₦ 286,768 (with a min of ₦ 10,928 and max of ₦ 297,696). The total employment effect was 0.6, with a 0.4 direct effect on employment, 0.1 indirect effect on employment, and 0.2 induced effect on employment. The total value added was ₦ 3,159,691; the mean value-added was ₦ 1,053,230; the median value added was ₦ 282,819; the range of the value-added was ₦ 2,352,583 (with a min of ₦ 262,144 and max of ₦ 2,614,727). The total output was ₦ 3,565,545; the mean output was ₦ 1,188,515; the median output was ₦ 325,560; the range of the output was ₦ 2,606,279 (with a min of ₦ 316,853 and max of ₦ 2,923,132). The economic impact of the AOIF donations shows that the total labor income of donations was ₦ 132,671; the mean labor income of donations was ₦ 44,223.67k; the median labor income of donations was ₦ 5,975; the range of the labor income of donations was ₦

117,724 (with a min of ₦ 4,486 and a max of ₦ 122,210). The total employment effect of donations was 0.3, and a 0.1 direct, indirect, and induced employment effect on the economy. The total value added of donations was ₦ 1,297,112; the mean value-added of donations was ₦ 432,370.7k; the median value-added of donations was ₦ 116,103; the range of the value-added of donations was ₦ 965,779 (with a min of ₦ 107,615 and a max of ₦ 1,073,394). The total output of donations was ₦ 1,463,722; the mean output of donations was ₦ 487,907.3k; the median output of donations was ₦ 133,648; the range of the output was ₦ 1,069,926 (with a min of ₦ 130,074 and max of ₦ 1,200,000).

Based on the AOIF activities, the top ten industry gainers are (see Table 19 in the AS). On the aggregate level of the top ten industries, the total labor income was ₦ 318,823; the mean labor income of the top ten industries was ₦ 31,882.3k; the median labor income of the top ten industries was ₦ 1,233; the range of the labor income of the top ten industries was ₦ 301,514 (with a min of ₦ 96 and a max of ₦ 301,610). The total value added of the top ten industries was ₦ 3,104,553; the mean value-added of the top ten industries was ₦ 310,455.3k; the median value-added of the top ten industries was ₦ 21,226; the range value-added of the top ten industries was ₦ 2,642,084 (with a min of ₦ 7,016 and a max of ₦ 2,649,100). The total output of the top ten industries was ₦ 3,482,581; the mean output of the top ten industries was ₦ 348,258.1k; the median output of the top ten industries was ₦ 28,851; the range output of the top ten industries was ₦ 2,948,798 (with a min of ₦ 12,762 and a max of ₦ 2,961,560). On the aggregate donations level of the top ten industries, the total donations labor income was ₦ 130,881; the mean donations labor income of the top ten industries was ₦ 13,088.1k; the median donations labor income of the top ten industries was ₦

506.5k; the range of the donations labor income of the top ten industries was ₦ 123,777 (with a min of ₦ 39 and max of ₦ 123,816). The total donations' value-added of the top ten industries was ₦ 1,274,475; the mean donations' value-added of the top ten industries was ₦ 127,447.5k; the median donations' value-added of the top ten industries was ₦ 8,713.5k; the range donations' value-added of the top ten industries was ₦ 1,084,625 (with a min of ₦ 2,880 and max of ₦ 1,087,505). The total donations output of the top ten sectors was ₦ 1,429,663; the mean donations output of the top ten industries was ₦ 142,966.3k; the median donations output of the top ten industries was ₦ 11,844; the range of donations' output of the top ten industries was ₦ 1,210,536 (with a min of ₦ 5,239 and a max of ₦ 1,215,775).

2020 Expenditure and Donation Economic Impact Results

Based on (AOIFFR, 2022), the economic impact of the AOIF activities in the year 2020 based on our empirical analysis (see Table 20, in the AS) shows that the total labor income was ₦ 127,146; the mean labor income was ₦ 42,382; the median labor income was ₦ 5,726; the range of the labor income was ₦ 112,822 (with a min of ₦ 4,299 and max of ₦ 117,121). The total employment effect was 0.3, with a 0.1 direct effect on employment, 0.1 indirect effect on employment, and 0.1 induced effect on employment. The total value added was ₦ 1,243,095; the mean value-added was ₦ 414,365; the median value added was ₦ 111,268; the range of the value-added was ₦ 925,559 (with a min of ₦ 103,134 and a max of ₦ 1,028,693). The total output was ₦ 1,402,767; the mean output was ₦ 467,589; the median output was ₦ 128,083; the range of the output was ₦ 1,025,370 (with a min of ₦

124,657 and a max of ₦ 1,150,027). The economic impact of the AOIF donations shows that the total labor income of donations was ₦ 995,031; the mean labor income of donations was ₦ 331,677; the median labor income of donations was ₦ 44,812; the range of the labor income of donations was ₦ 882,929 (with a min of ₦ 33,645 and a max of ₦ 916,574). The total employment effect of donations was 2: 1.1 direct, 0.4 indirect, and 0.5 induced employment effect on the economy. The total value added of donations was ₦ 9,728,338; the mean value-added of donations was ₦ 3,242,779; the median value-added of donations was ₦ 870,769; the range of the value-added of donations was ₦ 7,243,341 (with a min of ₦ 807,114 and a max of ₦ 8,050,455). The total output of donations was ₦ 10,977,920; the mean output of donations was ₦ 3,659,307; the median output of donations was ₦ 1,002,364; the range of the output was ₦ 8,024,444 (with a min of ₦ 975,556 and max of ₦ 9,000,000).

Based on the AOIF activities, the top ten industry gainers are (see Table 21 in the AS). On the aggregate level of the top ten industries, the total labor income was ₦ 125,432; the mean labor income of the top ten industries was ₦ 12,543.2k; the median labor income of the top ten industries was ₦ 485; the range of the labor income of the top ten industries was ₦ 118,622 (with a min of ₦ 38 and a max of ₦ 118,660). The total value added of the top ten industries was ₦ 1,221,402; the mean value-added of the top ten industries was ₦ 122,140.2k; the median value-added of the top ten industries was ₦ 8,350.5k; the range value-added of the top ten industries was ₦ 1,039,457 (with a min of ₦ 2,760 and a max of ₦ 1,042,217). The total output of the top ten industries was ₦ 1,370,128; the mean output of the top ten industries was ₦ 137,012.8k; the median output of the top ten industries was ₦ 11,351; the range output of the top ten industries was ₦

1,160,124 (with a min of ₦ 5,021 and a max of ₦ 1,165,145). On the aggregate donations level of the top ten industries, the total donations labor income was ₦ 981,620; the mean donations labor income of the top ten industries was ₦ 98,162; the median donations labor income of the top ten industries was ₦ 3796.5k; the range of the donations labor income of the top ten industries was ₦ 928,328 (with a min of ₦ 295 and max of ₦ 928,623).

Figure 7: Donation Reports
Source: (AOIFFR, 2022)

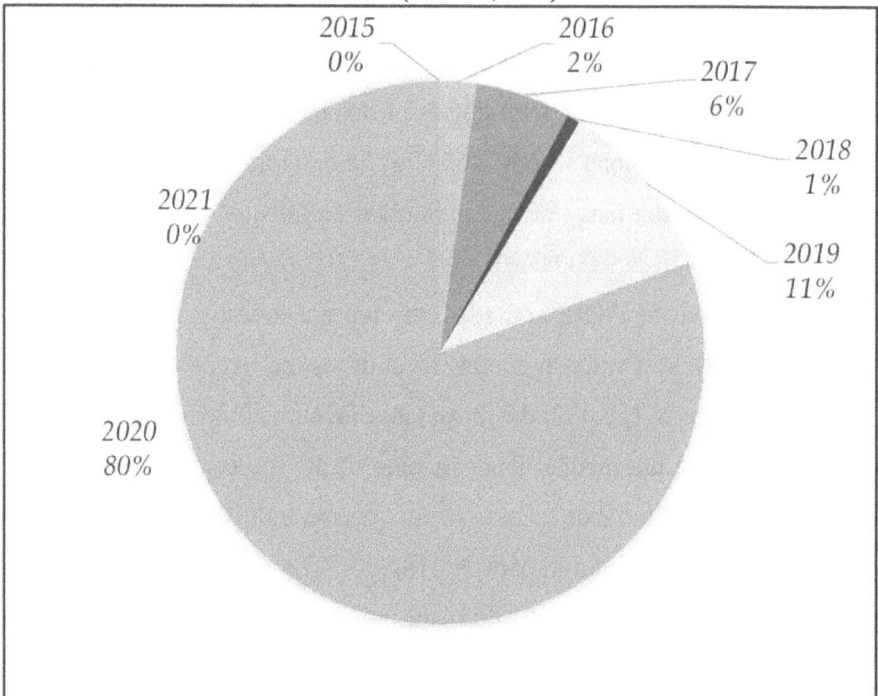

The total donations' value-added of the top ten industries was ₦ 9,558,572; the mean donations' value-added of the top ten industries was ₦ 955,857.2k; the median donations' value-added of the top ten industries was ₦ 65,352k; the range donations' value-added of the top ten industries was ₦ 8,134,685 (with a min of ₦ 21,602 and max of ₦ 8,156,287). The total donations output of the top ten industries was ₦ 10,722,476; the mean donations output of the top ten industries was ₦ 1,072,248; the median donations output of the top ten industries was ₦ 88,829.5k; the range of donations' output of the top ten industries was ₦ 9,079,022 (with a min of ₦ 39,292 and max of ₦ 9,118,314).

Figure seven shows the total donations to public schools made by the AOIF from 2015 to 2021. The pie chart shows 2020 at 80%, 2019 at 11%, 2017 at 6%, 2016 at 2%, 2018 at 1% and 2021 & 2015 at 0%.

2021 Expenditure and Donation Economic Impact Results

Based on (AOIFFR 2022), the economic impact of the AOIF activities in the year 2021 based on our empirical analysis (see Table 22, AS) shows that the total labor income was ₦ 1,658,385; the mean labor income was ₦ 552,795; the median labor income was ₦ 74,686; the range of the labor income was ₦ 1,471,547 (with a min of ₦ 56,076 and max of ₦ 1,527,623). The total employment effect was 3.3, with a 1.8 direct impact on employment, 0.7 indirect effect, and 0.8 induced effect on employment. The total value added was ₦ 16,213,895; the mean value-added was ₦ 5,404,632; the median value added was ₦ 1,451,281; the range of the value-added was ₦ 1,471,547 (with a min of ₦ 56,076 and max of ₦ 1,527,623). The total output was ₦ 18,296,532; the mean output was ₦ 6,098,844; the median output was ₦ 1,670,606; the range of the output was ₦ 13,374,074 (with a min of ₦ 1,625,926 and max of ₦ 15,000,000).

Based on the AOIF activities, the top ten industry gainers are (see Table 23 in the AS). On the aggregate level of the top ten industries, the total labor income was ₦ 1,636,033; the mean labor income of the top ten industries was ₦ 163,603.3k; the median labor income of the top ten industries was ₦ 6,327.5; the range of the labor income of the top ten industries was ₦ 1,547,213 (with a min of ₦ 492 and max of ₦ 1,547,705). The total value added of the top ten industries was ₦ 15,930,953; the mean value-added of the top ten industries was ₦ 1,593,095; the median value-added of the top ten industries was ₦ 108,920; the range value-added of the top ten industries was ₦ 13,557,808 (with a min of ₦ 36,003 and max of ₦ 13,593,811). The total output of the top ten industries was ₦ 17,870,793; the mean output of the top ten industries was ₦ 1,787,079; the median output of the top ten industries was ₦ 148,049; the range output of the top ten industries was ₦ 15,131,703 (with a min of ₦ 65,487 and a max of ₦ 15,197,190).

Figure 8: Estimated Cost
Source: (AOIFFR, 2022)

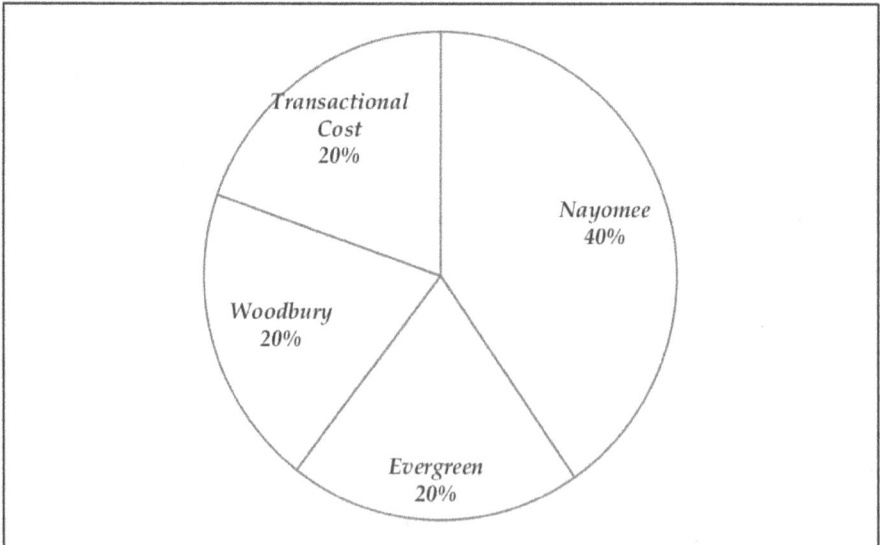

Figure eight shows the AOIF's unpublished estimated financial project activities that would have helped create new jobs and boost the Nigerian economy. However, the foundation moved its business activities to a more favorable business environment due to the unfavorable business environment plaguing the nation.

Anticipated Transactional Cost Economic Impact Results

Based on (AOIFFR 2022), the economic impact of the AOIF unpublished activities in the year 2022 based on our empirical analysis (see Table 24, in the AS) shows that the total labor income was ₦ 1,151,431; the mean labor income was ₦ 383,810; the median labor income was ₦ 382,567; the range of the labor income was ₦ 665,153 (with a min of ₦ 51,855 and max of ₦ 717,008). The total employment effect was 32.7, with a 28.8 direct effect on employment, 3.3 indirect, and 0.6 induced effect on employment. The total value added was ₦ 49,042,545; the mean value-added was ₦ 38,720,827; the median value added was ₦ 9,387,742; the range of the value-added was ₦ 37,786,851 (with a min of ₦ 933,976 and max of ₦ 38,720,827). The total output was ₦ 60,503,444; the mean output was ₦ 20,167,815; the median output was ₦ 10,343,528; the range of the output was ₦ 47,840,084 (with a min of ₦ 1,159,916 and max of ₦ 49,000,000).

Based on the AOIF activities, the top ten industry gainers are (see Table 26, in the AS). On the aggregate level of the top ten industries, the total labor income was ₦ 1,080,923; the mean labor income of the top ten industries was ₦ 108,092.3k; the median labor income of the top ten industries was ₦ 22,913.5k; the range of the labor income of the top ten industries was ₦ 716,556 (with a min of ₦ 583 and a max of ₦ 717,139).

The total value added of the top ten industries was ₦ 48,391,976; the mean value-added of the top ten industries was ₦ 4,839,198; the median value-added of the top ten industries was ₦ 365,635; the range value-added of the top ten industries was ₦ 38,685,256 (with a min of ₦ 42,640 and a max of ₦ 38,727,896). The total output of the top ten industries was ₦ 59,604,129; the mean output of the top ten industries was ₦ 5,960,413; the median output of the top ten industries was ₦ 440,959.5k; the range output of the top ten industries was ₦ 48,878,394 (with a min of ₦ 130,552 and a max of ₦ 49,008,946).

Anticipated Nayomee Project's Cost Economic Impact Results

Based on (AOIFFR 2022), the economic impact of the AOIF activities in the year 2022 based on our empirical analysis (see Table 24, AS) shows that the total labor income was ₦ 10,879,202; the mean labor income was ₦ 3,626,401; the median labor income was ₦ 1,238,822; the range of the labor income was ₦ 8,660,478 (with a min of ₦ 489,951 and max of ₦ 9,150,429). The total employment effect was 31.3, with a 12.6 direct effect on employment, 13.3 indirect, and 5.4 induced effect on employment. The total value added was ₦ 105,232,221; the mean value-added was ₦ 35,077,407; the median value added was ₦ 26,269,585; the range of the value-added was ₦ 61,313,431 (with a min of ₦ 8,824,603 and max of ₦ 70,138,034). The total output was ₦ 142,568,360; the mean output was ₦ 47,522,787; the median output was ₦ 30,608,987; the range of the output was ₦ 90,040,625 (with a min of ₦ 10,959,374 and max of ₦ 100,999,999).

Based on the AOIF activities, the top ten industry gainers are (see Table 25, in the AS). On the aggregate level of the top ten industries, the total labor income was ₦ 10,503,644; the mean labor income of the top ten industries was ₦ 1,050,364; the median labor income of the top ten industries was ₦ 132,943.5k; the range of the labor income of the top ten industries was ₦ 9,153,251 (with a min of ₦ 6,245 and max of ₦ 9,159,496). The total value added of the top ten industries was ₦ 105,232,221; the mean value-added of the top ten industries was ₦ 10,054,207; the median value-added of the top ten industries was ₦ 2,089,431; the range value-added of the top ten industries was ₦ 69,842,850 (with a min of ₦ 364,683 and a max of ₦ 70,207,533). The total output of the top ten industries was ₦ 136,425,010; the mean output of the top ten industries was ₦ 13,642,501; the median output of the top ten industries was ₦ 2,597,650; the range output of the top ten industries was ₦ 100,660,635 (with a min of ₦ 439,444 and a max of ₦ 101,100,079).

Anticipated Evergreen & Woodbury Project's Cost Economic Impact Results

Based on (AOIFFR 2022), the economic impact of the AOIF activities in the year 2022 based on our empirical analysis (see Table 24 AS) shows that the total labor income was ₦ 5,385,744; the mean labor income was ₦ 1,795,248; the median labor income was ₦ 613,278; the range of the labor income was ₦ 4,287,365 (with a min of ₦ 242,550 and max of ₦ 4,529,915). The total employment effect was 15.5, with a 6.2 direct effect on employment, 6.6 indirect, and 2.7 induced effect on employment. The total value added was ₦ 52,095,159; the mean value-added was ₦ 17,365,053; the median value added was ₦ 13,004,745; the range of the value-added was ₦ 30,353,184 (with a min of ₦ 4,368,615 and max of ₦ 34,721,799). The total output was ₦ 70,578,396; the mean output was ₦ 23,526,132; the median output was ₦ 15,152,964; the range of the output was ₦ 44,574,567 (with a min of ₦ 5,425,433 and max of ₦ 50,000,000).

Based on the AOIF activities, the top ten industry gainers are (see Table 25, in the AS). On the aggregate level of the top ten industries, the total labor income was ₦ 5,199,823; the mean labor income of the top ten industries was ₦ 519,982.3k; the median labor income of the top ten industries was ₦ 65,813.5k; the range of the labor income of the top ten industries was ₦ 4,531,313 (with a min of ₦ 3,091 and max of ₦ 4,534,404). The total value added of the top ten industries was ₦ 49,773,299; the mean value-added of the top ten industries was ₦ 4,977,330; the median value-added of the top ten industries was ₦ 1,034,372; the range value-added of the top ten industries was ₦ 34,575,668 (with a min of ₦ 180,536 and a max of ₦ 34,756,204). The total output of the top ten industries was ₦ 67,537,134; the mean output of the top ten industries was ₦ 6,753,713; the median output of the top ten industries was ₦ 1,285,965; the range output of the top ten industries was ₦ 49,831,997 (with a min of ₦ 217,547 and a max of ₦ 50,049,544).

CONCLUSION

An economic impact analysis story will not wholly show the picture to understand the Nigerian business environment. A psychologist, sociologist, and political scientist analysis is also needed. According to (Landes, 1998), the most significant resource a nation and its people should have is trust because the lack of that variable in the business equation will inevitably lead to a hostile business environment. According to the (Boston University

Global Development Policy Center (BUGDPC), 2022), in 2020, the Chinese loans to Africa database, which the BUGDPC manages, recorded eleven new loans to different African countries [with Nigeria making 5% of the pie] according to (Hwang et al., 2022).

Nigeria has borrowed over $6.5 billion from China since 2002 to build power plants and transportation systems and, in recent news, to pay for its state's works. The nation's infrastructure backbone II project currently uses about 55% of its annual revenue to service debts, which are projected to increase to 96% within the next decade. Today, Chinese loans represent 10% of Nigeria's debt stock and account for 80% of bilateral loans instead of multilateral institutions. The effects of COVID-19 on African economies led to a 77% reduction in the $8.2 billion agreement Chinese lending capacity, which may explain the drastic drop in Chinese lending amounts to Africa in 2020 and currently moving away from investing in Nigeria (Nyabiage, 2022).

The word motivation seems to be thrown around when inspiring young entrepreneurs. Nigeria is estimated to be the most populated nation by 2030, with youths making up about 65% of its population. Hence, the interesting question is, what motivates a nation to be trustworthy like Japan, and what makes a nation corrupt? Understanding the question well enough that you put oneself as a Japanese or Nigerian national may be the key for nations like Nigeria to create a more friendly business environment, which in turn will translate to economic growth and development as it is well known that Japan when compared to Nigerian, is a natural resource-poor nation but in comparison with Real Gross Domestic Product Japan is a wealthier nation. Evidence suggests that ordinary Nigerians can be as trustworthy as Japanese nationals, but how do we best achieve this? This is fundamentally an issue of individual psychology. One can not be motivated enough to put their country to the necessary degree [reducing brain drain, massive out-migration, and increased local corruption at every level of the economy] merely by being attracted to the thing the Western world [Norway, Finland, and Estonia] have or a potential African euphoria that might emerge as a consequence of Afriacaniess [a vision of heaven] no, a nation needs also be terrified of the hellish conditions its citizen faces of corruption is not reduced and the future of its next-generation on the world stage. Hence, the solution is "YOU [the everyday Nigerian that says no to participating in corruption in their little (area/office) of power]," not them but YOU. Because if YOU don't right and take yourself with enough seriousness, the nation will continue to be one with a hostile business environment.

Generally, as a country that prides itself as a religious country in its culture and beliefs, people from the outside might say the nation is not good at believing in what they believe (speaking from the laws of the Torah and the New Testament beliefs). Hence, one might argue with solid evidence that the nation is entirely of conflict and doubts and might not be able to articulate its culture, but its people's way of life is the bedrock of their culture. Hence, the ways of the Nigerian government are synonymous with the ways of the Nigerian people at the individual level. Some argue that "rights are attributed to YOU by the government, but the government is dependant on your actions [hence that statement of the Nigerian people (our government is corrupt)." To believe that statement is also to think that the state is an entity and the people are subordinates to the government. This can not be so in a democracy; "the state is dependent on the individual to the proportion that the individual is dependent on the government," making the individual and the government one. The failure to see Nigerians within the Nigerian system as one is a step in the wrong direction in solving the country's corruption issues and creating a friendly business environment that will promote economic growth and development because the individual is the active agent of the state (eyes, hands, mouth, and sense organs of the government).

REFERENCES

Ajie, H. A., & Wokekoro, O. E. (2012). The impact of corruption on sustainable economic growth and development in Nigeria. *International Journal of Economic Development Research and Investment*, 91-109.

Alesina, A., Devleeschauwer, A., Easterly, W., Kurlat, S., & Wacziarg, R. (2003). *Fractionalization. Journal of Economic Growth*, 155-194.
https://doi.org/10.1023/A:1024471506938

Ane Osiobe International Foundation. (2022, 3 10). Ane Osiobe International Foundation Financial Statements. Retrieved from Ane Osiobe International Foundation: https://aneosiobe.ngo/frmContentSecondary.aspx?NavID=26

Anokhin, S., & Schulze, W. S. (2009). Entrepreneurship, Innovation, and Corruption. *Journal of Business Venturing*, 465-476.
https://doi.org/10.1016/j.jbusvent.2008.06.001

Baha. (2022, 1 21). Retrieved from https://www.baha.com/?ts=1650387738384

Boston University Global Development Policy Center. (2022, 4 25). Chinese Loans to Africa During the COVID-19 Pandemic. Retrieved from BU Global Development Policy Center: https://www.bu.edu/gdp/2022/04/22/chinese-loans-to-africa-during-the-covid-19-pandemic/

Corruption Perceptions Index. (2022, 4 9). Retrieved from Transparency International: https://www.transparency.org/en/cpi/2021/index/nga

Easterly, W., & Levine, R. (1997). *Africa's Growth Tragedy: Policies and Ethnic Division. Quarterly Journal of Economics*, 1203-1250.
https://doi.org/10.1162/003355300555466

Egger, P., & Winner, H. (2005). *Evidence on Corruption as an Incentive for Foreign*

Direct Investment. European Journal of Political Economy, 932-952. https://doi.org/10.1016/j.ejpoleco.2005.01.002

Global Corruption Barometer Africa 2019: Citizen's Views and Experiences of Corruption. (2019, 7 11). Retrieved from Transparency International: https://www.transparency.org/en/publications/gcb-africa-2019

Hwang, J., Moses, O., Engel, L., & Shadbar, S. (2022). Chinese Loans to Africa During the COVID-19 Pandemic. Massachusetts: BU Global Development Policy Center.

Impaln. (2022, 4 11). Implan. Retrieved from Pricing and Data: https://implan.com/solutions/

Landes, D. S. (1998). *The Wealth and Poverty of Nations*. W. W. Norton & Company.

Leontief, W. (1966). *Input-Output Economics*. Oxford University Press.

Nyabiage, J. (2022, 5 10). *Nigeria looks to Europe for funding as Chinese lenders move away from costly projects in Africa*. Retrieved from South China Morning Post: https://www.scmp.com/news/china/diplomacy/article/3165844/nigeria-looks-europe-funding-chinese-lenders-move-away-costly

Osiobe, E. U. (2018). *The National Economic Impact from Agriculture*. Abuja: The Ane Osiobe International Foundation.

Osiobe, E. U. (2019). *The Economic Impact of Local Non-Government Direct Investment(s) on the Nigerian Economy: The Case of Lugbe, FCT, Nigeria*. The Ane Osiobe Trendsetters Series, 1-11.

Scully, G. W., & Slottje, D. J. (1991). *Ranking economic liberty across countries. Public Choice*, 121-152. https://doi.org/10.1007/BF00123844

Transparency International . (2015, 5 28). Transparency International. (Transparency International) Retrieved 4 9, 2022, from https://www.transparency.org/en/news/nigerias-corruption-challenge

Treisman, D. (2000). The causes of corruption: a cross-national study. *Journal of Public Economics*, 399-457. https://doi.org/10.1016/S0047-2727(99)00092-4

Vorhies, F., & Glahe, F. (1988). Political liberty and social development: An empirical investigation. *Public Choice*, 45-71. https://doi.org/10.1007/BF00183328

World Development Index. (2022, 4 20). World Bank. Retrieved from The World Bank: https://data.worldbank.org/country/nigeria?view=chart

APPENDIX

Table 5: The Production Account of the Nigerian Economy 2021
Source: (Implan 11 software and Database for Nigeria, 2022)

Industry Code	Description	Employment	Output ₦	Employee Compensation ₦	Proprietor Income ₦	Other Property Type Income ₦	Tax on Production and Imports ₦
3000	Total	57,833,308.60	44,705,258,363,281	1,722,474,518,005	566,252,337,265	32,793,545,446,289	24,189,853,139
3001	Agriculture	14,369,937.00	2,468,390,750,000	4,461,256,348	4,015,268,555	612,179,375,000	(173,294,128)
3002	Fishing	156,437.20	45,030,437,500	782,185,974	199,231,476	35,102,457,031	7,093,147
3003	Mining and Quarrying	2,730,308.00	3,323,925,250,000	21,027,123,047	17,120,103,516	1,958,215,000,000	4,676,562,012
3004	Food and beverages	622,433.30	1,396,554,875,000	22,300,917,969	9,257,606,445	900,987,187,500	1,321,530,640
3005	Textiles and wearing apparel	255,813.30	222,037,843,750	9,165,431,641	2,303,702,637	153,209,062,500	122,806,641
3006	Wood and paper	529,971.50	444,207,593,750	18,988,138,672	4,878,076,660	354,374,687,500	246,928,253
3007	Petroleum, Chemical, and Non-metal mfg.	951,748.50	1,315,054,750,000	34,099,824,219	11,624,273,438	1,054,070,250,000	1,925,015,747
3008	Metal products	573,480.80	358,452,781,255	20,547,017,578	4,578,950,195	268,071,937,500	346,151,459
3009	Electrical and machinery	1,611,277.50	1,161,742,875,000	57,729,824,219	13,176,477,539	834,692,000,000	433,713,318
3010	Transport equipment	532,395.50	594,186,250,000	19,074,988,281	5,377,593,750	351,898,750,000	170,056,488
3011	Other manufacturing	259,879.70	242,399,546,875	9,311,125,977	2,615,573,730	160,224,062,500	112,877,800
3012	Recycling	457,500.60	101,882,968,750	1,152,485,840	78,491,653	13,303,948,242	15,993,661
3013	Electricity, gas, and water	7,747,352.00	714,770,562,500	19,516,289,063	11,772,144,531	560,155,875,000	1,724,247,314
3014	Construction	573,480.80	1,540,281,750,000	114,411,054,688	25,135,867,188	929,758,437,500	321,706,482
3015	Maintenance and repair	280,635.30	100,227,640,625	5,174,949,707	1,493,704,590	69,572,023,438	292,449,036
3016	Wholesale Trade	5,620,884.50	1,945,014,125,000	103,649,804,688	26,986,919,922	1,467,793,875,000	4,401,108,887
3017	Retail Trade	6,195,669.50	2,601,097,250,000	114,248,914,063	35,396,062,500	1,474,668,125,000	6,882,103,027
3018	Hotels and restaurants	255,813.30	1,612,281,125,000	68,624,554,688	20,268,449,219	859,927,187,500	2,800,576,660
3019	Transport	529,971.50	1,351,310,000,000	70,394,031,250	15,319,787,109	833,171,812,500	965,149,414
3020	Post and telecommunications	1,142,569.00	1,585,894,750,000	53,897,160,156	20,334,052,734	1,295,790,000,000	923,219,971
3021	Financial intermediation and business services	9,497,830.00	13,811,901,000,000	233,043,187,500	129,677,648,438	12,952,378,000,000	(5,587,405,273)
3022	Public Administration	532,395.50	2,363,247,250,000	285,745,656,250	94,258,789,063	1,390,981,750,000	1,044,419,678
3023	Education, Health, and other services	1,868,165.40	5,178,001,000,000	422,495,000,000	104,840,570,313	4,103,201,750,000	1,158,900,024
3024	Private Households	226,039.80	49,607,050,781	11,077,000,000	4,498,473,145	21,976,345,703	31,766,306
3025	Others	311,319.30	177,758,937,500	1,556,596,191	1,044,518,921	137,841,546,875	26,176,577

Table 6: The Social Account of the Nigerian Economy 2021

Code	Description	Industry Commodity Production ₦	Institutional Commodity Production ₦	Total Commodity Supply ₦	Net Commodity Supply ₦	Intermediate Commodity Demand ₦	Institutional Commodity Demand ₦	Total Gross Commodity Demand ₦	Domestic Supply/ Demand Ratio	Avg RPC	Avg RSC
3000	Total	44,705,258.36 3,281	(2,688,946,45 4)	44,702.56 9,416,827	39,669.7 34,276.9 34	9,598.79 6,278.99 2	33,343, 992,37 4,877	42,942, 788,65 3,870	-	-	-
3001	Agriculture	2,468,390.750 ,000	(177,980,423)	2,468,212, 769,577	2,263,73 3,457,07 7	2,010,23 9,264,57 0	283,85 3,379,3 49	2,294,0 92,643, 918	98.6 8%	98.6 8%	91.72 %
3002	Fishing	45,030,437.50 0	(13,491,746)	45,016,94 5,754	43,807,1 05,178	37,231,8 01,382	10,626, 413,91 7	47,858, 215,29 8	91.5 4%	91.5 4%	97.31 %
3003	Mining and Quarrying	3,323,925.250 ,000	(74,973,648)	3,323,850, 276,352	6,649,27 6,352	6,625.44 7,189	8,496,3 30,551	15,121, 777,74 0	43.9 7%	43.9 7%	0.20%
3004	Food and beverages	1,396,554,875 ,000	(208,727,707)	1,396,346, 147,293	1,335,50 6,412,91 8	115,195, 529,480	1,348,9 98,630, 126	1,464.1 94,159, 606	91.2 1%	91.2 1%	95.64 %
3005	Textiles and wearing apparel	222,037,843,7 50	(33,319,256)	222,004,5 24,494	177,161, 801,838	15,611,5 99,941	193,38 9,536,1 25	209,00 1,136,0 66	84.7 7%	84.7 7%	79.80 %
3006	Wood and paper	444,207,593,7 50	(54,844,383)	444,152,7 49,367	428,793, 571,632	389,218, 790,839	136,83 4,791,8 93	526,05 3,582,7 32	81.5 1%	81.5 1%	96.54 %
3007	Petroleum, Chemical and Non-metal mfg.	1,315,054.750 ,000	(70,227,440)	1,314,984, 522,560	960,498, 522,560	573,550, 987,810	756,08 3,720,8 48	1,329,6 34,708, 659	72.2 4%	72.2 4%	73.04 %
3008	Metal products	358,452,781,2 50	(169,012,543)	358,283.7 68,707	343,637, 556,793	430,703, 113,739	49,012, 651,94 7	479,71 5,765,6 86	71.6 3%	71.6 3%	95.91 %
3009	Electrical and machinery	1,161,742,875 ,000	(426,447,113)	1,161,316. 427,887	1,129,65 5,257,96 5	491,116. 567,196	1,108,4 24,290, 863	1,599,5 40,858, 059	70.6 2%	70.6 2%	97.28 %
3010	Transport equipment	594,186,250,0 00	(580,486,938)	593,605,7 63,062	580,064, 094,116	82,016,6 21,381	736,62 6,088,5 01	818,64 2,709,8 82	70.8 6%	70.8 6%	97.72 %
3011	Other manufacturing	242,399,546,8 75	(58,812,054)	242,340,7 34,821	236,975, 717,243	63,219,9 07,199	226,48 2,288,6 16	289,70 2,195,8 16	81.8 0%	81.8 0%	97.79 %
3012	Recycling	101,882,968,7 50	(119,094,223)	101,763,8 74,527	97,534,9 96,597	1,782,92 9,129	98,675, 883,05 3	100,45 8,812,1 82	97.0 9%	97.0 9%	95.85 %
3013	Electricity, gas, and water	714,770,562,5 00	(160,046)	714,770,4 02,454	708,919, 408,313	219,184, 951,584	549,73 7,655,2 63	768,92 2,606,8 48	92.2 0%	92.2 0%	99.18 %
3014	Construction	1,540,281,750 ,000	(38,897)	1,540,281, 711,103	1,504,79 5,933,75 9	240,271, 707,866	1,445,9 49,780, 108	1,686,2 21,487, 974	89.2 4%	89.2 4%	97.70 %
3015	Maintenance and repair	100,227,640,6 25	(2,701,929)	100,224,9 38,696	94,430,2 41,430	6,761,51 5,691	93,212, 373,19 4	99,973, 888,88 5	94.4 6%	94.4 6%	94.22 %
3016	Wholesale Trade	1,945,014,125 ,000	(190,514,328)	1,944,823, 610,672	1,880,81 7,216,14 1	501,755, 487,610	1,521,7 37,164, 719	2,023,4 92,652, 329	92.9 5%	92.9 5%	96.71 %
3017	Retail Trade	2,601,097.250 ,000	(32,665)	2,601,097, 217,335	2,554,80 5,721,24 1	54,521,0 95,301	2,554,1 91,886, 791	2,608,7 12,982, 092	97.9 3%	97.9 3%	98.22 %

258

3018	Hotels and restaurants	1,612,281,125,000	(30,473)	1,612,281,094,527	1,498,039,414,839	31,718,184,946	1,562,548,271,535	1,594,266,456,481	93.96%	93.96%	92.91%
3019	Transport	1,351,310,000,000	(24,375,132)	1,351,285,624,868	937,067,531,118	385,955,646,861	738,704,006,968	1,124,659,653,829	83.32%	83.32%	69.35%
3020	Post and telecommunication	1,585,894,750,000	(2,175,288)	1,585,892,574,712	1,481,399,621,587	416,787,923,949	1,140,093,836,421	1,556,881,760,370	95.15%	95.15%	93.41%
3021	Financial intermediation and business services	13,811,901,000,000	(481,154,236)	13,811,419,845,764	13,758,686,240,295	3,429,157,042,684	10,628,106,302,673	14,057,263,345,357	97.88%	97.88%	99.62%
3022	Public Administration	2,363,247,250,000	(24,591)	2,363,247,225,409	2,347,405,312,323	2,163,830,302	2,680,704,059,748	2,682,867,890,049	87.50%	87.50%	99.33%
3023	Education, Health, and other services	5,178,001,000,000	(262,697)	5,178,000,737,303	5,074,350,651,365	49,327,865,230	5,275,884,063,479	5,325,211,928,708	95.29%	95.29%	98.00%
3024	Private Households	49,607,050,781	(17,008)	49,607,033,773	48,397,253,988	15,820,875	57,086,064,175	57,101,885,051	84.76%	84.76%	97.56%
3025	Others	177,758,937,500	(41,689)	177,758,895,811	176,601,960,264	44,662,646,239	138,532,904,015	183,195,550,254	96.40%	96.40%	99.35%

Source: (Implan 11 software and Database for Nigeria, 2022)

Where:

RPC = A Regional Purchase Coefficient (RPC) is the proportion of the total demand for a Commodity by all users in the chapter Area that is supplied by producers located within the chapter Area. Average RPC is the proportion of local demand for the Commodity that is currently met by local production.

RSC = The RSC, also known as the Local Use Ratio, indicates the proportion of the local supply of a Commodity that goes to meet local demands. It is calculated by dividing the Local Use of Local Supply by the Total Local Commodity Supply. Average RSC is the proportion of the Commodity's local supply that meets local demand.

Table 7: The Industry Account of the Nigerian Economy 2021
Source: (Implan 11 software and Database for Nigeria, 2022)

Code	Description	Household Demand ₦	Federal Government Demand ₦	Capital ₦	Inventory ₦	Foreign Exports ₦
3000	Total	24,659,713,678,178	3,554,503,279,812	2,678,719,313,926	2,206,621,819	5,033,015,641,993
3001	Agriculture	277,278,838,271	589,750,581	2,072,937,978	175,637,759	204,494,057,304
3002	Fishing	9,442,222,741	275,006,481	240,047	12,353,396	1,210,203,170
3003	Mining and Quarrying	3,533,823,314	74,876,402	94,382,906	2,967,800	3,317,275,823,665
3004	Food and beverages	1,230,428,602,580	141,888	168,202	190,411,127	60,848,828,781
3005	Textiles and wearing apparel	159,320,706,487	28,225,399	4,575,904,069	28,247,623	44,849,452,817
3006	Wood and paper	108,816,248,146	1,287,077,543	1,401,673,697	44,709,938	15,361,074,300
3007	Petroleum, Chemical and Non-metal mfg.	540,714,486,243	2,342,462,974	3,099,539,584	50,733,449	354,504,931,511
3008	Metal products	19,509,692,485	974,455,561	14,520,802,462	121,126,840	14,653,120,945
3009	Electrical and machinery	327,159,239,571	66,505,157,455	389,132,243,812	301,283,409	31,672,796,223
3010	Transport equipment	363,235,215,954	45,118,557,348	113,694,658,561	411,716,741	13,554,911,340
3011	Other manufacturing	149,748,781,695	8,075,909,422	27,434,130,392	48,119,797	5,366,319,578
3012	Recycling	94,897,730,640	902,411,930	172,359	115,763,350	4,233,826,984
3013	Electricity, gas, and water	506,838,285,482	141,778	185,144	147,557	5,850,995,451
3014	Construction	18,187,108,736	172,657,369,594	1,099,531,288,709	34,712	35,485,778,240
3015	Maintenance and repair	84,549,355,158	287,106,028	3,207,018,409	2,552,174	5,794,853,483
3016	Wholesale Trade	1,241,559,359,588	17,793,594,547	155,048,757,773	177,098,607	64,012,664,578
3017	Retail Trade	2,464,937,887,310	934,024,806	35,539,354,211	31,990	46,291,496,675
3018	Hotels and restaurants	1,468,232,371,611	3,130,511	179,201	28,634	114,241,681,847
3019	Transport	589,377,873,514	8,501,066,212	17,600,759,074	20,309,750	414,225,565,613
3020	Post and telecommunications	979,650,227,795	8,308,574,177	96,859,400,019	2,069,827	104,493,096,453
3021	Financial intermediation and business services	9,943,920,266,978	92,754,644,711	365,581,225,025	470,950,898	52,735,442,572
3022	Public Administration	71,417,536,498	1,982,946,902,918	291,147,608,237	21,516	15,841,913,251
3023	Education, Health, and other services	3,825,903,673,260	1,143,266,508,369	58,176,357,372	250,322	103,650,091,196
3024	Private Households	47,507,742,934	875,992,209	111,883	14,415	1,209,780,200
3025	Others	133,546,401,189	190,969	214,800	40,189	1,156,935,818
10001	Households	-	-	-	-	-
11001	Government	-	-	-	-	-
14001	Capital	-	-	-	-	-
14002	Inventory Additions/Deletions	-	-	-	-	-

Table 8: Multiplier by Top 25 sectors of the Economy in Nigeria
Source: (Implan 11 software and Database for Nigeria, 2022)

Code	Description	Direct Effects	Indirect Effects	Induced Effects	Total Effects	Type I Multiplier	Type SAM Multiplier
3001	Agriculture	1	2.265522	0.019125	3.284647	3.265522	3.284647
3002	Fishing	1	0.214165	0.030517	1.244682	1.214165	1.244682
3003	Mining and Quarrying	1	0.41285	0.032414	1.445264	1.41285	1.445264
3004	Food and beverages	1	0.677898	0.034659	1.712557	1.677898	1.712557
3005	Textiles and wearing apparel	1	0.293626	0.064353	1.357979	1.293626	1.357979
3006	Wood and paper	1	0.208316	0.062055	1.270371	1.208316	1.270371
3007	Petroleum, Chemical and Non-metal mfg.	1	0.16715	0.043117	1.210267	1.16715	1.210267
3008	Metal products	1	0.182179	0.081237	1.263416	1.182179	1.263416
3009	Electrical and machinery	1	0.217346	0.073315	1.29066	1.217346	1.29066
3010	Transport equipment	1	0.335836	0.060775	1.396611	1.335836	1.396611
3011	Other manufacturing	1	0.279664	0.065264	1.344928	1.279664	1.344928
3012	Recycling	1	0.789222	0.054936	1.844158	1.789222	1.844158
3013	Electricity, gas, and water	1	0.173745	0.053305	1.22705	1.173745	1.22705
3014	Construction	1	0.303059	0.108509	1.411568	1.303059	1.411568
3015	Maintenance and repair	1	0.244656	0.07947	1.324126	1.244656	1.324126
3016	Wholesale Trade	1	0.180461	0.077406	1.257867	1.180461	1.257867
3017	Retail Trade	1	0.389638	0.076328	1.465966	1.389638	1.465966
3018	Hotels and restaurants	1	0.51899	0.07527	1.594259	1.51899	1.594259
3019	Transport	1	0.320345	0.078807	1.399152	1.320345	1.399152
3020	Post and telecommunications	1	0.137649	0.05423	1.191879	1.137649	1.191879
3021	Financial intermediation and business services	1	0.038615	0.029505	1.068119	1.038615	1.068119
3022	Public Administration	1	0.256061	0.180207	1.436268	1.256061	1.436268
3023	Education, Health, and other services	1	0.108395	0.111374	1.219769	1.108395	1.219769
3024	Private Households	1	0.246828	0.340242	1.587071	1.246828	1.587071
3025	Others	1	0.211092	0.023672	1.234764	1.211092	1.234764

Type I Multipliers: These are representative of indirect effects. This type looks only at business-to-business purchases and does not include the effects of local household spending. This Multiplier is calculated as (Direct + Indirect Effects) / Direct Effect.

Type SAM Multiplier: (where SAM stands for Social Accounting Matrix) is calculated by dividing the sum of the Direct Effects, Indirect Effects, and Induced Effects by the Direct Effects.

Table 9: Industry Coefficient of the Top 25 Sectors of the Economy in Nigeria
Source: (Implan 11 software and Database for Nigeria, 2022)

Code	Description	Coefficient	Supply Demand Ratio / Regional Purchase Coefficient
3001	Agriculture	0.681365	0.986766
3002	Fishing	0.000041	0.915352
3003	Mining and Quarrying	0.000017	0.439715
3004	Food and beverages	0.005098	0.912110
3005	Textiles and wearing apparel	0.000125	0.847660
3006	Wood and paper	0.002760	0.815114
3007	Petroleum, Chemical, and Non-metal mfg.	0.011805	0.722378
3008	Metal products	0.000830	0.716336
3009	Electrical and machinery	0.001108	0.706237
3010	Transport equipment	0.000126	0.708568
3011	Other manufacturing	0.000133	0.817998
3012	Recycling	0.000001	0.970897
3013	Electricity, gas, and water	0.001624	0.921965
3014	Construction	0.000638	0.892407
3015	Maintenance and repair	0.000075	0.944549
3016	Wholesale Trade	0.006856	0.929491
3017	Retail Trade	0.000280	0.979336
3018	Hotels and restaurants	0.000035	0.939642
3019	Transport	0.003237	0.833201
3020	Post and telecommunications	0.000444	0.951517
3021	Financial intermediation and business services	0.031361	0.978760
3022	Public Administration	0.000014	0.874961
3023	Education, Health, and other services	0.000308	0.952892
3024	Private Households	0.000000	0.847560
3025	Others	0.000349	0.964008

Total Absorption Value	0.748629	
Value Added Coefficient	0.251371	
Total Production Function	1	

Table 10: Showing 2015 Expenditure Economic Impact
Source: (Author's Calculation, 2022)

Impact Type	Employment	Labor Income ₦	Value Added ₦	Output ₦
Direct Effect	0.1	80,592	707,859	791,350
Indirect Effect	0	2,958	76,565	85,778
Induced Effect	0	3,940	70,968	88,136
Total Effect	0.2	87,491	855,391	965,264

Table 11: Showing 2015 Top 10 Gainers
from the Foundation's Activities by sectors of the economy
Source: (Author's Calculation, 2022)

Sector	Description	Employment	Labor Income ₦	Value Added ₦	Output ₦
3023	Education, Health, and other services	0.1	81,652	717,164	801,753
3021	Financial intermediation and business services	0	2,352	86,298	89,555
3013	Electricity, gas, and water	0	178	3,379	4,071
301	Agriculture	0	26	1,899	7,556
3016	Wholesale Trade	0	566	6,942	8,424
3017	Retail Trade	0	435	4,747	7,569
3020	Post and telecommunications	0	388	7,159	8,282
307	Petroleum, Chemical and Non-metal mfg.	0	280	6,746	8,052
309	Electrical and machinery	0	249	3,186	4,086
306	Wood and paper	0	186	2,944	3,455

Table 12: 2016 Economic Impact
Source: (Author's Calculation, 2022)

	Showing 2016 Expenditure Impact				Showing 2016 Donation Impact			
Impact Type	Employment	Labor Income ₦	Value Added ₦	Output ₦	Employment	Labor Income ₦	Value Added ₦	Output ₦
Direct Effect	0.2	206,667	1,815,199	2,029,300	0	25,460	223,624	250,000
Indirect Effect	0.1	7,586	196,339	219,966	0	935	24,188	27,099
Induced Effect	0.1	10,104	181,986	226,011	0	1,245	22,420	27,843
Total Effect	0.4	224,357	2,193,524	2,475,277	0.1	27,640	270,232	304,942

Table 13: Showing 2016 Top 10 Gainers
from the Foundation's Activities by sectors of the economy source: (Author's
Calculation, 2022)

		Showing 2016 Expenditure Impact				Showing 2016 Donation Impact			
Sector	Description	Employment	Labor Income ₦	Value Added ₦	Output ₦	Employment	Labor Income ₦	Value Added ₦	Output ₦
3023	Education, Health, and other services	0.2	209,384	1,839,061	2,055,977	0	25,795	226,564	253,286
3021	Financial intermediation and business services	0.1	6,031	221,297	229,651	0	743	27,263	28,292
3013	Electricity, gas, and water	0	457	8,664	10,440	0	56	1,067	1,286
301	Agriculture	0	67	4,871	19,377	0	8	600	2,387
3016	Wholesale Trade	0	1,451	17,803	21,603	0	179	2,193	2,661
3017	Retail Trade	0	1,117	12,172	19,410	0	138	1,500	2,391
3020	Post and telecommunications	0	994	18,359	21,237	0	122	2,262	2,616
307	Petroleum, Chemical and Non-metal mfg.	0	718	17,299	20,648	0	88	2,131	2,544
309	Electrical and machinery	0	639	8,171	10,477	0	79	1,007	1,291
306	Wood and paper	0	476	7,549	8,860	0	59	930	1,091

Table 14: 2017 Economic Impact
Source: (Author's Calculation, 2022)

	Showing 2017 Expenditure Impact				Showing 2017 Donation Impact			
Impact Type	Employment	Labor Income ₦	Value Added ₦	Output ₦	Employment	Labor Income ₦	Value Added ₦	Output ₦
Direct Effect	0.3	247,536	2,174,162	2,430,603	0.1	66,197	581,422	650,000
Indirect Effect	0.1	9,086	235,166	263,465	0	2,430	62,889	70,457
Induced Effect	0.1	12,102	217,975	270,705	0	3,236	58,292	72,393
Total Effect	0.5	268,725	2,627,303	2,964,774	0.1	71,863	702,602	792,850

Table 15: Showing 2017 Top 10 Gainers
from the Foundation's Activities by sectors of the economy
Source: (Author's Calculation, 2022)

		Showing 2017 Expenditure Impact				Showing 2017 Donation Impact			
Secto r	Description	Employm ent	Labor Inco me ₦	Value Added ₦	Output ₦	Employm ent	Labo r Inco me ₦	Value Adde d ₦	Outp ut ₦
3023	Education, Health, and other services	0.3	250,7 90	2,202,7 44	2,462,5 56	0.1	67,06 7	589,0 65	658,5 45
3021	Financial intermediation and business services	0.1	7,224	265,06 0	275,06 5	0	1,932	70,88 3	73,55 9
3013	Electricity, gas, and water	0	547	10,378	12,505	0	146	2,775	3,344
301	Agriculture	0	80	5,834	23,209	0	21	1,560	6,207
3016	Wholesale Trade	0	1,738	21,323	25,875	0	465	5,702	6,920
3017	Retail Trade	0	1,338	14,579	23,248	0	358	3,899	6,217
3020	Post and telecommunica tions	0	1,191	21,990	25,437	0	318	5,881	6,803
307	Petroleum, Chemical and Non-metal mfg.	0	860	20,719	24,731	0	230	5,541	6,614
309	Electrical and machinery	0	766	9,787	12,549	0	205	2,617	3,356
306	Wood and paper	0	570	9,042	10,612	0	152	2,418	2,838

Table 16: 2018 Economic Impact
Source: (Author's Calculation, 2022)

		Showing 2018 Expenditure Impact				Showing 2018 Donation Impact			
Impact Type	Employme nt	Labor Income ₦	Value Added ₦	Output ₦	Employm ent	Labor Income ₦	Value Added ₦	Output ₦
Direct Effect	0.5	449,154	3,945,01 6	4,410,32 7	0.1	93,083	817,56 8	914,000
Indirect Effect	0.2	16,487	426,708	478,058	0	3,417	88,431	99,073
Induced Effect	0.2	21,959	395,515	491,194	0	4,551	81,967	101,796
Total Effect	1	487,601	4,767,23 9	5,379,57 9	0.2	101,051	987,96 7	1,114,869

265

Table 17: Showing 2018 Top 10 Gainers
from the Foundation's Activities by sectors of the economy
Source: (Author's Calculation, 2022)

		Showing 2018 Expenditure Impact				Showing 2018 Donation Impact			
Sect or	Description	Employ ment	Labor Incom e ₦	Value Adde d ₦	Outp ut ₦	Employ ment	Labo r Inco me ₦	Value Adde d ₦	Outpu t ₦
3023	Education, Health, and other services	0.5	455,05 9	3,996,8 77	4,468, 305	0.1	94,30 7	828,31 6	926,015
3021	Financial intermediation and business services	0.1	13,107	480,95 1	499,10 5	0	2,716	99,673	103,435
3013	Electricity, gas, and water	0.1	993	18,830	22,690	0	206	3,902	4,702
301	Agriculture	0.1	145	10,586	42,112	0	30	2,194	8,727
3016	Wholesale Trade	0	3,153	38,691	46,951	0	654	8,018	9,730
3017	Retail Trade	0	2,427	26,454	42,184	0	503	5,482	8,742
3020	Post and telecommunications	0	2,160	39,900	46,156	0	448	8,269	9,565
307	Petroleum, Chemical and Non-metal mfg.	0	1,560	37,595	44,875	0	323	7,791	9,300
309	Electrical and machinery	0	1,390	17,758	22,770	0	288	3,680	4,719
306	Wood and paper	0	1,035	16,406	19,255	0	214	3,400	3,990

Table 18: 2019 Economic Impact
Source: (Author's Calculation, 2022)

	Showing 2019 Expenditure Impact				Showing 2019 Donation Impact			
Impact Type	Employm ent	Labor Income ₦	Value Added ₦	Output ₦	Employme nt	Labor Income ₦	Value Added ₦	Output ₦
Direct Effect	0.4	297,696	2,614,72 7	2,923,13 2	0.1	122,210	1,073,39 4	1,200,00 0
Indirect Effect	0.1	10,928	282,819	316,853	0.1	4,486	116,103	130,074
Induced Effect	0.2	14,555	262,144	325,560	0.1	5,975	107,615	133,648
Total Effect	0.6	323,179	3,159,69 1	3,565,54 5	0.3	132,671	1,297,11 2	1,463,72 3

Table 19: Showing 2019 Top 10 Gainers
from the Foundation's Activities by sectors of the economy
Source: (Author's Calculation, 2022)

Sector	Description	Showing 2019 Expenditure Impact				Showing 2019 Donation Impact			
		Employment	Labor Income ₦	Value Added ₦	Output ₦	Employment	Labor Income ₦	Value Added ₦	Output ₦
3023	Education, Health, and other services	0.4	301,610	2,649,100	2,961,560	0.1	123,816	1,087,505	1,215,775
3021	Financial intermediation and business services	0.1	8,687	318,771	330,803	0	3,566	130,861	135,801
3013	Electricity, gas, and water	0.1	658	12,481	15,039	0	270	5,123	6,174
301	Agriculture	0.1	96	7,016	27,912	0	39	2,880	11,458
3016	Wholesale Trade	0	2,090	25,644	31,119	0	858	10,527	12,775
3017	Retail Trade	0	1,609	17,534	27,959	0	660	7,198	11,478
3020	Post and telecommunications	0	1,432	26,445	30,592	0	588	10,856	12,558
307	Petroleum, Chemical and Non-metal mfg.	0	1,034	24,918	29,743	0	425	10,229	12,210
309	Electrical and machinery	0	921	11,770	15,092	0	378	4,832	6,195
306	Wood and paper	0	686	10,874	12,762	0	?281	4,464	5,239

Table 20: 2020 Economic Impact
Source: (Author's Calculation, 2022)

Impact Type	Showing 2020 Expenditure Impact				Showing 2020 Donation Impact			
	Employment	Labor Income ₦	Value Added ₦	Output ₦	Employment	Labor Income ₦	Value Added ₦	Output ₦
Direct Effect	0.1	117,121	1,028,693	1,150,027	1.1	916,574	8,050,455	9,000,000
Indirect Effect	0.1	4,299	111,268	124,657	0.4	33,645	870,769	975,556
Induced Effect	0.1	5,726	103,134	128,083	0.5	44,812	807,114	1,002,364
Total Effect	0.3	127,146	1,243,095	1,402,767	2	995,031	9,728,338	10,977,919

267

Table 21: Showing 2020 Top 10 Gainers
from the Foundation's Activities by sectors of the economy
Source: (Author's Calculation, 2022)

Sector	Description	Showing 2020 Expenditure Impact				Showing 2020 Donation Impact			
		Employment	Labor Income ₦	Value Added ₦	Output ₦	Employment	Labor Income ₦	Value Added ₦	Output ₦
3023	Education, Health, and other services	0.1	118,660	1,042,217	1,165,145	1.1	928,623	8,156,287	9,118,314
3021	Financial intermediation and business services	0	3,418	125,412	130,146	0.2	26,747	981,459	1,018,506
3013	Electricity, gas, and water	0	259	4,910	5,917	0.2	2,027	38,426	46,304
301	Agriculture	0	38	2,760	10,981	0.2	295	21,602	85,937
3016	Wholesale Trade	0	822	10,089	12,243	0.1	6,435	78,955	95,810
3017	Retail Trade	0	633	6,898	11,000	0.1	4,953	53,985	86,084
3020	Post and telecommunications	0	563	10,404	12,036	0	4,409	81,422	94,189
307	Petroleum, Chemical and Non-metal mfg.	0	407	9,803	11,702	0	3,184	76,719	91,575
309	Electrical and machinery	0	362	4,631	5,937	0	2,836	36,238	46,465
306	Wood and paper	0	270	4,278	5,021	0	2,111	33,479	39,292

Table 22: Showing 2021 Expenditure Economic Impact
Source: (Author's Calculation, 2022)

Impact Type	Employment	Labor Income ₦	Value Added ₦	Output ₦
Direct Effect	1.8	1,527,623	13,417,425	15,000,000
Indirect Effect	0.7	56,076	1,451,281	1,625,926
Induced Effect	0.8	74,686	1,345,189	1,670,606
Total Effect	3.3	1,658,385	16,213,896	18,296,532

Table 23: Showing 2021 Top 10 Gainers
from the Foundation's Activities by sectors of the economy
Source: (Author's Calculation, 2022)

Sector	Description	Employment	Labor Income ₦	Value Added ₦	Output ₦
3023	Education, Health, and other services	1.8	1,547,705	13,593,811	15,197,190
3021	Financial intermediation and business services	0.4	44,579	1,635,766	1,697,510
3013	Electricity, gas, and water	0.3	3,378	64,044	77,173
301	Agriculture	0.3	492	36,003	143,228
3016	Wholesale Trade	0.2	10,725	131,591	159,684
3017	Retail Trade	0.1	8,254	89,974	143,473
3020	Post and telecommunications	0	7,348	135,704	156,981
307	Petroleum, Chemical and Non-metal mfg.	0	5,307	127,866	152,625
309	Electrical and machinery	0	4,727	60,396	77,442
306	Wood and paper	0	3,518	55,798	65,487

Table 24: Showing Anticipated Future Expenditure Economic Impact
Source: (Author's Calculation, 2022)

Impact Type	Nayomee Project				Woodbury & Evergreen Projects (Values X 2)				Transactions			
	Employ ment	Labor Income ₦	Value Added ₦	Output ₦	Employ ment	Labor Income ₦	Value Added ₦	Output ₦	Employ ment	Labor Income ₦	Value Added ₦	Output ₦
Direct Effect	12.6	9,150,429	70,138,034	100,999,999	6.2	4,529,915	34,721,799	50,000,000	28.8	717,008	38,720,827	49,000,000
Indirect Effect	13.3	1,238,822	26,269,585	30,608,987	6.6	613,278	13,004,745	15,152,964	3.3	382,567	9,387,742	10,343,528
Induced Effect	5.4	489,951	8,824,603	10,959,374	2.7	242,550	4,368,615	5,425,433	0.6	51,855	933,976	1,159,916
Total Effect	31.3	10,879,202	105,232,221	142,568,360	15.5	5,385,744	52,095,159	70,578,396	32.7	1,151,431	49,042,545	60,503,444

269

Table 25: Showing Anticipated Top 10 Gainers
from the Foundation's Project Activities by sectors of the economy
Source: (Author's Calculation, 2022)

| Sector | Description | Showing Nayomee Project Expenditure Impact | | | | Showing Woodbury & Evergreen Project Expenditure Impact | | | |
		Employment	Labor Income ₦	Value Added ₦	Output ₦	Employment	Labor Income ₦	Value Added ₦	Output ₦
3014	Construction	12.6	9,159,496	70,207,533	101,100,079	6.2	4,534,404	34,756,204	50,049,544
3021	Financial intermediation and business services	4.2	478,427	17,555,196	18,217,846	2.1	236,845	8,690,691	9,018,736
301	Agriculture	3.5	6,245	457,099	1,818,420	1.8	3,091	226,286	900,208
3016	Wholesale Trade	2.8	193,213	2,370,600	2,876,691	1.4	95,650	1,173,564	1,424,104
308	Metal products	1.6	212,609	2,483,884	3,033,123	0.8	105,252	1,229,645	1,501,546
3013	Electricity, gas, and water	1.6	19,236	364,683	439,444	0.8	9,523	180,536	217,547
309	Electrical and machinery	1.1	141,515	1,808,261	2,318,609	0.5	70,057	895,179	1,147,826
3017	Retail Trade	1	75,550	823,525	1,313,190	0.5	37,401	407,686	650,094
307	Petroleum, Chemical and Non-metal mfg.	0.9	124,372	2,996,725	3,577,006	0.4	61,570	1,483,527	1,770,795
306	Wood and paper	0.7	92,981	1,474,563	1,730,602	0.3	46,030	729,981	856,734

Table 26: Showing the Top 10
Foundation's Transactional Activities Impact by sectors of the economy
Source: (Author's Calculation, 2022)

Sector	Description	Employment	Labor Income ₦	Value Added ₦	Output ₦
3025	**Others**	28.8	717,139	38,727,896	49,008,946
3021	**Financial intermediation and business services**	1.6	181,704	6,667,364	6,919,034
3013	**Electricity, gas, and water**	0.5	5,715	108,342	130,552
301	**Agriculture**	0.3	583	42,640	169,629
306	**Wood and paper**	0.3	40,289	638,931	749,873
3020	**Post and telecommunications**	0.3	57,371	1,059,556	1,225,683
3016	**Wholesale Trade**	0.3	17,649	216,542	262,771
308	**Metal products**	0.2	28,178	329,200	401,993
309	**Electrical and machinery**	0.1	15,608	199,435	255,722
307	**Petroleum, Chemical and Non-metal mfg.**	0.1	16,687	402,070	479,926

Ejiro U. Osiobe